DATE DUE

NEWS
INCORPORATED

NEWS
INCORPORATED

CORPORATE MEDIA OWNERSHIP AND ITS
THREAT TO DEMOCRACY

Edited by

ELLIOT D. COHEN, PhD

PREFACE BY ARTHUR KENT

Prometheus Books

59 John Glenn Drive
Amherst, New York 14228-2197

4/05

Published 2005 by Prometheus Books

Inquiries should be addressed to
Prometheus Books
59 John Glenn Drive
Amherst, New York 14228–2197
VOICE: 716–691–0133, ext. 207
FAX: 716–564–2711
WWW.PROMETHEUSBOOKS.COM

09 08 07 06 05   5 4 3 2 1

Library of Congress Cataloging-in-Publication Data

News incorporated : corporate media ownership and its threat to democracy / edited by Elliot D. Cohen.
    p. cm.
Includes bibliographical references and index.
ISBN 1-59102-232-0 (hc)
    1. Broadcasting—United States. 2. Broadcasting—Political aspects—United States. 3. Mass media—Ownership. I. Cohen, Elliot D.

HE8689.8.N48 2005
302.23'0973—dc22

2004020147

Printed in the United States of America on acid-free paper

CONTENTS

5

II. MASS DECEPTION: HOW CORPORATE MEDIA ARE SYSTEMATICALLY MISLEADING AMERICANS

III. BREACH OF PROFESSIONAL STANDARDS: WHY CORPORATE MEDIA NEED TO INVESTIGATE THEMSELVES

PREFACE

ARTHUR KENT

ARTHUR KENT *is an independent journalist with his own production company, Fast Forward Films, based in London. In his thirty-year reporting career, he has reported for networks including the CBC, NBC, BBC News, CNN, and the History Channel, as well as London's* Observer *newspaper and the* Calgary Herald. *Kent won back-to-back Emmy Awards for NBC's 1989 coverage of the Tiananmen Square massacre and the Romanian uprising. During the 1991 Gulf War, he earned the name "The Scud Stud" by the first-ever live coverage of missile versus antimissile warfare. One year later, he was forced into a legal battle with NBC management over the intrusion of entertainment values into news. Kent won a record settlement from NBC and the right to publish the evidence in his book* Risk and Redemption: Surviving the Network News Wars. *Three months before the 9/11 terrorist attacks, his documentary about the Taliban,* Afghanistan: Captives of the Warlords, *was broadcast nationally in the United States by PBS, and following 9/11 the program was aired by the CBC.*

I f the journalistic universe is unfolding as it should, the US news media should be rocketing into an era of unbridled excellence. Sure, astronauts, not reporters, took the moonwalks of the twentieth century. But back on earth over the past hundred years, the men and women of the fourth estate accomplished one giant leap after another, advancing from the yellow journalism of the street corner to live reportage from anywhere on earth. By rights, the nation's journalists should have launched themselves into the new millennium as bold innovators, liberated by burgeoning technology and inspired by the challenge of reporting urgent crises at home and abroad.

But so far it's been a bumpy ride. Instead of boasts about going where no scribe has gone before, we're back to "Houston, we've got a problem." The forces of corporate gravity, warped by political pressures, have brought our craft and trade crashing down to earth. Corporate goliaths with no roots or belief in true journalism, but which are possessed of an insatiable hunger for revenue—increased income to be attained at any cost—dominate the mainstream media. For too many managers and editors, each news day has become a quest for a commercial narrative that will spike viewership or circulation: not the news as it is, but news you can use for higher share value.

Consequently, only the subjects and people that drive up the numbers are covered with any frequency and depth. Worse, more than a few proprietors are only too pleased to merge their commercial storyline with the administration's political narrative. Here, one word sums up the potential downside: Iraq.

In fact, since war and the coverage of war has become a key measure of competitive performance among big US media organizations, Iraq is a good place to start looking for evidence of managerial dysfunction. On that charred and chaotic landscape, one alarming fact looms above all others. Almost all the major scoops before, during, and for nearly a year after US forces invaded Iraq were produced not by dauntless reporters, but by administration insiders—political appointees who went public with their revelations in their own sweet time and for their own selfish reasons.

Following the grumblings of former treasury secretary Paul O'Neill, counterterrorism official Richard Clarke even more vividly exposed how the Bush administration's obsession with Saddam Hussein sucked energy and resources from the campaign against Osama bin Laden and al Qaeda. Similarly, the first man to attempt to manage postwar reconstruction, Gen. Jay Garner, who was abruptly replaced by Paul Bremer only weeks into the conflict, finally admitted some months later that his team had been hamstrung from the start. Defense Secretary Donald Rumsfeld's office had forced him to exclude State Department personnel—seasoned specialists on Iraq—from his operation. As a result, Garner, like the rest of the US military, was deprived of crucial advice—stratagems that could have reduced lawlessness after the regime's collapse, the cost of which, in lives and dollars, will be borne by both Iraqis and Americans for years to come.

Shamefully, both these sagas were ideal for journalistic overtures long before the whistle-blowers played their tunes. Ample evidence on the O'Neill/ Clarke themes existed in Washington well before the invasion of Iraq in March 2003. As for Garner, any of us on the ground in Kuwait and Iraq as US forces pushed northward (with Garner's hapless team lagging far, far behind) could watch with our own eyes the general's inelegant slide from the saddle.

At the time, a few of us managed to get these stories in print or on the air, sometimes by taking them to Canadian or British publications. But against a daily tidal wave of unquestioning coverage of White House and Pentagon briefings, what chance could there be that hard evidence from the field might dent the domestic consciousness? Bad enough that the nation's best-financed news organizations failed to come up with the answers. The real shame is that most of their reporters and editors didn't even ask the questions.

Why, your average consumer of news might ask, did the myth of a link between Saddam and al Qaeda go virtually unchallenged in the run-up to war? Why indeed: if there was one conclusion the rival Israeli and Saudi intelligence agencies shared in common after the 9/11 attacks, it was that no such link existed. Both let their findings become public in October 2001, and the story was widely reported. Likewise, if there was one set of facts established by even the most basic international news experience in the 1990s, it was that extreme Islamists such as Osama bin Laden despised Saddam as a blasphemer, and that he, in turn, feared and distrusted militant Islam.

But wait a minute. This thing, this resource, this legacy called "international news experience"—did big American news organizations put any kind of a premium at all on it in the 1990s? Not if a quick scan of the nation's media in the weeks prior to the 9/11 attacks is anything to go by. It was all Chandra Levy and shark attacks. One a tragic mystery, the other a phenomenon of nature, both were shamelessly exploited for ratings, readership, and revenue. Talk about intelligence failures—the FBI and the CIA have less to answer for than many of the dumbed-down organs of the nation's news industry.

Throughout the 1990s, the corrosive first decade of tabloid TV, the owners and managers of the nation's major broadcast networks slashed their foreign newsgathering assets. The news divisions of NBC, ABC, and CBS, the richest companies in the history of American broadcast journalism, were gutted of both newsgathering capability and institutional knowledge.

So it was, throughout 2003, that the network newscasts hummed along, evening upon evening, anchored by America's wealthiest journalists—all of whom boast of their personal editorial control of the broadcasts—while the administration propagated a lie of truly tragic proportions. Saddam, the president's men insisted, was in cahoots with Osama, so the hunt for the latter could be suspended while the Butcher of Baghdad was taken out of the equation. The networks, instead of fulfilling the role of a free press to help set the national agenda, were at best just along for the ride. At worst, wrapped in the flag, or blindfolded by it, they actively promoted the neoconservatives' flawed view of the world—while jacking up the ratings and their owners' share value.

The following chapters tell the story of how the rot first set in to News Incorporated, and how this decay is leeching steadily further into the core values of American journalism. These essays constitute a forensic examination of the loss of a nation's news virtue and the effect this decline is having on the body politic. The writers dare to ask: how can a people starved of information hope to keep their leading edge in the information age?

The answer is obvious. As the Iraq debacle shows, Americans must demand the restoration of their constitutional right to a free press, a news media free of managerial constraint and corruption. The nation's finances, its towns and cities and infrastructure, and especially it's sons and daughters in the US forces—none of these can be secure as long as the electronic marketplace of ideas and information is short-circuited by soulless conglomerates.

But let's take heart. There's a lot we can do, as citizens and reporters. A new generation of journalists is taking unprecedented risks to cover the deadly crossfire in Iraq and the Middle East. Their commitment and daring is a rallying call for us all. On the home front, as a people, Americans need to be more aware of their responsibilities as consumers of news. They need to turn off the trash and demand the straight goods. At the same time, American journalists need to reread the history of their craft to recharge the instincts and motivation that made them want to be reporters in the first place. The good news is that our teachers—our historic role models—are right here, waiting for us to reconnect.

There's Thomas Jefferson: given the choice between a country with a government and no press and one with a press but no government, he said he'd take the latter every time. And there's Mark Twain: "True patriotism," he wrote, "is loyalty to one's country, not its officeholders or institutions."

And how about Henry Louis Mencken and Isidor Feinstein Stone, two reporters who carved the bedrock of modern American journalism. Mencken said: "A good politician, under democracy, is as unthinkable as an honest burglar." I. F. Stone warned: "All governments are liars and we shouldn't believe a damned word they say."

What would Jefferson and Twain, Mencken and Stone have made of the Bush administration's policy, for instance, of concealing the return of dead Americans from Iraq? Here again, it wasn't the nation's most powerful media companies but an independent freedom of information campaigner who forced the administration to release photographs of the soldiers' coffins, allowing Americans to finally see the scope of individual sacrifice in Iraq. Would our forebears swallow the Pentagon's line about "sensitivity" toward the dead soldiers' families? No chance. They would recognize the lie and point to America's allies, like Britain, Italy, and Spain, whose news media are encouraged to witness the return of their fallen countrymen. They would help us realize that Americans deserve nothing less.

As you read the following analysis of what's gone wrong and why, keep in mind that these authors believe we can set things right. That's because they realize what's really at stake in reclaiming the independence and strength of the US news media: America's ability to clearly see both itself and the complex world it shares with other cultures. In these dangerous times, it's no exaggeration to say that the fourth estate is the first priority in succeeding in that age-old human struggle called survival.

ACKNOWLEDGMENTS

I am profoundly grateful to the many contributors to this book, whose talents, efforts, and steadfast devotion to democracy infuse its pages. Special thanks also goes to the following individuals for their kind assistance and support: the Honorable Michael Copps; James Fallows, National Correspondent, *Atlantic Monthly*; Mike Farrell, actor/producer; Bruce W. Fraser, freelance writer; Robert Greenwald, producer; Carol Hoenig, publicist; Alan Korn, National Lawyers Guild; Kate McArdle, executive director, Artists United; Steven L. Mitchell, editor in chief, Prometheus Books; Greg Palast, journalist/producer; and Chellie Pingree, president, Common Cause. Finally, a profound debt of gratitude is due to journalist Arthur Kent, who, in addition to crafting an eloquent preface, has emerged as an active partner in advancing this project, and its immensely important message.

Editor's Introduction

CORPORATE MEDIA'S
BETRAYAL OF AMERICA

T he mainstream media in America are owned and operated by a small elite group of Fortune 500 corporations. From General Electric's NBC, Viacom's CBS, News Corporation's Fox News, Disney's ABC, and AOL/Time Warner's CNN to Clear Channel's massive radio empire, American mainstream media have become the watchdog and guardian of the corporate bottom line instead of the vanguard of democracy and the public interest. What Americans see, hear, and read is now under the careful scrutiny of corporate headquarters, and, as a result, the public receives a homogenized, self-censored, self-serving version of reality.

Driven by profit maximization, these colossal, corporate media empires have cooperatively joined ranks with government offices and agencies at the highest federal levels, spinning off an intricate, seamless politico-corporate media web of deception. Instead of protecting against abuses of government power by keeping the public adequately informed, they have become complicit in destabilizing and undermining American democracy.

CONFLICT OF INTEREST IN CORPORATE MEDIA: WHY MAINSTREAM MEDIA LACKS CREDIBILITY

This betrayal of the public interest by corporate media, in pursuit of private gain, flies in the face of one of the most fundamental duties of journalism. Standards of journalistic practice in America have always, from their inception, demanded that journalists avoid even the *semblance* of conflict of interest. According to the Radio-Television News Directors Association *Code of Ethics*, radio and television journalists should "present the news with integrity and decency, avoiding real or perceived conflicts of interest."[1] Newspaper codes of ethics make similar ethical demands.[2] Yet it is such conflict that has become a defining mark of corporate media existence. As Arthur Kent has eloquently stated in the preface to this book, "the forces of corporate gravity, warped by political pressures, have brought our craft and trade crashing down to earth."

A conflict of interest arises because a trustee has a special interest that interferes with, or prevents, fulfillment of a trust.[3] In a democratic society, news organizations are trustees of the public and are expected to act in concert with the public interest, not some special, private interest. Like a fourth branch of the government (the so-called fourth estate), the media is entrusted with making sure that the public is adequately informed about the activities of government, thereby serving as a vital part of our system of "checks and balances." This vital, protective role of the media is enshrined in the annals of American constitutional law. Unfortunately, as Norman Solomon points out, the main form of "checks" that interest the corporate media are made payable to them, and the primary balance that interests them is their bottom line!

The conflicted nature of corporate media can be gleaned by raising some profoundly newsworthy questions which, not surprisingly, the media itself glosses over:

- Does a corporation have a real or apparent conflict of interest in reporting news that may embarrass corporate headquarters or quash a government contract? For example, does NBC have a real or apparent conflict of interest in covering the Iraq War when its parent company, General Electric, stands to increase its bottom line through military contracts?
- Is there a real or apparent conflict of interest in reporting on corporate lobbying for relaxed Federal Communication Commission (FCC) rules when the corporation so lobbying is also the owner of the news

corporation? Before the Iraq War began, corporate media successfully lobbied the FCC for such rule changes. Danny Schechter probes, "Did the FCC agree to waive the rules if the media companies agreed to wave the flag?"[4]

- Does Clear Channel have a conflict of interest, real or apparent, in reporting on the activities of the Bush administration when its chairman and vice chairman have well-documented financial/political ties to it? In 2003 Clear Channel not only reported on these activities, it also sponsored nationwide rallies ("Rally for America") aimed at supporting the Iraq War.
- Does Clear Channel have a conflict of interest, real or apparent, when it determines how much airtime an artist receives while the company is also in the live concert promotions business? It is at least the perception of some artists that their songs receive less airtime if they do not hire Clear Channel to promote their tours.[5]
- Does a Hollywood talent agency have a conflict of interest, real or apparent, in representing artists when it also has an interest in the production and distribution companies that employ these artists? When government fails to regulate the conduits through which the members of the creative community—independent producers, directors, writers, actors, and so on—speak, or are represented, their creative voices are silenced, sanitized, or otherwise melded to fit the narrow economic and political interests of the politico-corporate media establishment. As producer Len Hill explains, "the merger of Telemundo and NBC or the takeover of BET by Viacom . . . leads to an erosion of diversity. There are fewer corporate chieftains sitting on ever-more-exalted thrones. Both style and substance are pasteurized to meet the common requirement of corporate accountancy."[6]
- Did FCC chair Michael Powell have a real or apparent conflict of interest when he resisted requiring AOL and Time Warner to provide their competitors equal access to their cable TV system as a condition of their merger? Powell's father, Secretary of State Colin Powell, sat on AOL's board of directors and owned lucrative stock options in the company.[7]
- Was there a real or apparent conflict of interest when John Ellis, news director of Fox, called Florida in the 2000 presidential election for his first cousin, George W. Bush?
- And was there a conflict of interest, real or apparent, when Vice President Cheney's former company, Halliburton, received no-bid wartime

contracts worth hundreds of millions while Cheney was still receiving as much as one million dollars per year from this company?[8]

While this last question appears to be one of political conflict of interest, even raising it portends a conflict of interest, real or apparent, for news corporations, given their bottom-line interest in maintaining a symbiotic relationship with the government. How much careful investigation and reporting could the public expect this question to receive in the hands of such a press? And, short of editorializing from the Right by a Rush Limbaugh or a Bill O'Reilly, and from the Left by an Al Franken or a Paul Begala, mainstream media has not sincerely investigated the question of media fidelity to the public interest, despite persistent claims to being "fair and balanced." Indeed, how could it!

All of the above probing questions have an affirmative answer. Unfortunately, corporate media have a conflict of interest even in raising them. As Danny Schechter (quoting the writer Thomas Pynchon) reminds us, "If they can get you asking the wrong questions, they don't have to worry about the answers."

Conflict of interest (the reality as well as the appearance) is rampant in the politico-corporate media web. Like a cancer metastasizing, it has eaten away at the fabric of American democracy. This ubiquitous form of media treason has taken refuge behind a brand of corporate theology, the faith that somehow, by letting these corporate monolithic giants pursue their bottom line, the common good will be served in the end. According to this faith, it is extremely difficult to censor ideas because, sooner or later, they will "leak out."[9] According to this faith, by deregulating the corporate media, letting its bottom line freely expand, it will more efficiently deliver what viewers need and want. And while this self-serving faith is practiced and preached by Chairman Powell and the corporate media moguls, infotainment (entertainment disguised as news), infomercials (advertisements disguised as information), and editorials disguised as fact continue to supplant careful investigative reporting, once the pride of American journalism.

Unfortunately, too many journalists and editors have become congregants of this faith, sacrificing their journalistic souls to keep their jobs and to get "edited" versions of their stories out to the public. Some have caved to politico-corporate pressures. After 9/11, Dan Rather admitted that he and other journalists were intimidated about "asking the toughest of the tough questions" for fear of being branded unpatriotic.[10] One reactionary Web site calls such journalists who sell their journalistic integrity to satisfy their corporate bosses "Media Whores."[11]

Freedom of speech assumes an adequately informed public. Otherwise, talk about having such a right is empty rhetoric. But, unless Americans can, with confidence, trust their news sources to keep them adequately informed, this vital condition of freedom is undermined, and so, too, is the democracy that demands it. Nor is the problem of media censorship as simple as mega-media corporations trumping the journalists who work for them. The incorporation of journalism has ushered in a chilling new era in which media companies have even begun to censor the voices of *other* media companies. This phenomenon was the case when, on April 30, 2004, Sinclair Broadcasting Group, the nation's largest independent group owner of stations, covering 25 percent of the nation's television audience, trumped ABC when it ordered its ABC affiliates not to broadcast Ted Koppel's *Nightline* show. The show in question consisted entirely of Koppel reading the names of all the US servicemen and women killed in action in Iraq. Sinclair declared, "Despite the denials by a spokeswoman for the show, the action appears to be motivated by a political agenda designed to undermine the efforts of the United States in Iraq."[12] Yet, it is far from clear that Sinclair did not seek to advance its own "right-wing" political agenda in preempting the *Nightline* show. Since 1997, Sinclair had donated more than $200,000 to Republican candidates. Inserting its own "news" into its programming, it has referred to peace activists as "wack-jobs," the French as "cheese-eating surrender monkeys," progressives as "loony left," and "the liberal media" as the "hate-America crowd."[13] Sinclair also attempted to promote its own right-wing political agenda by requiring its affiliates to carry an anti-Kerry documentary just two weeks prior to the presidential election.[14] Under pressure from its affiliates, shareholders, and advertisers, Sinclair backed down.[15]

Democracy is not a contest to see which political ideology can most successfully prevent the other from being heard. Everyone in a democracy is entitled to express his or her political perspectives. The problem is not simply that Sinclair (or Fox, or any other news organization) chooses to air "right-wing" conservative (or "left-wing" liberal) views; the problem is far more complex than this. First, electronic journalists have an ethical duty to "clearly label opinion and commentary," thereby distinguishing it from "news reporting."[14] Second, they have an ethical duty to "present a *diversity* of expressions, opinions, and ideas in context."[16] Sinclair is in breach of both of these cardinal ethical duties to the public when, as a major gatekeeper of broadcast journalism, it chooses to exclude alternative views from being heard while boldly claiming to offer Americans a "fair and balanced news perspective" for broadcast just as Fox News does for cable.[18] Unfortunately, intolerance for diversity in the media, no less than in government, is a recipe for an anti-democratic, dictatorial regime.

In his classic essay "On Liberty," John Stuart Mill put the case against censorship in the form of a dilemma: if a belief is true and it is suppressed, then the public loses the opportunity to learn the truth. On the other hand, we can't be certain that a belief is false, and even if the suppressed belief is false, it may still contain some measure of truth or at least serve to challenge those with true beliefs to better defend themselves. So, true or false, the public suffers a loss when a belief is censored.[19] Whether or not Koppel was motivated by his own hidden antiwar agenda (something he emphatically denied) was plainly irrelevant. Moreover, Sinclair's move to prevent Americans from obtaining patently *factual* information about the casualties of the Iraq War was unequivocally undemocratic, and the status of America as a free nation was diminished to the extent that its citizens were denied the opportunity to see, hear, and judge for themselves.

Short of outright censorship, the corporate media climate has also fostered mindless parroting of what official government sources say. Issues are thereby "resolved" with an unsubstantiated, uninvestigated denial from officialdom. The *New York Times* has itself admitted having been guilty of such shallow reporting in its coverage of the weapons of mass destruction (WMD) issue prior to the US invasion of Iraq. Guardedly, it editorialized,

> But we do fault ourselves for failing to deconstruct the WMD issue with the kind of thoroughness we directed at the question of a link between Iraq and al Qaeda, or even tax cuts in time of war. We did not listen carefully to the people who disagreed with us. Our certainty flowed from the fact that such an overwhelming majority of government officials, past and present, top intelligence officials and other experts were sure that the weapons were there. We had a groupthink of our own.[20]

This admission followed a previous editor's note to the same effect. Still, the belted admission never made front-page news, and its self-defensive admission may have been unavoidable in light of the obvious faux pas of having supported a preemptive war based on faulty intelligence at best and the perpetration of a fraud at worst. Guarded admissions of wrongdoing by wrongdoers caught with their pants down are never noble, and this is even more regrettable when the wrongdoer is such a well-respected newspaper as the *New York Times*.

Thorough investigative reporting does not hang its hat on a denial by the very individuals under investigation. Instead, it vigorously pursues and follows up on any story portending important consequences for the public. A sad example of mainstream media's lack of such fortitude was in its coverage of the serious potential for voter fraud in the 2004 presidential election. Years prior, there had been reasonable concern that the security of electronic touch-screen voting machines might be breached. Experts in computer programming pointed to the ease at which malicious code could be installed into the thousands of lines of "spaghetti" code comprising an electronic voting program. In addition, the companies that tested and checked these programs were themselves hired by the makers of the voting machines. Opening the floodgates for conflict of interest.[21] Moreover, some voting machine companies appeared to have further conflicts of interest.

The most blatant example of such conflict concerned the Ohio-based company Diebold Election Systems, which supplied many states across the country with touch-screen voting machines, including key battleground states such as Ohio and Florida. Walden O'Dell, the company's chief executive, pledged "to help Ohio deliver its electoral votes to the president." Moreover, O'Dell had a history of giving generously to Republican candidates, was active in fundraising for Bush's reelection, and had been a guest of the president at his Texas ranch.[22] Whatever O'Dell may have meant by his remark that he would "help Ohio deliver its electoral votes to the president," the reliance on this company to supply many states with voting machines that left no verifiable paper trail, and which were not given reliable clearance by a testing agency not on Diebold's payroll, should have been carefully investigated and reported by mainstream media. Given the enormity of the stakes for a democratic society, and given the debacle of 2000 in Florida, the media had a duty to scrupulously investigate and to keep Americans fully informed about anything that had potential to compromise their right to vote. Unfortunately, the parroting of official government and corporate officials, save for an occasional editorial, paid lip service to this duty.[23] From Fox and CNN to the *New York Times* and Clear Channel, getting the word out about a potential problem brewing for the upcoming election should have been given abundantly more coverage than the Scott Peterson, Kobe Bryant, or Michael Jackson stories, which instead clogged the mainstream news hole.

In the aftermath of the 2004 presidential election, the media's duty to vigilantly pursue its role as fourth estate remains and may now be all the more urgent for the future survival of democracy in America. Hindsight is, of course, better than forethought. After the fact, the *New York Times* could not deny that it had fallen down on the job in its coverage of WMDs in Iraq. It remains to be seen whether its foresight will be improved in the challenges to democracy that lie ahead.

GOING ONLINE TO KEEP INFORMED:
CORPORATE MEDIA'S THREAT TO A FREE INTERNET

As the credibility gap of corporate media widens, it is small wonder that many Americans have sought out alternative sources of information besides mainstream TV, radio, and newspapers. Some have looked to the Internet as the answer to the problems of media consolidation with its growing number of alternative, independent news media sources with a Web presence such as *Mother Jones*, MediaChannel, and Salon.com.

In contrast to the more traditional communications conduits, the Internet involves communication from "the many" to "the many" since anyone with a Web site can be a media outlet. Such "open access" design of the Internet portends the prospect for a vibrant democratic media forum.

Unfortunately, corporations such as AOL/Time Warner and Comcast control the cables for delivery of broadband Internet and have, with FCC backing, vigilantly resisted allowing "common carriage" across these pipes. This means that they seek to bar competing Internet service providers (ISPs) from providing services through these cables. This is like a private company owning the interstate and not permitting other companies to transport their products on the highway. The impending danger is that the Internet will be transformed into yet another conduit of the politico-corporate media establishment. As the ACLU's Barry Steinhardt and Jay Stanley suggest, "when a handful of corporations control access to the Internet, and have the technical means to interfere with the free flow of information, they will do so. That is the case not only because they can make money . . . but also, potentially, because they have a political interest in certain issues or candidates, or because they have an interest in pleasing particular government officials who, for example, may have the power to decide regulatory proceedings affecting the company."[24]

Activist organizations such as the Center for Digital Democracy have attempted to get the word out to the public about this impending danger through their Web sites. The center's site contains an abundance of information on the broadband problem, and it is regularly updated. Fairness and Accuracy in Reporting (FAIR) provides Web-based investigative reporting aimed at scrutinizing and exposing media practices that jeopardize the public interest.

E-activist organizations such as the Free Press have worked diligently to enlist citizens in writing letters to their congresspersons to halt the spread of media consolidation, and there is a grassroots movement in America that is ever increasing. Its constituents are American citizens first; some are political conservatives; some are on the Left; some are Republicans and some Democrats. Groups as diverse as the National Organization for Women (NOW) and the National Rifle Association (NRA) have landed on the same side of the debate. In September 2003, the US Senate passed, with overwhelming bipartisan support, a "resolution of disapproval" to nullify the new relaxed FCC rules.[25] But the proportion of political conservatives and liberals, Republicans or Democrats, who have signed on is hardly the issue. Media consolidation is first and foremost a danger to the First Amendment right to freedom of speech—which is bereft of significance if speech is uninformed or worse, misinformed—and to the survival of democracy in America. The NRA fears that "gun-hating media giants like AOL/Time Warner, Viacom/CBS, and Disney/ABC could literally silence your NRA and prevent us from communicating with your fellow Americans by refusing to sell us television, radio, or newspaper advertising at any price."[26] NOW president Kim Gandy asks, "How will women learn about issues important to them if the media chooses to ignore those issues? Media democracy is crucial to the feminist and civil rights movements."[27] Americans of such diverse ideological perspectives agree on one thing: that an informed citizenry is crucial to the stability of a democracy, and that the increasing trend toward media consolidation undermines this essential condition.

THE POLITICO-CORPORATE MEDIA WEB: A VAST NETWORK OF CONFLICTING INTERESTS

Unfortunately, in just the past few years, corporate mergers have produced some of the most colossal alliances in media history, with mergers in such industries as cable, broadband (high-speed Internet conductivity), TV satellite, newspaper, and radio. In 2000, the merger of AOL, the world's largest Internet service provider, with Time Warner, a giant media conglomerate with massive cable holdings, gave the emerging company leverage over both content and conduit of broadband Internet and cable television. In 2000, the Times Mirror Co. and the Tribune Co. also merged, making it the third-largest newspaper in the nation with newspaper/television combinations in several major markets, including New York City and Los Angeles. In 2002, the merger of the two giant cable companies, AT&T and Comcast, created a corporate cable giant with the capacity to control the pipes for both cable TV and broadband Internet markets. In 2003, News Corporation (Fox) acquired General Motors' DirecTV, a system of direct broadcast satellites (DBS), which made it the gatekeeper for satellite television. In 2003 General Electric signed an agreement with Vivendi Universal to acquire its nonmusic assets, including its cable networks and Universal Pictures. In six years, Texas-based Clear Channel, the nation's largest radio station owner, has gone from owning just forty-four radio stations to a network of over twelve hundred. While these corporate players are in a constant state of flux—constantly merging and emerging—the one thing that has remained the same is the steady concentration of the awesome power of media in the hands of an ever-diminishing number of elite, profit-driven, private corporations.

The major media companies also have numerous other media holdings, from the world's largest music and publishing companies to movie production/distribution giants. For example, News Corporation owns HarperCollins Publishers, the *Weekly Standard*, and 20th Century Fox. Viacom owns Simon & Schuster, Paramount Pictures, and Blockbuster Video. Time Warner owns *Time* magazine, Warner Brothers (Television, Distribution, Theatres, and Music Group), and Castle Rock Entertainment.

In addition, these companies form an interlocking network with themselves, other giant corporations, and the US government. For example, General Electric, parent company of NBC, has seventeen direct corporate links to nine of the top ten media corporations.[28] General Electric is also one of the world's largest producers of jet engines and supplies Boeing, Lockheed Martin, and other military aircraft makers. Microsoft, co-owner with General Electric, of MSNBC, has a government division aimed at procurement of lucrative government contracts. Corporate media with twenty-four-hour news shows such as MSNBC, CNN, and Fox rely heavily on inside official government sources for an ongoing, steady stream of "inside information"—spun to the beat of the prevailing administration—to fill up their vast news holes. And these media companies are not willing to jeopardize their symbiotic relationships with the federal government.[29] Corporate media spend millions on lobbying in Congress and in the halls of regulatory agencies such as the FCC, and have been known to take government officials, including congresspersons and FCC employees, on all-expense-paid trips to meet with corporate media executives to discuss legislation and policy preferences.[30] As a result of this intricate politico-corporate media web, the "news" that Americans receive is largely a contrivance of favor trading, conflict of interest, and self-serving bottom-line corporate interests.

THE NEW FCC RULES:
MORE DEREGULATION, LESS DEMOCRACY

In June 2003, with the support of the Bush administration, the Federal Communications Commission (FCC), chaired by Michael Powell, opened the floodgate even wider for media consolidation by weakening the remaining regulations on media ownership. The new FCC rules let broadcast networks such as Fox and ABC own TV stations reaching 45 percent of the national market, a 10 percent increase from the earlier rule. They also let a single company own up to three TV stations in the largest cities, and, in all but the smallest markets, a company could have "cross-ownership" of both a newspaper and a radio or television station in the same city.

The earlier FCC rules had banned cross-ownership of broadcast and print media in the same market. They also permitted a broadcaster to own up to two stations in a single market if they are not large stations and there are at least eight other competitors. Under the leadership of Chairman Powell, the FCC revoked these regulations, replacing them with rules consistent with substantially increased media concentration and control.

The new FCC rules quickly came under fire by media activist organizations working through the courts. In August 2003, the Media Access Project (MAP), consisting of a skilled team of civil rights lawyers, acted on behalf of its client, Prometheus Radio Project, to challenge the new FCC rules in the Third US Circuit Court of Appeals in Philadelphia. MAP/Prometheus succeeded in getting the court to issue a stay on the new rules.[31]

In November 2003, amidst public outcry from millions of Americans petitioning lawmakers on Capital Hill to stop the new FCC rules from taking effect, the White House slipped a rider into a larger congressional bill, thereby rolling back the national broadcast cap from 45 percent to 39 percent, up 4 percent from the prior 35 percent cap. While this showed the power of American citizens to have their collective voices heard in Washington, the significance of this accommodation to the FCC rules was still largely symbolic.[32]

Congress's rollback of the national broadcasting cap to 39 percent was set at a percentage that would permit Viacom (CBS) and News Corp (Fox) to keep their current holdings. Both of these companies had already been operating above the earlier 35 percent cap and just under the new 39 percent in anticipation that the FCC or Congress would change the rules to make their illegal acquisitions legal. Moreover, this new legislation allows a company to violate the 39 percent broadcast cap without penalty for up to two years, which, once again, gives the company time to acquire new holdings above the national cap and to lobby for further FCC or legislative changes to raise the bar.

Not only does the new legislation provide a loophole for companies like Viacom and News Corporation to expand, other major media corporations operating substantially below the 39 percent cap, such as General Electric (NBC) and Disney (ABC), can also increase their holdings without violating the law. So this single legislative change still affords the major media corporations ample space to continue their campaign of acquisitions and mergers.

On June 24, 2004, the Third US Circuit Court of Appeals, which had issued the stay on the new FCC rules, acted in favor of the Prometheus Radio Project, sending these rules back to the commission to revisit. While the court did not deny the FCC's right to loosen existing regulations, it concluded that the present rules engendered an "arbitrary and capricious" bias toward deregulation, and it retained the stay until such time that the FCC produced a set of rules that were more defensible.[33]

Unfortunately, the court upheld the FCC's authority to lift the ban on newspaper/broadcast cross-ownership; and, given Congress's prior act of raising the media ownership cap to 39 percent, the arbitrariness of the FCC's expanded ownership cap may have become largely a moot point. Moreover, the FCC still has the option of appealing the case to the US Supreme Court in the hope that it will hear it.

Nevertheless, the court's decision still poses a blow to corporate media's quest for greater power and control over public information. In the first round, the Powell FCC refused to hear the voices of public dissent, and it was taken to task for it. In the second round, the FCC has an opportunity to listen more attentively.

REFORMING THE MEDIA: GETTING THE WORD OUT

In response to the immanent threat to democracy posed by corporate media consolidation, this book explores, in detail, the economic, political, and legal factors igniting the current corporate media crisis. It identifies crucial constitutional challenges in the light of historically significant FCC rulings, congressional legislation, and technological advances. It reveals how media manipulates and distorts reality to satisfy its obsession with the bottom line. It exposes, through telling contemporary examples—such as embedded journalism in coverage of the Iraq War—precisely how the new forms of American politico-media censorship work to undermine an informed public. It identifies the corporate media dynamics that threaten the future of open access to the Internet. It shows how corporate media is stifling the creative community of actors, musicians, writers, producers, and directors. It reveals the deceptive, systematic use of the slogan "the liberal media" as a means of political control.

Not only does this book present, in detail, the depth of the corporate media crisis, it makes suggestions to remedy the crisis through structural changes in the ways diverse media currently operate. It discusses the role of independent, alternative news sources and community and publicly owned media in developing a progressive, democratic media forum. It offers new technological possibilities for revamping conventional media, for example, Reed Hundt's innovative proposal to adapt certain broadcast media to wireless broadband Internet for television. It provides criteria for promoting nondiscriminatory media geared toward meeting public interest obligations and toward fulfilling media's watchdog function. In this regard, Cheryl Leanza and Harold Feld offer criteria for the FCC to apply in revamping their media ownership rules, using the common carrier, open-access Internet as a model. From a consumer's perspective, it gives guidance on how to best keep informed amid the current corporate media crisis. The proposals this book offers take into account current economic, legal, technological, and political realities. They come from individuals who work in the trenches and who are therefore sensitive to the obstacles that must be overcome.

In the end, accomplishing much of this needed reform will depend upon how vigilant we, the viewing public, are about the corporate media control of information. Complacency as opposed to protest can only assist in the selling out of American democracy. On the other hand, as Jay Harris suggests, the power of the public resides in its ability to seek news through alternative media sources. Without an audience, the corporate media cannot survive any more than can a parasite without a host.

THE TRUE MEDIA GIANTS AREN'T INCORPORATED

This book brings together, under one roof, contributions from many of the heroes of the media consolidation–opposition movement who through media activism, investigative reporting, and media criticism have courageously stood against the politico-corporate media establishment. Journalist Arthur Kent did not bow to corporate media pressures when, in 1992, he sacrificed his job at NBC's *Dateline* to protest NBC's manipulation of news in order to maximize its profit. Nor did Jay Harris, publisher of *Mother Jones*, when, in

1991, he resigned as publisher of the *San Jose Mercury News* to protest budget cuts by its parent company, Knight Ridder. Pete Tridish (pronounced "Petri dish," the name he acquired during his days as a radio pirate), founder of the Prometheus Radio Project, has devoted his life to traveling the nation and the world setting up community-based, low-power FM stations (LPFM), often without pay, in order to advance the cause of a more democratic media. Former FCC chair Reed Hundt did not mince words when he recently went on record calling the Powell commission's stance "the most radical view of media consolidation that any democracy has ever supported . . . exclusively driven by ideology and business interests." When Mark Cooper, research director of the Consumer Federation of America, the nation's largest consumer advocacy group, petitioned the FCC to block the merger of AOL and Time Warner unless it conducted its cable business without discrimination, his goal was to defend open access to the Internet.

In editing this book, I have taken great pains to commission authors who have earned their distinction, not through fear of being branded unpatriotic by their politico-corporate commanders, but through their consistent and demonstrable dedication to freedom of speech and of the press. While the corporate media has lost its credibility for many Americans, my hope is that the torchbearers speaking in this book will be received in the spirit of their dedication to democracy, unfettered by the clouds of hypocrisy and fraud pervading today's mainstream media. For Americans who prize democracy, I hope this book will stand as a wake-up call to look carefully behind the superficial slogans of a free America and the stars and stripes strategically displayed on the TV monitor.

NOTES

1. Radio-Television News Directors Association (RTNDA), *Code of Ethics*, http://www.rtndf.org/ethics/coe.shtml (accessed May 1, 2004).

2. American Society of Newspaper Editors (ASNE), *Code of Ethics*, http://www.asne.org/kiosk/archive/principl.htm (accessed May 1, 2004).

3. Michael Davis and Andrew Stark, eds., *Conflict of Interest in the Professions* (New York: Oxford University Press, 2001).

4. Danny Schecter, chapter 6 in this volume.

5. "One Thing Is Crystal Clear: Clear Channel Is a Subsidiary of Bush, Inc.," *BuzzFlash.com*, April 18, 2003, http://www.buzzflash.com/analysis/03/04/18_clear.html (accessed April 22, 2004).

6. Len Hill, chapter 10 in this volume.

7. Janine Jackson, "Their Man in Washington: Big Media Have an Ally in New FCC Chair Michael Powell," *FAIR* (September–October 2001), http://www.fair.org/extra/0109/powell.html (accessed April 22, 2004).

8. Pratap Chatterjee, "Halliburton Makes Big Killing on Iraq War," *Alternet.org*, March 23, 2003, http://www.alternet.org/story.html?StoryID=15445 (accessed April 22, 2004).

9. Mark Cooper, chapter 8 in this volume.

10. Mathew Engle, "U.S. Media Cowed by Patriotic Fever, Says CBS Star," *Guardian*, September 17, 2002, http://www.guardian.co.uk/bush/story/0,7369,717097,00.html (accessed April 24, 2004).

11. http://www.mediawhoresonline.com/nonwhores.htm.

12. Sinclair Broadcast Group, "ABC Nightline Pre-emption," http://www.sbgi.net/.

13. Paul Schmeizer, "The Death of Local News," *AlterNet.org*, April 23, 2003, http://www.alternet.org/story.html?StoryID=15718 (accessed April 30, 2004).

14. "TV Group to Show Anti-Kerry Film on 62 Stations," *New York Times*, October 11, 2004.

15. "Sinclair Won't Air Full Anti-Kerry Film," *Morning Edition*, October 20, 2004.

16. RTNDA, *Code of Ethics.*

17. Ibid., my italics.

18. Wes Vernon, "Sinclair, The Next Fox, 'Fair and Balanced'," *NewsMax.com*, January 29, 2004, http://www.newsmax.com/archives/articles/2004/1/28/150537.shtml (accessed May 1, 2004).

19. John Stuart Mill, "On Liberty," in *Philosophical Issues in Journalism*, ed. Elliot D. Cohen (New York: Oxford University Press, 1994).

20. "A Pause for Hindsight," *New York Times*, July 16, 2004, http://www.commondreams.org/views04/0716-15.htm (accessed November 28, 2004).

21. "Who Tests Voting Machines?" *New York Times*, May 30, 2004, http://www.nytimes.com/2004/05/30/opinion/30SUN1.html (accessed November 5, 2004).

22. Bob Fritrakis and Harvey Wasserman, "Diebold's Political Machine," *MotherJones.com*, http://www.motherjones.com/commentary/columns/2004/03/03_200.html (accessed November 5, 2004).

23. Paul Krugman, "Hack the Vote," *New York Times*, December 2, 2003, http://www.nytimes.com/2003/12/02/opinion/02KRUG.html (accessed November 5, 2004).

24. Steinhardt and Stanley, chapter 11 in this volume.

25. "Media Regulation Timeline," *NOW with Bill Moyers*, January 30, 2004, http://www.pbs.org/now/politics/mediatimelineupdate.html (accessed April 20, 2004).

26. "Gun Foes on Same Side in FCC Media Fight," *Join Together Online*, June 2, 2003, http://www.jointogether.org/gv/news/summaries/reader/0,2061,563555,00.html (accessed April 22, 2004).

27. Lisa Bennett-Haigney, "Will the Media Merger Free-for-All Extinguish

Women's Voices?" *National NOW Times* (Fall 2001), http://www.now.org/nnt/fall-2001/mediamerger.html (accessed April 22, 2004).

28. Peter Phillips, chapter 1 in this volume.

29. Peter Phillips and Jay Harris, chapters 1 and 3, respectively, in this volume.

30. *Off the Record: What Media Corporations Don't tell You about Their Legislative Agendas* (Washington, DC: Center for Public Integrity, 2000), http://www.public-i.org/dtaweb/downloads/otr.pdf (accessed April 21, 2004).

31. For information and updates on the status of this case, *Prometheus Radio Project v. FCC*, see MAP's Web site, http://www.mediaaccess.org.

32. See the Free Press's update on "Media Ownership Rules," http://www.mediareform.net/rules/ (accessed April 24, 2004).

33. "Court Orders Rethinking of Rules Allowing Large Media to Expand," *New York Times*, June 25, 2004. For information and updates on the status of this case, see MAP's Web site, http://www.mediaaccess.org.

POSTSCRIPT: POWELL LEGACY

The authors of this book speak collectively to a national crisis, the very survival of democracy itself. Without a vigilant press to keep us informed about affairs of state, we are divested of our freedom. Whether mainstream media will eventually respond to this vital need depends on many factors broached in this book, not the least of which is the determination of the American people. When FCC chair Michael Powell refused to listen to the collective voice of many Americans, this voice only grew louder. In the midst of this growing opposition, Powell has resigned, leaving it to his successor to carry the torch. The legacy of Powell, if nothing else, is that the voice of the American people cannot be ignored. The new FCC chair would do well to take this lesson seriously. There is now a new opportunity for Americans to once again decry the threat to democracy posed by the corporate media, and for the new FCC to listen.

Elliot Cohen
January 25, 2004

I

CENSORSHIP

How News Has Become Largely a Paid Political Announcement and What Consumers Can Do about It

1

BEYOND THE
NEW AMERICAN CENSORSHIP

PETER PHILLIPS
PROJECT CENSORED

PETER PHILLIPS, *professor and chair of sociology at Sonoma State University, is director of Project Censored, an investigative sociology and media analysis project dedicated to the freedom of information throughout the United States. In his work with Project Censored, he has published seven editions of* Censored: Media Democracy in Action *(Seven Stories Press) and the* Project Censored Guide to Independent Media and Activism 2003 *(Seven Stories Press). The national and international news editor of the* North Bay Progressive *newspaper in Santa Rosa, California, he also writes op-ed pieces for independent media nationwide, including Z maga-zine,* Counterpunch, Common Dreams, Social Policy, *and* Briarpatch, *and frequently speaks on media censorship and various sociopolitical issues on radio and TV talks shows, including* Talk of the Nation, Public Interest, Talk America, World Radio Network, Democracy Now!, *and the* Jim Hightower Show.

An earlier version of this article appears in Peter Phillips, *Censored 2005: The Top 25 Censored Stories* (New York: Seven Stories Press, 2005). Reprinted by permission of the publisher.

Election 2004 was a serious test of democracy in the United States. Perhaps we failed the test. At no other time since the 1930s have we been so dangerously close to institutionalized totalitarianism. No-fly lists, prison torture, domestic spying, mega–homeland security agencies, suspension of habeas corpus, global unilateralism, and military adventurism interlocked with corporate profit taking are all spurred on by a media-induced citizen paranoia.

Corporate media is in the entertainment business and fails to cover important news stories voters need to make election decisions. We need information about our country's leaders. These are the people making decisions that impact all of our lives. We need to know who our leaders are and what they are doing. What are their backgrounds, their motivations? What policies and laws are they enacting? What actions are they undertaking, with or without our consent? We don't need to like them, but we do need to know about them. A participatory democracy needs people to be aware of issues in order to have active, engaged voters.

The real winners on November 2, 2004, were the military-industrial complex, which will continue to feed at the five-hundred-billion-dollar military trough, and the corporate media, whose coffers were filled with billions of dollars for campaign ads. And can we be sure we actually had a fair election among those who did vote? Election Systems & Software (ES&S), Diebold, and Sequoia are the companies primarily involved in implementing the new voting stations throughout the country. All three have strong ties to the Bush administration. The largest investors in ES&S, Diebold, and Sequoia are government defense contractors Northrup-Grumman, Lockheed-Martin, Electronic Data Systems (EDS), and Accenture. Diebold hired Scientific Applications International Corporation (SAIC) of San Diego to develop the software security in its voting machines. A majority of officials on SAIC's board are former members of either the Pentagon or the CIA, including:[1]

- Army Gen. Wayne Downing, formerly on the National Security Council
- Bobby Ray Inman, former CIA director
- Retired Adm. William Owens, former vice chairman of the Joint Chiefs of Staff
- Robert Gates, another former director of the CIA

Might the fifty million voters who cast their ballots on electronic voting machines be concerned that the major investors in the voting machine companies are some of the top defense contractors in the United States and that the firm that developed the security software for electronic voting is made up of former CIA and NSA directors? They will never know unless the mass corporate media tells them.

Might many Americans be more willing to vote if they knew that a conservative right-wing organization has replaced the American Bar Association as the main vetting group for federal judge appointments? Or would there be concern for our returning military vets if it were widely known that many are permanently contaminated with high levels of radioactive depleted uranium (DU)? Might this concern increase among young people if they knew the extent of government plans to reinstate the military draft in the United States?

These news stories and hundreds like them are ignored or dismissed by the corporate media in the United States. The First Amendment of the US Constitution, guaranteeing freedom of the press, was established to maximize citizen cognition of critical issues in society. It was clearly perceived by the founders that democracy could only be maintained through an informed electorate.

A daily newspaper, along with the three major TV networks—ABC, CBS, and NBC, as well as CNN, MSNBC, and Fox—are the major sources of news and information for most Americans. News stories and the invidious entertainment segments from these corporate sources generally have similar themes and common frames of understanding. This concentration of access to media sources leaves most Americans with very narrow parameters of news awareness and an almost complete lack of competing opinions.

Democracy in the United States is only a shadow in a corporate media cave of deceit, lies, and incomplete information. We stand ignorant of what the powerful are doing in our name and how the corporate media ignores key issues affecting us all.

Democracy is the people making decisions about the important issues in their lives. Freedom is the ability to act on these decisions. Without an electoral choice, democracy is nonexistent and freedom only means the right to choose your own brand of toothpaste. Without an active independent media informing on the powerful, we lack both freedom and democracy.

The corporate media agenda of maximum profits undermines the public purpose of a free press by creating the fiscal necessity for cutting costs and increasing the entertainment content. Ratings and audience share translate to higher advertising value and higher profits. This structural arrangement of corporate media results in what Robert McChesney calls rich media, poor democracy.[2]

The United States is involved in global empire building at a level about which most people in the country are uninformed. The United States intervenes daily in the internal affairs of other countries around the world and the corporate media seldom report on our activities.

On February 29, 2004, Richard Boucher from the US Department of State released a press report claiming that Jean-Bertrand Aristide had resigned as president of Haiti and that the United States facilitated his safe departure. Within hours the major broadcast news stations in the United States, including CNN, Fox, ABC, NBC, CBS, and NPR, were reporting that Aristide had fled Haiti. An Associated Press release that evening said, "Aristide resigns, flees into exile." The next day headlines in the major newspapers across the country, including the *Washington Post*, *USA Today*, *New York Times*, and *Atlanta Journal Constitution*, all announced, "Aristide Flees Haiti." The *Baltimore Sun* reported, "Haiti's first democratically elected president was forced to flee his country yesterday like despots before him."

However on Sunday afternoon, February 29, Dennis Bernstein with Pacifica News Network was interviewing reporters live in Port-au-Prince, Haiti, who were claiming that Aristide was forced to resign by the United States and taken out of the presidential palace by armed US marines. On Monday morning Amy Goodman with *Democracy Now!* news show interviewed Congresswoman Maxine Waters. Waters said she had received a phone call from Aristide at 9:00 AM EST, March 1, in which Aristide emphatically denied that he had resigned and said that he had been kidnapped by US and French forces. Aristide made calls to others, including TransAfrica founder Randall Robinson, who verified Congresswoman Waters's report.

With this situation, mainstream corporate media was faced with a dilemma. Confirmed contradictions to headlined reports were being openly revealed to hundreds of thousands of Pacifica listeners nationwide. By Monday afternoon, March 1, mainstream corporate media began to respond to charges. Tom Brokaw on NBC *Nightly News* voiced, "Haiti in crisis. Armed rebels sweep into the capital as Aristide claims US troops kidnapped him; forced him out. The US calls that nonsense." Brit Hume with Fox News Network reported Colin Powell's comments: "He was not kidnapped. We did not force him on to the airplane. He went on to the airplane willingly, and that's the truth." Mort Kondracke, executive editor of *Roll Call* (the Capitol Hill newspaper) added, "Aristide, . . . was a thug and a leader of thugs and ran his country into the ground." The *New York Times* in a story buried on page 10 reported that "President Jean-Bertrand Aristide asserted Monday that he had been driven from power in Haiti by the United States in 'a coup,' an allegation dismissed by the White House as 'complete nonsense.'"

Still, mainstream/corporate media had a credibility problem. Their original story was openly contradicted. The kidnap story could be ignored or back-paged as was done by many newspapers in the United States. Or it could be framed within the context of a US denial and dismissed. Unfortunately, the corporate media seemed not at all interested in conducting an investigation into the charges, seeking witnesses, or verifying contradictions. Nor was the mainstream media asking or answering the question of why they fully accepted the State Department's version of the coup in the first place. Corporate media certainly had enough prewarning to determine that Aristide was not going to willingly leave the country. Aristide had been saying exactly that for the past month during the armed attacks in the north of Haiti. When Aristide was interviewed on CNN on February 26, he explained that the terrorists and criminal drug dealers were former members of the Front for the Advancement and Progress of Haiti (FRAPH), which had led the coup in 1991, killing five thousand people. Aristide believed they would kill even more people if a coup was allowed to happen. It was also well known in media circles that the US undersecretary of state for Latin America, Roger Noriega, had been senior aide to former senator Jesse Helms, who as chairman of the Senate Foreign Affairs Committee was a longtime backer of Haitian dictator Jean-Claude Duvalier and an opponent of Aristide. These facts alone should have been a red flag regarding the State Department's version of Aristide's departure. Weeks later most news stories on Haiti published in the United States still claimed that Aristide "fled" Haiti while reporting the ongoing civil unrest in the country.

The corporate media's recent coverage of Haiti is an example of how the new American censorship works. If news stories contradict the official sources of news, they tend to be downplayed or ignored. Corporate/mainstream media has become dependent upon the press releases and inside sources from government and major corporations for their twenty-four-hour news content and are increasingly unwilling to broadcast or publish news that would threaten ongoing relationships with official sources.

This means that freedom of information and citizen access to objective news is fading in the United States. In its place is a complex entertainment-oriented news system, which protects its own bottom line by servicing the most powerful military-industrial complex in the world. Corporate media today is interlocked and dependent on government sources for news content. Gone are the days of deep investigative reporting teams challenging the powerful. Media consolidation has downsized newsrooms to the point where reporters serve more as stenographers than as researchers.[3]

The twenty-four-hour news shows on MSNBC, Fox, and CNN are closely interconnected with various governmental and corporate sources of news. Maintenance of continuous news shows requires a constant feed and an ever-entertaining supply of stimulating events and breaking news bites. Advertisement for mass consumption drives the system, and prepackaged sources of news are vital within this global news process. Ratings demand continued cooperation from multiple sources for ongoing weather reports, war stories, sports scores, business news, and regional headlines. Print, radio, and TV news also engage in this constant interchange with news sources.

The preparation for and following of ongoing wars and terrorism fits well into the visual kaleidoscope of preplanned news. Government public relations specialists and media experts from private commercial interests provide ongoing news feeds to the national media distribution systems. The result is an emerging macrosymbiotic relationship between news dispensers and news suppliers. Perfect examples of this relationship are the Iraq War press pools organized by the Pentagon both in the Middle East and in Washington, DC, which give prescheduled reports on the war to selected groups of news collectors (journalists) for distribution through their respective corporate media organizations. The Pentagon's management of the news has become increasingly sophisticated with restrictions and controls being cumulatively added to each new military action or invasion in which the United States is involved.[4]

During the Iraq War, embedded reporters (news collectors) working directly with military units in the field were required to maintain cooperative working relationships with unit commanders as they fed breaking news back to the US public. Cooperative reporting was vital to continued access to government news sources. In addition, rows of news story reviewers back at corporate media headquarters were used to rewrite, soften, or spike news stories from the field that threatened the symbiotics of global news management or might be perceived by the Pentagon as too critical.

Journalists working outside of this approved mass media system faced ever-increasing dangers from "accidents" of war and corporate-media dismissal of their news reports. Massive civilian casualties caused by US troops, extensive damage to private homes and businesses, and reports that contradict the official public relations line were downplayed, deleted, or ignored by corporate media, while content was analyzed by experts (retired generals and other approved collaborators) from within the symbiotic global news structure.

Symbiotic global news distribution is a conscious and deliberate attempt by the powerful to control news and information in society. It is the overt

manifestation of censorship in our society. The Homeland Security Act, Title
II Section 201(d)(5), specifically asks the directorate to "develop a comprehensive plan for securing the key resources and critical infrastructure of the
United States including . . . information technology and telecommunications
systems (including satellites) . . . [and] emergency preparedness communications systems." Corporate media's cooperation with these directives insures
an ongoing transition to inevitably tighter controls over news content in the
United States. From a Homeland Security agency perspective, total information control would be the ideal state of maximized security for the media systems in the United States.

Corporate media today is perhaps too vast to enforce complete control
over all content twenty-four hours a day. However, the government's goal
and many multinational corporations' desires are for the eventual opera-
tionalization of a highly controlled news system in the United States. The
degree to which corporate media is hastening moves in this direction is
directly related to the high-level embeddedness of the media elite within the
corporate power structure in the United States.

This new American censorship is facilitated by the continuing consolidation of the corporate media. Since the passage of the Telecommunications
Act of 1996, a gold rush of media mergers and takeovers has been occurring
in the United States. Over half of all radio stations have been sold in the past
eight years, and the repeatedly merged AOL/Time Warner (CNN) is the
largest media organization in the world. Less than a handful of major media
corporations now dominate the US news and information systems. Clear
Channel owns over twelve hundred radio stations. Ninety-eight percent of all
cities have only one daily newspaper and huge chains like Gannett and
Knight Ridder increasingly own these.[5]

Media corporations have been undergoing a massive merging and
buyout process that is realigning the sources of information in America. Conglomeration changes traditional media corporate cultures. Values such as
freedom of information and belief in the responsibility of keeping the public
informed are adjusted to reflect policies created by bottom-line-oriented
CEOs. These structural arrangements facilitate the new censorship in America today. It is not yet deliberate killing of stories by official censors, but a
rather subtle system of information suppression in the name of corporate
profit and self-interest.

The big corporations that now dominate media in America are princi-
pally in the entertainment business. The corporate media is narrowing its
content with news reports often looking very much the same. Between media

consolidation, the primacy of bottom-line considerations, and the ignoring of important but complex political issues, it is now believed that Americans are the most entertained, least informed people in the world.[6]

Media owners and managers are economically motivated to please advertisers and upper-middle-class readers and viewers. Journalists and editors are not immune to management influence. Journalists want to see their stories approved for print or broadcast, and editors come to know the limits of their freedom to diverge from the bottom-line view of owners and managers. The results are an expansion of entertainment news, infomercials, and synergistic news all aimed at increased profit taking.

Corporate media are multinational corporations in their own right, with all the vested interests in free-market capitalism and top-down control of society. In 1997 the eleven largest or most influential media corporations in the United States were General Electric Company (NBC), Viacom Inc. (cable), the Walt Disney Company (ABC), Time Warner Inc. (CNN), Westinghouse Electric Corporation (CBS), the News Corporation Ltd. (Fox), Gannett Co. Inc., Knight Ridder Inc., New York Times Co., Washington Post Co., and the Times Mirror Co. Collectively, these eleven major media corporations had 155 directors in 1996. These 155 directors also held 144 directorships on the boards of Fortune 1,000 corporations in the United States. These eleven media organizations have interlocking directorships with each other through thirty-six other Fortune 1,000 corporations creating a solid network of overlapping interests and affiliations. All eleven media corporations have direct links with at least two of the other top media organizations. General Electric, owner of NBC, has the highest rate of shared affiliations with seventeen direct corporate links to nine of the ten other media corporations.[7]

These directors are the media elite of the world. While they may not agree on abortion and other domestic issues, they do represent the collective vested interests of a significant portion of corporate America and share a common commitment to free-market capitalism, economic growth, internationally protected copyrights, and a government dedicated to protecting their interests.

Given this interlocked media network, it is more than safe to say that major media in the United States effectively represent the interests of corporate America, and that the media elite are the watchdogs of acceptable ideological messages, parameters of news content, and general use of media resources.

Corporate media promote free-market capitalism as the unquestioned American ideological truth. The decline of communism opened the door for unrestrained free-marketers to boldly espouse market competition as the final solution for global harmony. Accordingly, corporate media have become the

mouthpiece of free-market ideology by uncritically supporting the underlying assumption that the marketplace will solve all evils and that we will
enjoy economic expansion, individual freedom, and unlimited bliss by fully
deregulating and privatizing society's socioeconomic institutions.

The corporate media have been fully supportive of the US policy of
undermining socialist- or nationalist-leaning governments and pressuring
them into ideological compliance. The full force of US-dominated global
institutions—WTO, World Bank, IMF, and NAFTA—focus on maximizing
free-market circumstances and corporate access to every region of the world.
Economic safety nets, environmental regulations, labor unions, and human
rights take second place to the free flow of capital and investments. The corporate media elites are in the forefront of this global capital movement with
an unrelenting propaganda agenda that gives lip service to democracy while
refusing to address the contradictions and hypocrisies of US global policies.

A closer examination of this American media–supported ideology
reveals that "free market" essentially means constant international US government intervention on behalf of American corporations. This public-private
partnership utilizes US embassies, the CIA, FBI, NSA, US military, Department of Commerce, USAID, and every other US government institution to
protect, sustain, and directly support our vital interest—US business.

This ideological mantra affects the US population as well. We are still
riding on the betterments from the first three quarters of the twentieth century
and have not faced the full impacts of the economic bifurcation that has
occurred in the past thirty years. Poverty levels are rising, the numbers of
working poor expanding, and homelessness one pay check away for many. In
the last quarter century economic conditions have declined for the bottom sixty
million Americans, and most of the next one hundred million have barely held
their own, while the corporate and media elites have socked away fortunes.[8]

In the past few years, corporate media outlets, under pressure from powerful corporate/government officials, have fired or disciplined journalists for
writing critical stories about the powerful in the United States. These termi-
nations have sent a chilling message to journalists throughout the United
States: if you attack the sacred cows of powerful corporate/governmental
institutions, your career is on the line. Journalists who fail to recognize their
role as cooperative news collectors are disciplined in the field or barred from
reporting, as in the Second Iraq War celebrity cases of Geraldo Rivera and
Peter Arnett.

In a well-known case of pressure by powerful institutions, Fox TV news
reporters Steve Wilson and Jane Akre were fired by WTVT in Tampa for

refusing to change their story on the dangers of Monsanto's bovine growth hormone (rBGH) in the Florida milk supply. Scientific research has shown that rBGH, when injected into cows to expand milk production, results in the increase of the insulin-like growth factor IGF-I in milk. IGF-I has been linked to breast and prostate cancer. Monsanto claims that the milk is safe, but new scientific evidence suggests otherwise. Monsanto put pressure on Fox Television in New York, WTVT's parent company, threatening dire consequences if the story ran. When Wilson and Akre refused to say the milk was unchanged, they were fired by the Fox station general manager, who was quoted as saying, "We paid $3 billion for these stations: we'll decide what the news is. The news is what we tell you it is."[9]

Perhaps the most infamous case of media willingly succumbing to external pressures by the government is the retraction by CNN of the story about the US military's use of sarin gas in 1970 in Laos during the Vietnam War. CNN producers April Oliver and Jack Smith, after an eight-month investigation, reported on CNN on June 7, 1998, and later in *Time* magazine that sarin gas was used in operation Tailwind in Laos and that American defectors were targeted. The story was based on eyewitness accounts and high military command collaboration.

Under tremendous pressure from the Pentagon, Henry Kissinger, Colin Powell, and Richard Helms, CNN and *Time* retracted the story, saying that "the allegations about the use of nerve gas and the killing of defectors are not supported by the evidence," and fired Oliver and Smith. Columnists and pundits across the nation attacked Oliver and Smith for their alleged unprofessional journalism. *Newsweek* even wrote on July 20, 1998, that the allegations were "proven wrong." Oliver and Smith have steadfastly stood by their original story as accurate and substantiated. What is troubling about this issue is the speed with which CNN/*Time* withdrew their support for Oliver and Smith, after having fully approved the release of the story only weeks before.

Tailwind can perhaps best be understood in the context of the new Vietnam War revelations published in the *Toledo Blade* in October 2003[10] and widely ignored by the corporate media. The *Toledo Blade* story discloses the unrestricted savaging of hundreds of civilians in the Central Highlands by an elite American Tiger Force during a several-month period in 1967. This free-fire force was given authority to massacre at will anyone found in the region. Newly available government documents disclose how an army war crimes investigation in 1971 encouraged solders to keep quiet and how the case was closed in 1975.

The eight-month investigation by Michael Sallah, Joe Mahr, and Mitch

Weiss for the *Toledo Blade* is similar to the investigation of the Tailwind story by CNN reporters April Oliver and Jack Smith in 1997–1998. Both stories reveal deadly illegal war crimes by US forces in Southeast Asia, both stories were covered up by higher authorities in the Pentagon, and both stories challenge the fictionalized storyline of average GIs caught up in a lousy misunderstood war, who in isolated incidents made low-level field decisions that resulted in My Lai–type mistakes. The Tailwind and Tiger Force stories reveal much higher-level policies of a vicious win-at-any-cost war officiated by Pentagon and high-level government officials. It is the revelation of these policies that the Pentagon seems strongly motivated to suppress.

For the Tailwind story, April Oliver and Jack Smith conducted an eight-month investigation into the use of sarin gas in Laos during the Vietnam War. As Oliver states in *Censored 1999*,[11] "We stand by the story. We are not novices at news-gathering. . . . The Tailwind story was carefully researched and reported over eight months, with our bosses' [CNN] approval of each interview request and each line of the story's script. It was based on multiple sources, [six eyewitnesses] from senior military officials to firsthand participants . . . in addition to half a dozen on-camera sources more than a dozen pilots told us of the availability or use of a special 'last resort' gas . . . gb (the military name for sarin), or cbu-15 (a sarin cluster bomb)."

After the airing of the Tailwind story in June of 1998, CNN came under a firestorm of pressure from the Pentagon, veteran groups, and other media to retract the story. CNN president Rick Kaplan told Oliver and Smith that CNN did not want to end up in congressional hearings across from Colin Powell and that the story had become a "public relations problem." A CNN investigation into Oliver and Smith's story by attorney Floyd Abrams and CNN's vice president David Kohler resulted in a recommendation for retraction, claiming that the evidence did not support the use of sarin gas. On July 10, 1998, Ted Turner made a public apology for airing the Tailwind story before the Television Critics Association. Oliver and Smith were fired and CNN retracted the story.

Anyone who actually reads CNN's investigative report can see the overwhelming evidence that supports the original version of the story.[12] However, the CNN report uses a new standard of absolute proof by saying that the ability to stand up in a court of law is the criterion for airing stories. Such a standard, if enforced, would essentially eliminate investigative journalism, and stories like Watergate would never have been published. It is the responsibility of media to stand firm on solid evidence and tell the truth about important social issues, but it is not journalistically feasible to research each story as if it were to be presented in a court of law. The fact that CNN failed to uphold a commitment to the First Amendment speaks more about the symbiotic relationship between corporate media and sources of news than it does about erroneous reporting.

Oliver eventually won a large settlement from her lawsuit for wrongful termination. Numerous media critics including Fairness and Accuracy in Reporting, Alexander Cockburn, Project Censored, *Democracy Now!*, and MediaChannel reported her side of the story, including how CNN caved in to pressure from the Pentagon.[13] CNN officials clearly understood that they might not be invited to the next war unless a retraction occurred. CNN faced more than a public relations problem; they faced a bottom-line profitability problem if they were refused access to military cooperation on future broadcasts. Kohler and Turner knew full well the necessity of cooperation with official sources.

Corporate media has also ignored many important questions related to 9/11, which would offend their sources of news in the government. Corporate news star Dan Rather in an interview with Matthew Engel for the *Guardian* admitted that the surge of patriotism after 9/11 resulted in journalists failing to ask the tough questions. Rather stated, "It starts with a feeling of patriotism within oneself. I know the right question, but you know what? This is not exactly the right time to ask it."[14]

When was the right time to question the levels and intensity of civilian deaths during and after the bombings of Afghanistan? According to CNN chairman Walter Isaacson there was never a good time. In a memo to his CNN correspondents overseas Isaacson wrote, "We're entering a period in which there's a lot more reporting and video from Taliban-controlled Afghanistan. You must make sure people [Americans] understand that when they see civilian suffering there, it's in the context of a terrorist attack that caused enormous suffering in the United States." Isaacson later told the *Washington Post*, "It seems perverse to focus too much on the causalities of hardship in Afghanistan." This is the same Walter Isaacson who, when assuming the chairmanship of CNN in August 2001, claimed that news needed to be redefined: "There would be a greater focus on entertainment, technology, health and fitness," he said. "The goal should be to make the news smart, but also fun and fascinating."[15]

Marc Herold, an economics professor at the University of New Hampshire, compiled a summation of the death toll in Afghanistan, concluding that over four thousand civilians died from US bombs—more than died at the World Trade Center. Yet only a handful of newspapers covered his story.

Time magazine reviewed Herold's report but dismissed it, stating, "In compiling the figures, Herold drew mostly on world press reports of questionable reliability." *Time* went on to cite the Pentagon's unsubstantiated claim that civilian casualties in Afghanistan were the lowest in the history of war.[16]

At times, the corporate media starts in on a story and realizes that it may lead into areas of concern to their sources of news. Numerous papers in the country including the *San Francisco Chronicle* on September 29, 2001, reported how millions of dollars were made buying pre-9/11 put-options on United and American Airlines stocks. Yet by mid-October nothing else was ever printed on the subject. The director of the Chicago office of the FBI, Tom Kneir, admitted on August 17, 2002, at the American Sociological Association annual meeting that the FBI conducted an investigation into the pre-9/11 stock options, but he refused to disclose who bought the stock, and the corporate media has never asked.

At times, the hypocrisy of corporate media news coverage is overwhelming. During the first week of December 2003, US corporate media reported that American forensic teams were working to document some forty-one mass graves in Iraq to support future war crime tribunals in that country. Broadly covered in the media as well was the conviction of Gen. Stanislav Galic by a UN tribunal for war crimes committed by Bosnian Serb troops under his command during the siege of Sarajevo in 1992–1994.

These stories show how corporate media likes to give the impression that the US government is working diligently to root out evildoers around the world and to build democracy and freedom. This theme is part of a core ideological message in support of our recent wars in Panama, Serbia, Afghanistan, and Iraq. Governmental spin transmitted by a willing US media establishes simplistic mythologies of good versus evil, often leaving out historical context, special transnational corporate interests, and prior strategic relationships with the dreaded evil ones.[17]

The hypocrisy of US policy and corporate media complicity is evident in the coverage of Donald Rumsfeld's stopover in Mazar-e Sharif, Afghanistan, on December 4, 2003, to meet with regional warlord and mass killer Gen. Abdul Rashid Dostum and his rival Gen. Ustad Atta Mohammed. Rumsfeld was there to finalize a deal with the warlords to begin the decommissioning of their military forces in exchange for millions of dollars in international aid and increased power in the central Afghan government.

Few people in the United States know that Gen. Abdul Rashid Dostum fought alongside the Russians in the 1980s, commanding a twenty-thousand-man army. He switched sides in 1992 and joined the mujahideen when they took power in Kabul. For over a decade, Dostum was a regional warlord in charge of six northern provinces, which he ran like a private fiefdom making millions by collecting taxes on regional trade and international drug sales. Forced into exile in Turkey by the Taliban in 1998, he came back into power as a military proxy of the United States during the invasion of Afghanistan.

Charged with mass murder of prisoners of war in the mid-1990s by the UN, Dostum is known to use torture and assassinations to retain power. Described by the *Chicago Sun Times* as a "cruel and cunning warlord,"[18] he is reported to use tanks to rip apart political opponents or crush them to death. Dostum, a seventh-grade dropout, likes to put up huge pictures of himself in the regions he controls, drinks Johnnie Walker Blue Label, and rides in an armor-plated Cadillac.

A documentary entitled *Massacre at Mazar*, released in 2002 by Scottish film producer Jamie Doran, exposes how Dostum, in cooperation with US special forces, was responsible for the torturing and deaths of approximately three thousand Taliban prisoners of war in November of 2001. In Doran's documentary, two witnesses report on camera how they were forced to drive into the desert with hundreds of Taliban prisoners held in sealed cargo containers. Most of the prisoners suffocated to death in the vans and Dostum's soldiers shot the few prisoners left alive. One witness told the London *Guardian* that a US Special Forces vehicle was parked at the scene as bulldozers buried the dead. A soldier told Doran that US troops masterminded a cover-up. He said the Americans ordered Dostum's people to get rid of the bodies before satellite pictures could be taken.

Dostum admits that a few hundred prisoners died, but asserts that it was a mistake or that they died from previous wounds. He has kept thousands of Taliban as prisoners of war since 2001 and continues to ransom them to their families for ten to twenty thousand dollars each.

Doran's documentary was shown widely in Europe, prompting an attempt by the UN to investigate, but Dostum has prevented any inspection by saying that he could not guarantee safety for forensic teams in the area.

During the recent meeting with Dostum, Donald Rumsfeld was quoted as saying, "I spent many weeks in the Pentagon following closely your activities, I should say your successful activities."[19] The *Post* reported that General Dostum was instrumental in routing Taliban forces from northern Afghanistan in the early weeks of the war two years ago, but said nothing about General Dostum's brutal past. Nor has US broadcast media aired Doran's documentary.

A number of other questions remain unasked and unresolved regarding events surrounding the 9/11 attacks. Both the BBC and the *Times of India* published reports several months before 9/11 that the United States was then planning an invasion of Afghanistan. The Unocal oil pipeline from the Caspian Sea region was to be built through Afghanistan and the United States needed a cooperative government in power. Agence France-Press in March 2002 reported that the US-installed interim leader of Afghanistan, Hamid Karzai, had worked with the CIA since the 1980s and was once a paid consultant for Unocal.

A report from France, still unacknowledged by the US press, reveals how the Bush administration, shortly after assuming office, slowed down FBI investigations of al Qaeda and terrorist networks in Afghanistan in order to deal with the Taliban on oil. The ordered slowdown resulted in the resignation of FBI deputy director John O'Neill, expert in the al Qaeda network and in charge of the investigation. O'Neill later took a job as chief of security at the World Trade Center where he died "helping with rescue efforts."[20]

An October 31, 2002, report in the French daily *Le Figaro* disclosed that Osama bin Laden had met with a top CIA official while in the American hospital in the United Arab Emirates to receive treatment for a kidney infection earlier that summer. CBS news reported on January 28, 2002, that Osama bin Laden was in a Pakistani military hospital on September 10, 2001.

On 9/11, four planes are hijacked and deviate from their flight plans, all the while on Federal Aviation Administration (FAA) radar. The planes are all hijacked between 7:45 and 8:10 AM Eastern time. It is a full hour before the first plane hits the World Trade Center. But it is an hour and twenty minutes later—after the second plane hits—that the president becomes officially informed. Then he gives no orders. He continues to listen to a student talk about her pet goat. It's another twenty-five minutes until he makes a statement.[21]

Because of corporate media's failure to investigate questions around 9/11, conspiracy theories abound in America. Corporate media chooses instead to offer mindless entertainment in place of deeper investigations into important national questions. The result is that the general public knows more about Winona Ryder's shoplifting trial and the Laci Peterson murder case than it does about the history of US involvement in Afghanistan and Iraq.

The First Amendment provides for freedom of the press and was established to protect our democratic process by guaranteeing an informed electorate. Yet we hold national elections in which millions of voters refuse to participate. We denigrate and blame nonvoters for being uncaring citizens, yet the corporate media has failed to address core issues affecting most people in this country. Voter participation levels are directly related to issues that the citizenry feels are important. Many people no longer trust the corporate media to provide the full truth. This opens people's susceptibility to believing in conspiracies and plots to explain unanswered questions. Cynicism has deterred voting for many.

How can we free ourselves from this dilemma? We can advocate strongly for corporate media to invest in democracy by supporting deep investigative reporting on key national issues. We can advocate for full and clear reporting on the policies and plans emerging from the public and private policy circles of the American corporate and governmental elites. Full analysis and disclosure of the published plans of the Trilateral Commission, the Council on Foreign Relations, the Hoover Institute, the Heritage Foundation, the Cato Institute, the World Bank, and the Project for the New American Century would go a long way in showing the road maps that the policy elites are building for the world. We don't need macroconspiracy theories to understand that powerful people sit in rooms and plan global change with private advantage in mind.

If open debate on sociopolitical policies were offered nationwide, it would certainly draw wider voter participation. Imagine a Silicon Valley computer programmer thinking about social policies that would prevent outsourcing of his job to foreign firms. Imagine his enthusiasm voting for representatives who would work to protect his livelihood.

Recognition of corporate media compliance with sources of news is an important step in understanding our new American censorship. A full media reform movement that challenges continued corporate media consolidation is underway in the United States, and tens of thousands of people are involved.[22]

Knowing the importance of the role of media in the continuation of democracy, we have a huge task before us. We must mobilize our resources to redevelop our own news and information systems from the bottom up, while at the same time attempting reform at the top. We can expand distribution of news via small independent newspapers, local magazines, independent radio, and cable access TV. By using the Internet we can interconnect with like-minded grassroots news organizations to share important stories globally.

Emerging in the corporate media news vacuum are hundreds of independent news sources. Independent newspapers, magazines, Web sites, radio, and TV are becoming more widely available. Independent media centers (www.Indymedia.org) have sprung up in over two hundred cities in the past five years. Thousands of alternative news organizations already exist and are listed in Project Censored's *Guide to Independent Media and Activism*.[23]

There is a compelling need to encourage activists and concerned citizens to avoid the propaganda of corporate news and to focus instead on news from independent sources. The more corporate news you watch, the less you really know.[24]

Imagine *real news* as media information that contributes to the lives and sociopolitical understandings of working people. Such real news informs, balances, and awakens the less powerful in society. Real news speaks truth to power and challenges the hegemonic top-down corporate entertainment news systems. Real news empowers and keeps key segments of working people in America tuned in, informed, and active. Real news cannot be measured with Arbitron ratings. It is not there for the selling of materialism or capitalist propaganda. It is not there for nationalistic grandioseness. Nor is it there to provide entertaining stimulation to the alienated suburbs. Real news can only be measured through its success in building democracy, stimulating grassroots activism, and motivating resistance to top-down institutions.

Real news builds movements for social change. It keeps the 5 percent radical vanguard aware of our power and our collective ability to influence positive change. Real news is about stimulating social activism in our daily lives and making each act deliberate and heart centered. Real news reports to the center of self, and helps us find the collective for shared action. Real news organizes movement toward betterment, shapes policy for equality, and stands in the faces of the robber-baron corporate power brokers.

NOTES

1. Mark Lewellen Biddle, "Voting Machines Gone Wild," *In These Times*, January 5, 2004.

2. Robert McChesney, *Rich Media, Poor Democracy* (Urbana: University of Illinois Press, 1999).

3. David Barsamian, *Stenographers to Power: Media and Propaganda* (Monroe, ME: Common Courage Press, 1992).

4. Robin Andersen, "The Made-for-TV 'Reality' War on Iraq," chapter 6 in *Censored 2004* (New York: Seven Stories Press, 2003).

5. Ben H. Bagdikian, *The New Media Monopoly* (Boston: Beacon Press, 2004).

6. Neil Postman, *Amusing Ourselves to Death: Public Discourse in the Age of Show Business* (New York: Penguin, 1986).

7. Peter Phillips, "Self-Censorship and the Homogeneity of the Media Elite," in *Censored 1998* (New York: Seven Stories Press, 1998).

8. H. Sklar, L. Mykyta, and S. Wefald, *Raise the Floor: Wages and Policies That Work for All of Us* (Cambridge, MA: South End Press, 2002).

9. Steve Wilson and Jane Akre, http://www.foxbghsuit.com, 2000.

10. "Elite Unit Savaged Civilians in Vietnam," *Toledo Blade*, 2003, www .toledoblade.com/apps/phcs.dll/article?AID=/20031002/SRTIGERFORCE.

11. April Oliver, "The Censored Side of the CNN Firings over Tailwind," in *Censored 1999*, ed. Peter Phillips (New York: Seven Stories Press, 1999).

12. *Tailwind Report*, CNN, 1998, http://www.cnn.com/US/9807/02/tailwind .findings/index.html.

13. Martin McLaughlin, "The Evidence of US Nerve Gas Use in Operation Tailwind," *World Socialist*, http://www.wsws.org/news/1998/july1998/cnn2-j24.

14. Matthew Engel, "War on Afghanistan: American Media Cowed by Patriotic Fever, Says Network News Veteran," *Guardian*, May 17, 2002, p. 4.

15. Matthew Engel, "Media: Has Anything Changed?" *Guardian*, September 2, 2002, p. 2.

16. Marc Herold, "Truth about Afghan Civilian Casualties," chap. 9 in *Censored 2003* (New York: Seven Stories Press, 2002).

17. Norman Solomon, "Media Fog of War," in *Censored 2004*.

18. Jan Cienski, "Uncle Sam's Shifty New Ally," *Chicago Sun Times*, October 21, 2001, p. 19.

19. Bardley Graham, "Rumsfeld Meets Warlords: Feuding Afghans Urged to Disarm, Yield to Rule from Kabul," *Washington Post*, December 5, 2003, p. A18.

20. Jean-Claude Brisard and Guilluame Basquie, *Forbidden Truth: US Taliban and Secret Oil Diplomacy and the Failed Hunt for bin Laden* (New York: Thunder's Mouth Press, 2002).

21. David Ray Griffin, *The New Pearl Harbor: Disturbing Questions about the Bush Administration and 9/11* (Northampton, MA: Olive Branch Press, 2004).

22. Robert McChesney, *The Problem of the Media* (New York: Monthly Review Press, 2004).

23. Peter Phillips ed., *Project Censored Guide to Independent Media and Activism* (New York: Seven Stories Press, 2003); see also http://www.projectcensored.org.

24. Danny Schechter, *The More You Watch, the Less You Know* (New York: Seven Stories Press, 1997).

2

BIG MONEY, SELF-CENSORSHIP, AND CORPORATE MEDIA

NORMAN SOLOMON
INSTITUTE FOR PUBLIC ACCURACY

NORMAN SOLOMON, *a nationally syndicated columnist on media and politics, is founder and executive director of the Institute for Public Accuracy (a national consortium of policy researchers and analysts) and a longtime associate of the media watch group FAIR (Fairness & Accuracy in Reporting). His weekly column, distributed by Creators Syndicate, has been in national syndication since 1992. Solomon is also a senior advisor to the National Radio Project, which produces the weekly public-affairs program "Making Contact," heard on 160 noncommercial radio stations in North America. He is the author of eleven books, most recently,* War Made Easy: How Presidents and Pundits Keep Spinning Us to Death *(Wiley, 2005). Solomon's op-ed articles have appeared in a range of newspapers including the* Washington Post, Los Angeles Times, Newsday, New York Times, Boston Globe, Miami Herald, USA Today, Philadelphia Inquirer, *and* Baltimore Sun, *and he has appeared as a guest on many media outlets including the PBS* NewsHour with Jim Lehrer, *CNN, MSNBC, Fox News Channel, C-SPAN, public radio's* Marketplace, *and NPR's* All Things Considered, Morning Edition, *and* Talk of the Nation.

"HOW MUCH ARE YOU WORTH?"

Half a century ago, sociologist C. Wright Mills warned of "a creeping indifference and a silent hollowing out." In the United States, he observed, "money is the one unambiguous criterion of success," and behind the obvious fact that people "want money" lurked the more unsettling reality that "their very standards are pecuniary."[1] A few years later, author Vance Packard asked a key question: "By encouraging people constantly to pursue the emblems of success, and by causing them to equate possessions with status, what are we doing to their emotions and their sense of values?"[2]

Today that question echoes more ominously than ever. While advertising and other commercial messages keep extending their reach, news coverage routinely gives fuel to society's preoccupation with financial assets. Fixated on money and what it might bring, the media fascination with purchasing power never stops. Mainstream news organizations have steadily shifted resources and priorities to the business of business. When PBS launched *Wall Street Week* with Louis Rukeyser in 1970, the program was conspicuous. Now there are dozens of national TV shows—most of them daily—devoted to the quest for high returns.

After *Moneyline* premiered on CNN in 1980, cable television news grew while embracing the world of investment. In 1989, General Electric opted to dedicate much of its startup news channel, CNBC, to coverage of and commentary about the stock market. A decade later, when host Lou Dobbs left *Moneyline* in spring 1999 at the start of his two-year absence from CNN, it was the leading cable network's most profitable show. By then, broadcast networks were fervently targeting the same lucrative demographics, and not only with expressly financial programs. Between the mid-1980s and the late 1990s, the main TV networks doubled the amount of airtime devoted to the New York Stock Exchange and Nasdaq. Regular news shows got accustomed to lavishing attention on minor business developments not because of significant economic implications for the general public, but because of decisions being made by management executives with oversight of news departments.

Some viewers, the ones with plenty of disposable income, became far more equal than others. When CNN revamped its daytime schedule in mid-1999 to make room for three and a half hours of programs about commerce and investment, the cable giant's president Richard Kaplan explained: "We look at business and finance as something we have to cover on a general interest news network. It's like the Cold War in the '50s. You just have to do it."[3] And the unstated goal was not simply to attract a higher number of viewers. As the

Associated Press reported in April 2001, noting intense competition between *Moneyline* and CNBC's *Business Center* program: "The audiences are small, but affluent, so advertisers pay a premium to run commercials."[4]

Many news stories now amount to little more than human interest narratives about the glories and tribulations of entrepreneurs, financiers, and CEOs. At networks owned by multibillion-dollar conglomerates like General Electric, Viacom, and Disney, the news divisions solemnly report every uptick or downturn of the markets. In contrast, when was the last time you heard Peter Jennings report the latest rates of on-the-job injuries or the average wait times at hospital emergency rooms? While many viewers assume that coverage reflects the considered judgment of journalistic pros, those journalists are enmeshed in a media industry dominated by corporate institutions with enough financial sway to redefine the meaning of functional professionalism.

In theory, noncommercial TV and radio outlets are insulated from the inordinate power of money. But across the country, each year, "public broadcasting" relies on hundreds of millions of dollars from corporations that are pleased to provide underwriting to burnish their images among upscale viewers and listeners. Whatever other benefits accrue, those firms buy some valuable PR with their de facto commercials, known euphemistically in the trade as "enhanced underwriter credits."

Along with the politically appointed board of the nonprofit Corporation for Public Broadcasting, corporate donors exert hefty influence on programs by "underwriting"—and, in some cases, literally making possible—specific shows. Private money is a big determinant of what's on "public" broadcasting. Without corporate funding for specific programs, many current shows would not exist. While public television airs the *Nightly Business Report*, viewers can search in vain for a regular show devoted to assessing the fortunes of working people. At PBS, no less than at avowedly commercial networks, the operative assumption seems to be that wealth creates all labor, not the other way around. Back in the 1770s, Adam Smith articulated a more progressive outlook, writing: "It was not by gold or by silver, but by labor, that all the wealth of the world was originally purchased."[5]

By the start of the twenty-first century, National Public Radio was locked into airing "NPR business updates" to supplement newscasts many times each day on stations nationwide. Listeners will be disappointed if they wait for an "NPR labor update." Various public radio stations feature *Marketplace*, a national daily program, and the weekly *Sound Money* show, but there is no broadcast such as "Workplace" or "Sound Labor."

Meanwhile, major print outlets are loaded with obsessions about profits. *Time* and *Newsweek* have often done cover stories on the race to amass wealth: upbeat or even ecstatic in bullish times, and somber when the news is hard for investors to bear. While fattening their business sections, daily newspapers have turned more and more newsprint over to targeting the affluent readers most coveted by business advertisers. Around the country the pattern has been similar, with dailies vastly enlarging their financial coverage —at the expense of other news. The "general circulation" press has become transfixed with the investor.

Along the way, these trends have transformed basic concepts of what it really means to be a journalist. "As the 1980s rocketed along, our 'readers' became 'consumers,'" recalls *New York Times* reporter Diana B. Henriques. "As the 1990s unfolded, those 'consumers' morphed into 'investors.' And today, some of us are speaking only to investors who also own computer modems."[6] The quality of mainstream journalism has always suffered because of the power of big money in the form of ownership and advertising, but flawed bygone eras are apt to evoke fond nostalgia in the present day. "As our intended audience has gotten narrower, so have we," Henriques lamented in *Columbia Journalism Review*'s last issue of 2000. "Business news today rarely sounds the sonorous chords or heart-lifting themes of great journalism. Most of it simply buzzes and squeaks, a reedy clarinet against a rhythm section of cash registers and ticker tape."[7]

Back in 1989, business reporter David Cay Johnston, then at the *Philadelphia Inquirer*, told me: "The financial pages of the newspapers of this country see the world through the eyes of bankers as opposed to through the eyes of bank customers."[8] These days, his words also apply to many other pages of newspapers—as well as to other types of media outlets. With business stories migrating so extensively across the media board, the accompanying sensibilities and priorities have drastically shifted mind-sets about "news." Idolatry of high-tech magnates, from Bill Gates on down, harmonizes with a prevalent tone that presents dollar assets as tacit measures of human value. Unless or until they appear to be headed for prison, top executives and shrewd big investors are good bets to emerge as media heroes. In sharp contrast, across the mass-media landscape, average workers hardly qualify as noble. Often, their very human needs come across as clunky impediments to economic progress.

Contemporary journalists are accustomed to depicting the "cost" of the work force as a barrier to wealth creation. In the midst of the decade's great boom, on April 30, 1997, a cheery article about the latest economic news appeared under this headline on the front page of the *New York Times*: "Markets Surge as Labor Costs Stay in Check." (For nonaffluent readers, the headline might as well have read, "Great News: Your Wages Aren't Going Up.") "The stock market rocketed yesterday to its greatest gain in more than five years," the *Times* reported. Why? Because important people were happy that wages had barely increased in the United States, and employers had not shelled out more for "benefits like health insurance and pensions." The story spotlighted the jubilant comment of a senior economist at Goldman Sachs: "There is no question this is a better labor cost report than we had anticipated." Indeed, the conditions were "better" for employers. How about employees? Well, they didn't merit any ink. The eighteen-paragraph article quoted a few current and former government economists without a word from workers, their representatives, or labor advocates.

Monologues of mass media keep confronting viewers, listeners, and readers with a demand that is frequently implicit: "How much are you worth?" The usual response provided to us: "Not enough."

At the same time, big money tilts reporting and punditry. While envelope-pushing investors, shady executives, and firms with cooked books (Martha Stewart, Tyco execs, Enron) are fair game, we rarely hear strong voices speaking against the outsized systemic power of large corporations. The cracks in the media walls include some tough stories about corporate influence and manipulation that could hardly please their targets. But the essence of propaganda, as any ad exec knows, is repetition. When certain stories and themes are repeated endlessly, the odds are stacked heavily against occasional muckraking journalism reverberating inside the national media's echo chamber.

Much of journalism now routinely wields monetary yardsticks. Even the most esteemed daily newspapers often cover cultural offerings by using dollar figures as overarching benchmarks, highlighting the financial earnings of various films, plays, books, paintings, CDs, and music videos. The internalization of dollars as markers for human worth and artistic achievement has insidiously skewed how we view the meaning of culture and creativity. And the deep concern that Vance Packard voiced many years ago is rendered silent, in part by the unwillingness of most American journalists to keep his question in mind. Yet it is a question that, if asked, could alter the steady drumbeat of today's reporting. "By encouraging people constantly to pursue the emblems of success, and by causing them to equate possessions with status, what are we doing to their emotions and their sense of values?"

BIG AND BEHOLDEN

Don't worry, we've been told countless times: media outlets are diverse enough to maintain vigilance.

"I have yet to see a piece of writing, political or non-political, that doesn't have a slant," E. B. White observed in a 1956 essay. To that candid assessment he added a more dubious one: "The beauty of the American free press is that the slants and the twists and the distortions come from so many directions, and the special interests are so numerous, the reader must sift and sort and check and countercheck in order to find out what the score is. This he does."[9]

I thought of White's claim one day while passing through the National Press Building lobby. Eight networks were on eight television screens. With the possible exception of the Weather Channel, they all certainly had slants. Two eminent members of the punditocracy occupied two screens. The odious Don Imus was on another. Investor news was also profuse. Lots of slants. But not from many directions.

The media industry—no less than the political campaign system—is awash in oceans of dollars. Commercial broadcasters siphon huge profits from frequencies that theoretically belong to the public. Cable TV conglomerates expand under the protection of federal regulations placing severe limits on the power of municipalities to charge franchise fees for the use of public rights-of-way. Station owners proceed to cash in on their free portions of a digital spectrum worth billions of dollars. We hear a lot about the need for campaign finance reform, but how often have we heard the phrase "media finance reform"?

Assurances about the present-day media system often resemble the more complacent defenses of how politicians get elected. In March 2001, lauding "the classic Madisonian structure of American democracy," syndicated columnist Charles Krauthammer wrote: "Madison saw 'factions,' what we now call interests, not only as natural, but as beneficial to democracy because they inevitably check and balance each other."[10]

But the phrase "check and balance" deserves another look—in a financial context. The big checks and big (bank) balances are hardly reassuring. Complacency rests on mythology, as when Krauthammer cited Madison: "His solution to the undue power of factions? More factions. Multiply them—and watch them mutually dilute each other." However, when we "watch them," any such "solution" becomes implausible. Power is steadily more concentrated, not diluted.

The media establishment has a hefty stake in the status quo. A curb on campaign spending would eat into profits. In 2000, an estimated $1 billion in campaign-ad revenue flowed to TV stations. And during the year's election cycle, "soft money" campaign contributions totaled more than $5.5 million from the corporate owners of five powerhouse networks—Time Warner (CNN), Walt Disney (ABC), News Corp. (Fox), Viacom (CBS), and General Electric (NBC). But even if big donors vanished from campaign financing, we'd still be left with the crying need for media finance reform. If those who pay the piper call the tune, why is that any less true in news media than in politics?

Midway through the Senate debate on the McCain-Feingold campaign finance reform bill, a *Washington Post* editorial declared: "The goal should be to reduce the flow of funds, the extent to which offices and policies now are all but openly bought by the interest groups that the policies affect." The newspaper added that with so much big money flowing into the coffers of senators, "There is no way they cannot be beholden."[11] That's true. And when you consider America's major media outlets—and the massive corporate ownership and advertising involved—the same conclusion should be inescapable. "There is no way they cannot be beholden."

Free and open discourse is essential to democracy. But amid all the talk about the sanctity of the First Amendment, we don't hear politicians or mainstream pundits insisting that multibillion-dollar conglomerates be pushed off its windpipe. As a practical matter, the top guarantee in the Bill of Rights is gasping for breath. Free speech is of limited value when freedom to be heard requires big bucks.

GREATNESS OF WEALTH

Like most people, American journalists are apt to look at the very rich with awe. Names like Bill Gates, George Soros, and Warren Buffett have the ring of modern-day royalty—high above the rest of us, and maybe even vaguely immortal.

The inclination to see wealth as a gauge of human worth goes back a long way. "They measure everything by the gold standard, men as well as mules," Joshua Speed observed during a visit to California in 1876. "You never hear of Mr. Smith as a good man, or Mr. Brown as an honest man, or Mr. Jones as a Christian, but Mr. S has twenty thousand million and so on. The more he has, the better he is—and it matters not how he got it, so he has it."[12]

Speed, who was a close friend of Abraham Lincoln, might not be any more upbeat now. These days, in a society eager to condemn an Enron debacle or a Global Crossing scandal, we might want to conclude that decent standards ultimately prevail. But media censure comes down hard on financial mismanagement, flagrant skullduggery, and collapse—not on zeal to keep maximizing profits and riches while the human consequences for many people are grim.

If Enron had kept scrupulous accounts instead of fabricating its financial books, it might still be considered a model corporate citizen. After all, while Enron was riding high on Wall Street, national media coverage was generally favorable as the company gorged itself on electricity privatization—heralded as "reform" and boosted by political influence-leasing from California to India.

In 1993, Enron wrangled an agreement with India's state government of Maharashtra for a 695-megawatt plant. "The Enron project was the first private power project in India," Arundhati Roy recalled in her book *Power Politics*. Lots of cash lubricated the fix. "Enron had made no secret of the fact that, in order to secure the deal, it had paid out millions of dollars to 'educate' the politicians and bureaucrats involved in the deal," Roy wrote. For India, the size of the scheme was unprecedented: "Experts who have studied the project have called it the most massive fraud in the country's history."[13] The project's gross profits were set to exceed $12 billion.

Not that such massive gouging bothered US media. On the contrary. For the journalistic mainstream, privatization—whether in western India or northern California—was beneficent. Ken Lay and the rest of Enron's smart guys were ahead of the curve. Visionary hotshots.

THE PULL OF GREED

By mid-2002 just about every politician and pundit was eager to denounce wrongdoing in business: sinners had defiled the holy quest for a high rate of return. Damn those who left devoted investors standing bereft at corporate altars!

On the surface, media outlets were filled with condemnations of avarice. The July 15 edition of *Newsweek* featured a story headlined "Going After Greed," complete with a full-page picture of George W. Bush's anguished face. But after multibillion-dollar debacles from Enron to WorldCom, the usual media messages were actually quite equivocal—wailing about greedy CEOs while piping in a kind of hallelujah chorus to affirm the sanctity of the economic system that empowered them.

At a Wall Street pulpit, Bush declared America's need for business leaders "who know the difference between ambition and destructive greed." (Presumably, other types of greed are fine and dandy.) During his much-ballyhooed speech, the president asserted that "all investment is an act of faith." With that spirit, a righteous form of business fundamentalism is firmly in place. The great god of capitalism is always due enormous tribute. Yet wicked people get most of the blame when things go wrong. "The American system of enterprise has not failed us," Bush proclaimed. "Some dishonest individuals have failed our system."

Corporate theology about "the free enterprise system" readily acknowledges bad apples while steadfastly denying that the barrels are rotten. After all, every large-scale racket needs enforceable rules. Rigid conservatives may take their faith to an extreme. ("Let's hold people responsible—not institutions," a *Wall Street Journal* column urged.)[14] But pro-corporate institutional reform went on the mainstream agenda, as media responses to Bush's sermon on Wall Street made clear. The *Atlanta Constitution* summarized a key theme with its headline over an editorial: "Take Hard-Line Approach to Restore Faith in Business."[15] Many newspapers complained that Bush had not gone far enough to crack down on corporate malfeasants. "His speech was more pulpit than punch," lamented the *Christian Science Monitor*.[16] A July 10 editorial in the *Washington Post* observed that "it is naive to suppose that business can be regulated by some kind of national honor code."[17] But such positions should not be confused with advocacy of progressive social policies.

"There is one objective that companies can unite around," the *Post* editorial said, "and that is to make money. This is not a criticism: the basis of our market system is that, by maximizing profits, firms also maximize the collective good." Coming from media conglomerates and other corporate giants, that sort of rhetoric is notably self-serving. It takes quite a leap of faith to believe that when firms maximize profits they also "maximize the collective good." A much stronger case could be made for opposite conclusions.

The Washington Post Co. itself has long served as a good example. Midway through the 1970s, the media firm crushed striking press workers at its flagship newspaper. That development contributed to "maximizing profits" but surely did nothing to "maximize the collective good"—unless we assume that busting unions, throwing people out of work, and holding down wages for remaining employees is beneficial for all concerned.

During the first several years of the twenty-first century, despite its newly trumpeted antigreed ethos, news coverage did not really challenge the goal of amassing as much wealth and power as possible. For Enron's Ken Lay and similar executives, falling from media grace was simultaneous with their loss of wealth and power. Such corporate hotshots would still be media darlings if they'd kept their greed clearly within legal limits—adding still more money to their hundreds of millions or billions of dollars in personal riches—while, every day, thousands of other human beings continued to die from lack of such necessities as minimal health care and nutrition.

One day a few decades ago, at a news conference, I asked Nelson Rockefeller how he felt about being so wealthy while millions of children were starving in poor countries. Rockefeller, who was vice president of the United States at the time, replied a bit testily that his grandfather John D. Rockefeller had been very generous toward the less fortunate. As I began a follow-up, other reporters interrupted so that they could ask more news-savvy questions.

Basic questions about wealth and poverty—about economic relations that are glorious for a few, adequate for some, and injurious for countless others—remain outside the professional focus of American journalism. In our society, prevalent inequities are largely the results of corporate function, not corporate dysfunction. But we're encouraged to believe that faith in the current system of corporate capitalism will be redemptive.

Leaving no pixel unturned, entrepreneurial genius has found endless ways to innovate on behalf of the eternal quest for more capital. Just as the highest monetary achievers among us have learned to seem to do good while doing extraordinarily well for themselves, the TV networks teach us that the most pristine values are to be achieved by, not coincidentally, spending money. Every priceless moment, as MasterCard commercials have often reminded us, somehow seems to coincide with financial expenditures.

To better live in a society that treasures individuality, you can learn how to be more in step with everyone else who matters. Glancing at a TV screen for scarcely more than a second, you have the potential to absorb the latest data from key stock market indicators as well as glimpse snippets of headlines crawling across the bottom of the screen, take in computer-generated graphics, listen to voices, hear background music—and, of course, keep an eye on the big picture.

The legends of the corporate-driven community, laid down by conventions of commerce and politics, are suitable for compliance with never-never lands of public pretense. Contrived narratives that provide maximum profits can have little to do with authentic experience. To guide the expenditures of time and resources for enhancement of cash flow, our powerful institutions must function as arbiters of social meaning. And first among equals of those institutions are the powerhouses of mass media. As Marshall McLuhan observed, "All media exist to invest our lives with artificial perceptions and arbitrary values."[18]

BUBBLING BULL

With the *new economy* in shambles, it was easy for media outlets to look back and disparage the illusions of the late 1990s—years crammed with high-tech mania, fat stock options, and euphoria on Wall Street. But the media retrospectives had little to say about the fact that much of the bubble was filled with hot air from hyperventilating journalists.

Traveling back on a time machine, we would see mainstream reporters and pundits routinely extolling the digitally enhanced nirvana of huge profits and much more to come. The new economy media juggernaut was not to be denied. Sure, journalists occasionally offered the commonsense observation that the boom would go bust someday. But it was a minor note in the media's orchestral tributes to the new economy. And the bullish pronouncements included an awful lot of hyped bull.

In summer 1997, *BusinessWeek*'s July 28 edition was scorning "economic dogma" for its failure to embrace the glorious future at hand. "The fact is that major changes in the dynamics of growth are detonating many conventional wisdoms," the magazine declared in an editorial that concluded: "It is the Dow, the S&P 500, and Nasdaq that are telling us old assumptions should be challenged in the New Economy."[19] A column published that same week in the very conservative *Washington Times*, by economist Lawrence Kudlow, rang the same bell: "Actually, information age high-tech breakthroughs have undreamed of spillovers that impact every nook and cranny of the new economy." Kudlow was upbeat about "even higher stock prices and even more economic growth as far as the eye can see."[20]

In 1998, the July 20 issue of *Time* was one of many touting the economic miracles of the Internet. "The real economy exists in the thousands—even tens of thousands—of sites that together with Yahoo are remaking the face of global commerce," *Time* reported. The magazine could not contain its enthusiasm: "The real promise of all this change is that it will enrich all of us, not just a bunch of kids in Silicon Valley."[21]

When the last July of the 1990s got underway, *Newsweek* was featuring several pages about the national quest for riches: "The bull market, powered by the cyberboom, is a pre-millennium party that's blowing the roof off the American Dream. It's just that some of us can't seem to find our invitations. And all this new wealth is creating a sense of unease and bewilderment among those of us who don't know how to get in touch with our inner moguls."[22]

Meanwhile, insightful analysis of the new economy received scant mass-media exposure. But it certainly existed. While *Newsweek* was fretting about "inner moguls," for instance, the progressive magazine *Dollars & Sense* published an article by economist Dean Baker warning that the country was in the midst of "a classic speculative bubble."[23] A crash was on the way, Baker pointed out, and it would financially clobber many working people. With the stock market near its peak, Baker anticipated grim financial realities: "Many moderate-income workers do have a direct stake in the market now that the vast majority of their pensions take the form of tax-sheltered retirement accounts such as a 401(k). These plans provide no guaranteed benefit to workers. At her retirement, a worker gets exactly what she has managed to accumulate in these accounts. Right now, a large percentage of the assets in these retirement accounts is in stock funds."

Overall, Baker contended, "the post-crash world is not likely to be a pretty one. The people who take the biggest losses will undoubtedly be wealthy speculators who should have understood the risks. The yuppie apostles of the 'new economy' will also be humbled by a plunging stock market. But these people can afford large losses on their stock holdings and still maintain a comfortable living standard." Baker concluded his in-depth article by predicting a foreseeable tragedy that major media outlets rarely dwelled on ahead of time: "The real losers from a stock market crash will be the workers who lose most of their pensions, and the workers who must struggle to find jobs in the ensuing recession. Once again, those at the bottom will pay for the foolishness of those at the top."

In late September of 1999, the enthralling title of *Time*'s twenty-page cover story—"GetRich.com"—heralded scenarios for wondrously swift elevation into the ranks of the wealthy.[24] The spread had its share of wry digs and sardonic asides, but reverence for the magnitude of quick money in dot-comland seemed to dwarf any misgivings. Although the magazine explained that "it's not all about the money," the punch line arrived a few dozen words later: "But mostly, it's the money." And there was plenty of it moving into new digital enterprises. "In the second quarter of this year, venture-capital funding in the US increased 77 percent, to a record $7.6 billion. More than half went to Internet start-ups." At the time, Silicon Valley executives were holding stocks and options valued at $112 billion—a few billion dollars more than the gross domestic product (GDP) of Portugal. Computer-literate job seekers were riding high: "Never before have the unemployed been so cocky. . . . E-commerce niches are getting claimed so quickly that there might not be time for business school anymore." Said one Stanford grad who was enjoying the rush of launching his own dot-com firm: "It's all about the buzz. I can't explain it. It's like magic."

While *Time* and other media outlets were simply reporting on the dot-com phenomenon, they were also hyping the phenom—glorifying it and egging it on. They did so repeatedly during the last few years of the twentieth century. That coverage makes for sad reading now. But, truly, it was just as sad then. The hollowness of excessive monetary dreams is scarcely mitigated when they are being fulfilled.

Although the departed Internet boom became the stuff of some fond memories, its heyday came in a dubious economic context. The tech bounties were hardly being shared equitably. In a book titled *Economic Apartheid in America*, authors Chuck Collins and Felice Yeskel pointed out: "Between 1977 and 1999, the average after-tax income of the wealthiest 1 percent of households went up 119.7 percent. The bottom fifth of households lost 12 percent and the middle fifth lost 3.1 percent."[25] And corporations were carrying a shrunken proportion of the tax burden. In spring 2004 a Bryn Mawr College professor emeritus of economics, Richard Du Boff, noted that "corporate tax payments have fallen below 8 percent of all federal tax revenues from 13 percent in 1980 and 23 percent in 1960."[26]

Those kinds of enormous disparities rarely seem to trouble the journalists who avidly recount the ups and downs of big investors. The sensibilities that major media outlets bring to bear on economic reporting are not far afield from the goals that preoccupy the media moguls who are yearning to gain even greater market share and even more humongous profits. "We can have democracy in this country or we can have great wealth concentrated in the hands of a few," Supreme Court Justice Louis Brandeis commented, "but we can't have both."[27] This observation applies fully to the news media.

When cable TV was spreading with great fanfare in the early 1980s, the upbeat futurist Alvin Toffler foresaw the emergence of "a truly new era—the age of the de-massified media." In theory, the country would be cable-wired for democracy. But today, as Americans can see by clicking through the corporate-dominated fare, the realities of economic power have implemented very different plans for cable television. A snapshot of the trend appeared in the *Wall Street Journal* on September 15, 2003, when an article mentioned in passing: "Of the top 25 cable channels, 20 are now owned by one of the big five media companies."[28]

The likes of Viacom, Disney, News Corp. (which includes Fox), Time Warner, and General Electric continue to promote values similar to the ones that were implicit in countless news stories celebrating the dot-com boom. Fixations on getting rich are the propellants of profit-driven media conglomerates. When the subject is zeal to accumulate wealth, they'll be the last to focus on the downsides: for individuals and for democracy.

Inked onto parchment and chiseled into stone, the First Amendment is not really a guarantee. It's a promissory ideal that can be redeemed only by our own vitality in the present. If freedom of speech can be augmented by freedom to be heard, media outlets are the lifeblood of the body politic. Extensive circulation of ideas, information, analysis, and debate must exist— not just once in a while, but all the time—or the consequences are severe, even catastrophic.

You can gauge our society's political and social health by checking some vital media signs: scrutinize the programming of stations that fall under the purview of the Federal Communications Commission. Watch a few dozen TV channels. Listen to all the radio stations on the AM and FM bands. If the dominant content doesn't make you feel sick, then you're probably not paying close attention.

By any measure, since the 1980s, media ownership in the United States has steadily moved in only one direction—toward greater concentration in fewer and fewer corporate hands. Former *Washington Post* assistant managing editor Ben Bagdikian sketched out the nation's terrain of media ownership in 1983, when his book *The Media Monopoly* first appeared: "50 corporations dominated most of every mass medium." With each new edition of the book, that number kept dropping—to 29 media firms in 1987, 23 in 1990, 14 in 1992, and 10 in 1997. Published in 2000, the sixth edition of *The Media Monopoly* documented that just a half-dozen corporations were supplying most of the United States' media fare. "It is the overwhelming collective power of these firms, with their corporate interlocks and unified cultural and political values, that raises troubling questions about the individual's role in the American democracy," Bagdikian wrote.[29]

SPLASH WITHOUT ECHO

Of course there is exceptional journalism that disrupts the overall patterns of media coverage. But the problem is that they are such exceptions.

In February 2000, *Time* magazine offered some notable journalism in the form of a fourteen-page investigative report—"Big Money and Politics: Who Gets Hurt?"—providing extensive coverage of how government decisions really get made in the nation's capital. The cover story, by Donald Barlett and James Steele, was terrific. But the mass media's response to the new exposé was dismal.

Barlett and Steele didn't bother with the fluff and psychoblather that dominate political reporting. They bypassed the styles and personal traits of politicians. Instead, in the February 7 issue of *Time*, the two journalists illuminated a process that normally remains in shadows. Money doesn't talk. It screams. And it gets heard. The crux of the real story is that "Washington extends favorable treatment to one set of citizens at the expense of another," Barlett and Steele wrote. For those with megabucks behind them, the doors swing wide. For others, the portals of democracy are unlikely to open more than a crack. "If you know the right people in Congress and in the White House, you can often get anything you want. And there are two surefire ways to get close to those people: Contribute to their political campaigns. Spend generously on lobbying."[30]

As a case study of how big money purchases big favors, *Time* devoted several pages to shrewd efforts by Carl Lindner, the chair of Chiquita Brands International. He poured a few million dollars into the coffers of key politicians in Washington, while US trade policies vital to his firm's banana fortunes hung in the balance.

People who send large checks to politicians and top lobbyists "enjoy all the benefits of their special status," Barlett and Steele explained. For example: "If they make a bad business decision, the government bails them out. If they want to hire workers at below-market wage rates, the government provides the means to do so. If they want more time to pay their debts, the government gives them an extension. If they want immunity from certain laws, the government gives it." Meanwhile, lacking deep pockets, most Americans "pick up a disproportionate share of America's tax bill . . . pay higher prices for a broad range of products, from peanuts to prescription drugs . . . pay taxes that others in a similar situation have been excused from paying . . . are compelled to abide by laws while others are granted immunity from them."

The well-documented account of "Big Money and Politics" couldn't have been more timely. As Barlett and Steele noted, "In this presidential election year, companies and industries that hope for special treatment in the new decade are busy making their political contributions and their connections."

The fact that such intrepid journalism made a splash in *Time* magazine was encouraging. But other media—including wire services, big daily newspapers, and broadcast networks—failed to pick up on the superb cover story. Days later, no interview with Barlett or Steele had aired on any major TV or radio outlets. In effect, national media reacted with a yawn.

MISSING CANDOR

Let's imagine that the CEO of a leading media conglomerate felt the need to come clean about the firm's overall activities. The public statement might go something like this:

> While revenues are down in our broadcasting division, we've done our best to wring every last dollar out of the airwaves that the parent company has been able to hijack from the public. Fortunately, these days, the FCC—we call it the "Federal Complicity Cabal" around the office—is giving us just about everything we demand.
>
> In some urban areas, we now own at least half a dozen radio stations, plus a couple of TV outlets. And the restrictions against also owning local newspapers are on their way out, too.
>
> On television, we've been able to flood the market with more junky old shows than ever. The newer sitcoms and dramas continue to push the boundaries of exploiting sexuality to spike ratings (in sync with like-minded commercials). Most of the movers and shakers on our board of directors are big supporters of conservative moralizers in Washington, but that's no conflict with their commitment to profitable sleaze. Whatever works!
>
> Meanwhile, our TV news division is paring down to the essentials. (Rest assured there'll be no skimping on wardrobes and hair spray.) We've cut back on producers, researchers, and those still eager to engage in actual journalism. And we've brought additional talent on board with reliable devotion to our corporate model. Prodded by management, boat-rockers have walked the plank.
>
> After buying several hundred radio stations across the country since enactment of the bipartisan telecommunications law in 1996, we're able to clone our sound with just enough trickery to make most people think they're listening to a station with a local staff. For those who don't care for our daily offerings of Rush Limbaugh, Dr. Laura, and various imitators, we provide the free-market choice of insipid oldies and present-day pop to help listeners wile away their pitiful consumptive lives.
>
> We're excited about the expanding revenue stream for product placements in our movies. Showing the brand on a can of beer or a pack of cigarettes can really help us meet our shooting budgets. Only half in jest, we're wondering if we might be able to get some marquee stars to temporarily adopt nicknames during a movie's release. There's no telling how much we might be able to fetch from a three-way deal with Julia "Marlboro" Roberts.
>
> Speaking of cigarettes, our magazine division now does a better job of going light on smoking-and-health articles. The firm relies on many millions of ad dollars from tobacco companies, and it would be financially irre-

sponsible to publish lots of stories about the horrors of lung cancer and emphysema due to smoking. In that spirit, during the past year, our print outlets have downplayed the strong new evidence of serious hazards from secondhand smoke.

On the Internet, while revenues are down, we've been filling people's screens with enough pop-up ads and other obnoxious features to partly compensate. Also, our search-engine department has been taking plenty of payoffs—all perfectly legal—from site owners who'd rather be in the top 10 listings instead of showing up as number 247. Ha ha.

Our book division is finding better ways to communicate with the biggest chains before we sign up new authors. If the key execs who place orders for Borders or Barnes & Noble stores aren't enthusiastic about particular manuscripts, we ought to think twice or three times about sinking our capital into publishing them. It's far smarter to fatten the advertising budget for the next blockbuster by Tom Clancy (or whoever the heck he hired to write "his" latest book) than to roll the dice for a dozen works of purported art by earnest nobodies.

At the media outlets owned by our conglomerate, quite a few employees are sincerely dedicated to the finest principles of journalism, artistic expression, and public service. To be honest, such dedication can impede the maximization of profits that our shareholders have every right to expect. But, over time, clear rewards and tacit punishments are apt to result in wondrous transformations. As we move forward into a brave new multimedia world, surely the best is yet to come.

NEWS TRAFFIC

Listeners don't get much news these days if they tune into commercial radio stations. Coverage of national and global events is scant at best, while local news—once the pride of many AM radio stations—is now an endangered species. The remaining community news is usually the "rip and read" variety from wire services.

But let's give credit where it's due. In the United States, thousands of radio outlets are doing a good job of gathering one particular type of news. The coverage is often meticulous and dependable as stations devote substantial resources to providing reliable up-to-the-minute information: if you want the latest news about traffic, in all kinds of weather, turn on the radio.

Using an array of helicopters, mobile phones, and other assorted information relay systems, radio stations keep listeners posted on vehicular fender-benders, glitches, snarls, and alternative routes. Where I live, a local "all news" CBS affiliate—owned by the giant Infinity broadcasting conglomerate—hypes "traffic and weather together" every ten minutes, around the clock. And the quality of the traffic reports is impressive.

But what if thousands of radio stations across the country were augmenting their fine reporting on the latest road conditions with comparable from-the-sky breaking news coverage of social conditions in local communities? The result might sound something like this:

"Now for the latest, we go to Dan in Skyview Copter One over downtown."

"Things don't look good from here. Already this morning we've seen several dozen homeless people clutching their blankets in the downtown area. Apparently they had no place to sleep indoors overnight, even when the mercury plunged below twenty degrees. Right now we're hovering near City Hall, with its gold-plated dome sparkling in the early light, and from this height we can see a number of children huddled on sidewalk grates along with some adults, apparently trying to stay warm. Now back to the studio."

"Thanks, Dan. We go now to Skyview Copter Two, southwest of the city. Ben, what's the latest?"

"Well, Jill, I can't say the news is positive. Looks like the homeless encampment in Maple Park has gotten quite a bit bigger since yesterday morning. Apparently the shelters—public and private—just can't keep up with the demand. And from here I can see that most people don't seem to have much to eat this morning in the area of the park. Some are simply wandering from one trash can to another, evidently searching for bottles to cash in for the deposits."

"OK, Ben, sounds like a bad scene out there. Thanks for the update. Now over to Melissa in Skyview Copter Three, somewhere above skid row."

"That's right—since just before dawn we've been circling over some of the most economically depressed neighborhoods of the city, and I wish we had some better news to report. But our informal Day Labor index is quite downbeat at this hour. Ordinarily by now most of the low-income people waiting on sidewalks and street corners have been picked up by the slew of independent contractors who cruise the main thoroughfares to hire day laborers on the cheap. But in an apparent sign of the slowing economy, many more men than usual are still standing along the curbs at this hour. Hands in pockets, they seem unlikely to get offered a day's work today, even at low wages."

"All right, Melissa. And now, for a change of pace, we go to Skyview Copter Four, currently aloft and eyeing the upscale Buckingham Ridge neighborhood."

"Quite a bit of activity in evidence this morning, Jill, and I can tell you the mayor has just stepped into the sleek black limo that's been parked in front of his house since he staggered home late last night. He's headed to a news conference to announce further plans for the tax-supported downtown Convention Center complex being built by a team of renowned Italian architects. Now back to the studio."

"Thanks. And please keep your eyes open up there for the comings and goings of the rich and famous this morning. We could sure use some upbeat news."

CORPORATE HEALTH

A special issue of *Time* was filled with health information in mid-January 2003, offering plenty of encouragement under the rubric of medical science with an ethereal twist: "How Your Mind Can Heal Your Body."

The spread on "The Power of Mood" begins with this teaser: "Lifting your spirits can be potent medicine. How to make it work for you." An article about "Mother Nature's Little Helpers" is a discussion of alternative remedies. Other pieces probe techniques of psychotherapy, investigate high-tech ways of scanning the brain, and ponder "Are Your Genes to Blame?"

Of course, more than altruism was at work. While the January 20 issue of *Time* contained page after page of informative journalism, it also included dozens of lucrative full-color ads pegged to the theme of health. There were elaborate pitches for laxative capsules, a purple pill for heartburn, over-the-counter sinus medication, and prescription drugs for allergies and Alzheimer's. On a preventative note, there was even a full-page ad for an inhaler that "helps you beat cigarette cravings one at a time" and another for a "stop smoking lozenge."

While all this was going on inside *Time* magazine, the same kind of advertising appeared in *Newsweek* to harmonize with its cover's keynote: "What Science Tells Us About Food and Health."

We may feel that it's nice of America's largest-circulation newsweekly to print so much healthful information. But if you picked up the previous week's *Time* and turned past the cover, the first thing you saw was a two-page layout for Camels, with the heading "Pleasure to Burn." Like the multi-entendre slogan, the ad's graphic is inviting; a handsome guy, presumably quite debonaire as he stands next to a liquor shelf, lights up a cigarette as he eyes the camera.

And so it goes. Many big media outlets tell us how to make ourselves healthy while encouraging us to make ourselves sick. They offer us tips and new scientific data on how to maximize longevity. But overall complicity with the lethal cigarette industry—whether through glamorization or silence —is widespread and ongoing.

The media's mixed messages about health are unabashedly self-contradictory, but they're also customary to such an extent that they're integral to a media cycle that never quits. The same news organizations that produce innumerable downbeat stories about obesity in America are beholden to huge quantities of ad revenue from fast food—and usually wink at the most popular artery-clogging chains. If most people are ignorant of the deep-fried dangers posed by McDonald's and Burger King, they can thank the news media for dodging the matter.

With television, radio, and print media now devoting plenty of coverage to health concerns, and with aging baby boomers serving as a massive demographic target, the media emphasis is tilted toward high-end health expectations. But we need much more than news about the latest theories and scientific findings on preventative measures, palliatives, and cures.

Until news outlets shift their commitments, they will continue to undermine public health as well as promote it. The present-day contradictions are severe: journalists do not equivocate about cancer; we all understand that there's nothing good about the disease. Yet journalists routinely go easy on proven causes of cancer, such as cigarettes and an array of commercially promoted chemicals with carcinogenic effects.

Air pollution from gas-guzzling vehicles certainly qualifies as cancer causing. But for every drop of ink that explores such causality, countless gallons are devoted to convincing Americans that they should own air-fouling trucks or SUVs. While the health-oriented front covers of *Time* and *Newsweek* on the stands were similar, the back covers were identical—an advertisement for Chevy's Silverado diesel truck. The headline trumpeted the appeal: "A Sledgehammer in a Ballpeen World."

In a 1986 essay, the American writer Wallace Stegner wrote: "Neither the country nor the society we built out of it can be healthy until we stop raiding and running, and learn to be quiet part of the time, and acquire the sense not of ownership but of belonging."[31]

Such outlooks are antithetical to the functional precepts of the media industry. It is largely dedicated to "raiding and running." It perceives quiet as dead air and squandered space. It portrays ownership as the essence of success and human worth. How healthy can such operative values be?

MEDIA MERGERMANIA

Four months after stunning news about plans to combine Viacom and CBS, 2000 began with the announcement of an even more spectacular merger—America Online and Time Warner. Faced with those and other giant steps toward extreme concentration of media power, journalists mostly responded with acquiescence.

When the Viacom-CBS story broke, media coverage depicted a match made in corporate heaven: at more than $37 billion, it was the largest media merger in history. With potential effects on the broader public kept outside the story's frame, what emerged was a rosy picture. "Analysts hailed the deal as a good fit between two complementary companies," the Associated Press reported flatly. The news service went on to quote a media analyst who proclaimed: "It's a good deal for everybody."[32]

"Everybody"? Well, everybody who counts in the mass-media calculus. For instance, the media analyst quoted by AP was from the PaineWebber investment firm. "You need to be big," Christopher Dixon explained. "You need to have a global presence." Dixon showed up again the next morning in the lead article of the September 8, 1999, edition of the *New York Times*, along with other high-finance strategists. An analyst at Merrill Lynch agreed with his upbeat view of the Viacom-CBS combination. So did an expert from ING Barings: "You can literally pick an advertiser's needs and market that advertiser across all the demographic profiles, from Nickelodeon with the youngest consumers to CBS with some of the oldest consumers."[33]

In sync with the prevalent media spin, the *New York Times* devoted plenty of ink to assessing advertiser needs and demographic profiles. But during the crucial first day of the *Times*'s coverage, foes of the Viacom-CBS consolidation did not get a word in edgewise. There was, however, an unintended satire of corporate journalism when a writer referred to the bygone era of the 1970s: "In those quaint days, it bothered people when companies owned too many media properties."[34]

The *Washington Post*, meanwhile, ran a front-page story that provided similar treatment of the latest and greatest media merger, pausing just long enough for a short dissonant note from media critic Mark Crispin Miller: "The implications of these mergers for journalism and the arts are enormous. It seems to me that this is, by any definition, an undemocratic development. The media system in a democracy should not be inordinately dominated by a few very powerful interests."[35] It wasn't an idea that the *Post*'s journalists pursued.

Overall, the big media outlets—getting bigger all the time—offer narrow and cheery perspectives on the significance of merger mania. News accounts keep the focus on market share preoccupations of investors and top managers. Numerous stories explore the widening vistas of cross-promotional synergy for the shrewdest media titans. While countless reporters are determined to probe how each company stands to gain from the latest deal, few of them demonstrate much enthusiasm for exploring what is at stake for the public.

With rare exceptions, news outlets covered the Viacom-CBS merger as a business story. But more than anything else, it should have been covered, at least in part, as a story with dire implications for possibilities of democratic discourse. And the same was true for the announcement that came a few months later—on January 10, 2000—when a hush seemed to fall over the profession of journalism.

A grand new structure, AOL/Time Warner, was unveiled in the midst of much talk about a wondrous *new media* world to come, with cornucopias of bandwidth and market share. On January 2, just one week before the portentous announcement, the head of Time Warner had alluded to the transcendent horizons. Global media "will be and is fast becoming the predominant business of the 21st century," Gerald Levin said on CNN, "and we're in a new economic age, and what may happen, assuming that's true, is it's more important than government. It's more important than educational institutions and non-profits."[36]

Levin went on: "So what's going to be necessary is that we're going to need to have these corporations redefined as instruments of public service because they have the resources, they have the reach, they have the skill base. And maybe there's a new generation coming up that wants to achieve meaning in that context and have an impact, and that may be a more efficient way to deal with society's problems than bureaucratic governments." Levin's next sentence underscored the sovereign right of capital in dictating the new direction. "It's going to be forced anyhow because when you have a system that is instantly available everywhere in the world immediately, then the old-fashioned regulatory system has to give way," he said.

To discuss an imposed progression of events as some kind of natural occurrence is a convenient form of mysticism, long popular among the corporately pious, who are often eager to wear mantles of royalty and divinity. Tacit beliefs deem the accumulation of wealth to be redemptive. Inside corporate temples, monetary standards gauge worth. Powerful executives now herald joy to the world via a seamless web of media. Along the way, the rest of us are not supposed to worry much about democracy. On January 12, 2000, AOL chief Steve Case assured a national PBS *NewsHour* television audience: "Nobody's going to control anything." Seated next to him, Levin declared: "This company is going to operate in the public interest." By happy coincidence, they insisted, the media course that seemed likely to make them much richer was the same one that held the most fulfilling promise for everyone on the planet.

Journalists accustomed to scrutinizing the public statements of powerful officials seem quite willing to hang back from challenging the claims of media magnates. Even when reporting on a rival media firm, journalists who work in glass offices hesitate to throw weighty stones; a substantive critique of corporate media priorities could easily boomerang. And when a media merger suddenly occurs, news coverage can turn deferential overnight.

On March 14, 2000—the day after the Tribune Company announced its purchase of the *Los Angeles Times* and the rest of the Times Mirror empire— the acquired newspaper reported on the fine attributes of its owner-to-be. In a news article that read much like a corporate press release, the *Times* hailed the Tribune Company as "a diversified media concern with a reputation for strong management" and touted its efficient benevolence. Tribune top managers, in the same article, "get good marks for using cost-cutting and technology improvements throughout the corporation to generate a profit margin that's among the industry's highest." The story went on to say that "Tribune is known for not using massive job cuts to generate quick profits from media properties it has bought."[37]

Compare that rosy narrative to another news article published the same day, by the *New York Times*. Its story asserted, as a matter of fact, that "the Tribune Co. has a reputation not only for being a fierce cost-cutter and union buster but for putting greater and greater emphasis on entertainment and business."[38]

"It is not necessary to construct a theory of intentional cultural control," media critic Herbert Schiller commented in 1989. "In truth, the strength of the control process rests in its apparent absence. The desired systemic result is achieved ordinarily by a loose though effective institutional process." In his book *Culture, Inc.*, subtitled *The Corporate Takeover of Public Expression*, Schiller went on to cite "the education of journalists and other media professionals, built-in penalties and rewards for doing what is expected, norms presented as objective rules, and the occasional but telling direct intrusion from above. The main lever is the internalization of values."[39]

Self-censorship has long been one of journalism's most ineffable hazards. Waves of mergers that periodically rock the media industry are likely to heighten the dangers. To an unprecedented extent, large numbers of American reporters and editors now work for just a few huge corporate employers, a situation that hardly encourages unconstrained scrutiny of media conglomerates as they assume unparalleled importance in public life.

The mergers also put a lot more journalists on the payrolls of megamedia institutions that are very newsworthy as major economic and social forces. But if those institutions are paying the professionals who provide the bulk of the country's news coverage, how much will the public learn about the internal dynamics and societal effects of these global entities?

Many of us grew up with tales of journalistic courage dating back to Colonial days. John Peter Zenger's ability to challenge the British Crown with unyielding articles drew strength from the fact that he was a printer and publisher. Writing in the *New York Weekly*, a periodical burned several times by the public hangman, Zenger asserted in November 1733: "The loss of liberty in general would soon follow the suppression of the liberty of the press; for it is an essential branch of liberty, so perhaps it is the best preservative of the whole."[40]

In contrast to state censorship, which is usually easy to recognize, self-censorship by journalists tends to be obscured. It is particularly murky and insidious in the emerging media environment, with routine pressures to defer to employers that have massive industry clout and global reach. We might wonder how Zenger would fare in most of today's media workplaces, especially if he chose to denounce as excessive the power of the conglomerate providing his paycheck.

Americans are inclined to quickly spot and automatically distrust government efforts to impose prior restraint. But what about the implicit constraints imposed by the hierarchies of enormous media corporations and internalized by employees before overt conflicts develop?

"If liberty means anything at all," George Orwell wrote, "it means the right to tell people what they do not want to hear."[41] As immense communications firms increasingly dominate our society, how practical will it be for journalists to tell their bosses—and the public—what media tycoons do not want to hear about the concentration of power in few corporate hands? Orwell's novel *1984* describes the conditioned reflex of "stopping short, as though by instinct, at the threshold of any dangerous thought . . . and of being bored or repelled by any train of thought which is capable of leading in a heretical direction."[42]

In the real world, bypassing key issues of corporate dominance is apt to be a form of obedience: in effect, self-censorship. "Circus dogs jump when the trainer cracks his whip," Orwell observed more than half a century ago, "but the really well-trained dog is the one that turns his somersault when there is no whip."[43] Of course, no whips are visible in America's modern newsrooms and broadcast studios. But if Orwell were alive today, he would surely urge us to be skeptical about all the somersaults.

NOTES

1. C. Wright Mills, *The Power Elite* (New York: Oxford University Press, 1956), pp. 345, 346.

2. Vance Packard, *The Status Seekers* (1959), quoted in Leonard Roy Frank, ed., *Influencing Minds* (Portland, OR: Feral House, 1995), p. 133.

3. Stephen Battaglio, "CNN Bullish on Business News," *Hollywood Reporter*, July 19, 1999.

4. David Bauder, "Lou Dobbs to Return to Anchor CNN's 'MoneyLine,'" Associated Press, April 10, 2001.

5. Adam Smith, *The Wealth of Nations* (Amherst, NY: Prometheus Books, 1991).

6. Diana B. Henriques, "Business Reporting: Behind the Curve," *Columbia Journalism Review* (November/December 2000).

7. Ibid.

8. Martin A. Lee and Norman Solomon, *Unreliable Sources: A Guide to Detecting Bias in News Media* (New York: Carol Publishing Group, 1990), p. 182.

9. E. B. White, *Essays of E. B. White* (New York: Harper & Row, 1977), p. 84.

10. Charles Krauthammer, "McCain's Costly Crusade," *Washington Post*, March 23, 2001.

11. "First Say No," *Washington Post*, March 23, 2001.

12. James Brook, Chris Carlsson, and Nancy J. Peters, eds., *Reclaiming San Francisco: History, Politics, Culture* (San Francisco: City Light Books, 1998), pp. 102–103.

13. Arundhati Roy, *Power Politics* (Cambridge, MA: South End Press, 2001), pp. 53, 54, 55.

14. "The Market Can Police Itself," *Wall Street Journal*, June 28, 2002.

15. "Take Hard-Line Approach to Restore Faith in Business," *Atlanta Journal-Constitution*, July 10, 2002.

16. Editorial, "Just Bad Apples? Or Bad Trees?" *Christian Science Monitor*, July 10, 2002.

17. "Capitalism and Conscience," *Washington Post*, July 10, 2002.

18. Marshall McLuhan, *Understanding Media* (1964), quoted in George Seldes, ed., *The Great Thoughts* (New York: Ballantine Books, 1996), p. 308.

19. "Old Dogmas and the New Economy," *BusinessWeek*, July 28, 1997.

20. "New Paradigm with Bountiful Effects," *Washington Times*, July 24, 1997.

21. "Click Till You Drop," *Time*, July 20, 1998.

22. "They're Rich (and You're Not)," *Newsweek*, July 5, 1999.

23. "Too Much of the Bubbly on Wall Street?" *Dollars & Sense*, July 1, 1999.

24. "Get Rich.com: Secrets of the New Silicon Valley, *Time*, September 27, 1999.

25. Chuck Collins and Felice Yeskel, *Economic Apartheid in America: A Primer on Economic Inequality and Security* (New York: New Press, 2000).

26. Du Boff statement in "Bush's Housing Policies; Kerry's Corporate Tax Cut," news release, Institute for Public Accuracy, March 26, 2004.

27. Louis Brandeis, quoted in George Seldes, ed., *The Great Quotations* (New York: Lyle Stuart, 1960).

28. "How Media Giants Are Reassembling the Old Oligopoly," *Wall Street Journal*, September 15, 2003.

29. Ben Bagdikian, *The Media Monopoly*, 6th ed. (Boston: Beacon Press, 2000), p. xxi.

30. Donald L. Barlett and James B. Steele, "How the Little Guy Gets Crunched," *Time*, February 7, 2000.

31. Wallace Stegner, "A Sense of Place," quoted in Seldes, *The Great Thoughts*, p. 437.

32. Seth Sutel, "CBS and Viacom to Combine in Biggest Media Deal Ever," Associated Press, September 7, 1999.

33. Lawrie Mifflin, "Viacom to Buy CBS, Forming 2d Largest Media Company," *New York Times*, September 8, 1999.

34. Floyd Norris, "The New, Improved Redstone Still Knows How to Get His Way," *New York Times*, September 8, 1999.

35. Paul Farhi, "Viacom to Buy CBS, Uniting Multimedia Heavyweights," *Washington Post*, September 8, 1999.

36. "Millennium 2000: Media in the New Century," CNN, January 2, 2000.

37. James F. Peltz and Eric Slater, "Tribune-Times Mirror Merger; Tribune Strategy Melds 'Old' with 'New,'" *Los Angeles Times*, March 14, 2000.

38. David Barboza, "A New Approach to Old Media; Tribune Company Feeds Content to Diverse Outlets," *New York Times*, March 14, 2000.

39. Herbert I. Schiller, *Culture, Inc.: The Corporate Takeover of Public Expression* (New York: Oxford University Press, 1989), p. 8.

40. Zenger quoted in Seldes, ed., *The Great Thoughts*, p. 512.

41. Orwell, from his suppressed introduction to his satiric book *Animal Farm*, quoted in ibid., p. 350.

42. George Orwell, *1984* (New York: Signet, 1977), pp. 174–75.

43. Orwell's circus-dog analogy quoted in Michael Shelden, *Orwell: A Biography* (New York: HarperCollins, 1991), p. 367.

3

TO BE OUR OWN GOVERNORS

The Independent Press and the
Battle for "Popular Information"

JAY HARRIS
PUBLISHER, *MOTHER JONES*

JAY HARRIS *is the publisher of* Mother Jones *magazine and chief executive officer of* Mother Jones' *nonprofit parent, the Foundation for National Progress. During his tenure, the organization has built on its tradition of groundbreaking public interest reporting while growing circulation to unprecedented levels. Believing that* Mother Jones' *investigative content has audience potential beyond print media, he has overseen the 1993 launch and development of MotherJones.com,* Mother Jones' *popular Web site, and has negotiated deals to supply* Mother Jones *material to both* Inside Edition *and PBS's* Frontline.

Harris is vice chair of the Independent Press Association and recently joined the board of advisors of Free Speech TV. Before joining Mother Jones *in 1991, he was general manager of* Newsweek's *Pacific edition, based in Hong Kong, with oversight of circulation programs in twenty-four Asian and South Pacific nations.*

Harris is married to Marcia Cohen, who is Assistant Dean for Fiscal Affairs at the Stanford University School of Medicine. They have two daughters, Amelia (13) and Charlotte (11).

W hatever we might think about the failings of contemporary news media, there's no denying that we're swimming in it. News—at least someone's idea of news—is available through any and every delivery medium we use or contemplate using. It's a vast topic with so many facets that there's no one best place to start. So, keeping it personal, I'll enter from my own backyard—California. Or, as we say nowadays, Cahleefornia.

Despite all of the media hype about Arnold Schwarzenegger's election to the governorship of California in 2003—the national political significance of electing a Republican in a large Democratic state, blah, blah, blah—at the end of the day I don't believe that what happened in California is terribly strange. After all, what did it tell us but that Californians were pissed off at politics as usual? Democratic governor Gray Davis was never an easy guy to warm up to, but the last four weeks of his campaign to avoid recall sealed his doom. That last month put on a superconcentrated display of everything people *dis*liked about him. Every morning Gray was there on the front page of the newspaper, signing some new law or issuing some executive order calculated to win favor with some stripe or another of the California electorate. In both scope and intensity, it was a grotesque display of pandering. Never mind that much of what he did—for immigrants, for gays and lesbians, for the environment—was perfectly fine public policy: his timing told the voters all they needed to know about his character. Perhaps if he'd done those things *out of principle* sometime during his first four years in office, he'd have engendered some of the loyalty needed to help him beat the recall. But by cramming these acts into the last four desperate weeks, he came off like a pimp. In the face of that, I can understand how lots of people, including many Democrats, voted for the Governator.

I was surprised at the size of Arnold's victory, but—with the benefit of hindsight—I am convinced that the anger that drove the California recall election fits with many conversations I've had recently, with smart people from across the country and across much of the political spectrum— committed lefties, liberal and centrist Dems, moderate and even conservative Republicans. They're angry that they're being lied to, they're angry with blatant cronyism, with policy to the highest bidder, and, frankly, they're angry at "the media," too, for being so vacuous when the stakes seem so high.

Call me a cockeyed optimist, but I believe this is a moment of huge opportunity. The stakes *are* high—the 9/11 attacks, a preemptive war, record state deficits, spectacular corporate scandals, a jobless recovery, and a ballooning national debt have brought the public sphere to public attention to a much greater degree than during the Clinton years. But the potential this has for rallying the public's attention and engagement will work to the benefit of our country if and only if we can connect popular concern with better "popular information." To my mind there is no escaping the need for a radical rethinking of how America's news needs—fundamental to a functioning democracy—are met.

The term "popular information," by the way, is from founding father James Madison. More than two hundred years ago, Madison said that "popular government without popular information is a prologue to a farce or a tragedy, or perhaps both."[1] Oh, Jimmy, what would you say if you were around today?

Consider the widening gap between the policy direction of this country and popular values. On issue after issue—health care, jobs and the economy, taxes, international cooperation, the environment—polls show that a majority of Americans express values that are closer to "progressive" policy stances than to those of the current administration and the Republican majority in Congress. What explains that?

Certainly politics is part of it. This Administration understands those popular values—they watch polls, too—and they are shameless about and adept at exploiting them.

The Iraq War was sold as a necessary response to an imminent threat posed by a madman with weapons of mass destruction.

That 2003 tax cut—the one which even the blatantly Tory *Financial Times* characterized as "the inmates running the asylum"—was sold as an economic stimulus and a jobs creation package.[2]

Logging in National Forests—the "Healthy Forests" initiative—was unveiled to uncritical TV reporters as a necessary response to the threat of forest fires.

An amnesty for air polluters was labeled the "Clear Skies" initiative.

But those stories are just the tip of a very large iceberg—most of it missing from the ten o'clock news. How much of the gap between public values and voting behavior is related to the state of our most-read, most-watched news media? Plenty.

Perhaps you'll recall how, in his 2003 State of the Union address, President Bush spun out his bold, "green" initiative for a hydrogen car? Within twenty years, the president said, fuel-cell cars will "make our air significantly cleaner, and our country much less dependent on foreign sources of oil." That is a truly fabulous sound bite.

Only here's the catch: according to a nice bit of reporting that came out in *Mother Jones*, the administration's plan for producing hydrogen, the National Hydrogen Energy Road Map, calls for 90 percent of the hydrogen for the fuel cell program to be cracked from oil and natural gas in a process that burns oil, coal, and natural gas. (The remaining 10 percent will be cracked from water using nuclear energy.) This, of course, is the very same "road map" that was drafted in concert with the energy industry.[3]

The administration has also made "judicial reform" a priority—they want to rescue the courts from "liberal activist" judges. But one critically important aspect of their reform drive has stayed largely under the radar of the press: the business agenda. *Mother Jones* Washington correspondent Michael Scherer recently reported that "since 1998, major corporations— Home Depot, Wal-Mart, and the insurance giant AIG to name a few—have spent more than $100 million through front groups to remake the courts. . . . By targeting incumbent judges in state elections, they have tilted state supreme courts to pro-business majorities and ousted aggressive attorneys general."[4] That pool of conservative judges in state courts creates a farm team from which appointees to the federal bench can be plucked.

To the extent that conservative court-packing has been covered in the mainstream news, the coverage has almost always emphasized the social conservatism of new judges—the business agenda has remained unexplored. Even conservatives have been surprised at this huge hole in the coverage: "The *New York Times* understands sex," conservative leader Grover Norquist explained to *Mother Jones*. "It doesn't understand money."[5]

There's another gap in the news when it comes to stories that make overt connections between policies and the lives of regular people. Reporter Stephanie Mencimer wrote a story for *Mother Jones* about Henderson, North Carolina, a textile mill town that has fallen on hard times.[6]

One of the key figures in her story is Sam Jefferson, a forty-eight-year-old father of three and a thirty-year employee of Harriet and Henderson Yarns. When the Bush administration, seeking basing rights for an air assault on Iraq, cut a deal with Turkey and Pakistan to increase textile imports from those countries, those imports pushed Harriet and Henderson into bankruptcy, and Sam Jefferson lost his job. For the first time in his life, he went on unemployment insurance from the state. But the state has problems, too: North Carolina's income tax rates are tied to federal rates, so the state has lost nearly a half a billion in revenue as a result of the Bush tax cuts. After he lost his job, Sam looked into a state job-training program for aspiring truck drivers, but the program had been eliminated in the face of state deficits.

The plot gets thicker—and more heartrending. Sam Jefferson has three kids; when the article was written, his oldest girl was a senior in high school, a good student aspiring to go to college. Because of the state's budget situation, tuitions at state colleges have been dramatically raised, and now the least expensive state college costs $7,000 a year. That's still too much for Sam to afford, especially now that the Bush Department of Education has changed the formula for calculating federal tuition aid eligibility and frozen the funding for Pell grants, the federal program created to assist low-income students with college tuition. Back in the 1970s these grants covered an average of 84 percent of tuition at public universities; today they cover an average of 40 percent. When his daughter asked him what was going to happen, Jefferson had to reply, "It doesn't look too good."

The human story behind the sound bites—"compassionate conservatism," "job creation," "leave no child behind"—has human interest as well as public importance. Yet news coverage of current issues is often little more than made-for-TV sound bites from officials and politicians; the meatier, more complicated stories about human consequences rarely make news, much less headlines. Why aren't the substantive stories also "headline news"?

Part of the answer is related, I believe, to the profit and stock price concerns of a few gigantic media companies, the few behemoths that dominate the entertainment industry after three decades of dramatic consolidation. When a former *Washington Post* managing editor named Ben Bagdikian published the first edition of his classic book *Media Monopoly* in 1983, he made the case that public understanding had suffered when a mere fifty companies controlled 90 percent of what Americans read, see, and hear for news. Seventeen years later that number of controlling companies was down to six.

What does consolidation do to *the news*? In the spring of 2003, days before the FCC voted to ease restrictions on cross-ownership between newspapers, TV, and radio, Ted Turner wrote an op-ed in the *Washington Post*: the proposed changes, he argued, "will extend the market dominance of the media corporations that control most of what Americans read, see, or hear" and "give them more power to cut important ideas out of the public debate."[7]

Now that's interesting. Turner said what few media moguls have copped to publicly, that the news business selects the ideas they'll let into the public debate, and that ideas are, in effect, screened by large private companies. So let's think for a minute about what filters the decision makers use.

Certainly, bottom-line interests—profits and stock price—are everyday concerns driving news executives, and many news decisions flow, not from any obligation felt to the public and their need to know, but from what drives business results. Bottom-line concerns eliminate stories that might offend advertisers (for instance, the failure of the national newsmagazines to cover the health effects of cigarette smoking during the 1970s and 1980s). They drive producers and reporters to cover celebrity fluff and scandal (those stories are cheap to produce, and they tend to draw strong ratings and support ad sales efforts). Bottom-line interests lead to cuts in newsroom staffs and bureaus. (A producer who had worked for CNN since its founding says that one of the first things AOL did when it acquired CNN was to gut the investigative reporting staff of the network—from thirty people down to ten, and most of those assigned to do what he called "*People* magazine stories.") Business concerns can sap not only the wallet but the will needed for investigative reporting. Investigations are expensive, yes, but equally problematic is the potential for old-fashioned muckraking to complicate the business and political life of management. ("You send someone out for six months on expenses," a former managing editor of the *Wall Street Journal* told *Mother Jones*, "And then the roof falls in.")[8]

The problem of consolidation, though, goes deeper than the obvious factors of budgets, audience, and advertising. Large, publicly traded media companies have complicated and multilevel relationships with many of the industries and with the government they are supposed to cover. Like any big industry, Big Media wants good relations with banks and Wall Street. They want favors from government including preferential access to broadcast spectrum, easier license renewals, less regulation, and, of course, permission to consolidate still further. Their reporters need access to industry leaders and government officials—access that can be denied if coverage isn't appropriately deferential. The impact of these relationships on the quality of news is devastating, all the more so because the influence can be hard to see.

In April 2003 all of the national newspapers and the news networks covered the $1.4 billion settlement reached between state and local securities regulators and ten Wall Street firms. These were the banking and securities companies whose stock analysts had, during the early days of the 1999–2000 stock market bust, fudged evaluations of various stocks in order to win and sustain business for their investment banking arms. The list included Merrill Lynch, Credit Suisse First Boston, Morgan Stanley, Citigroups' Salomon Smith Barney, Piper Jaffray, Goldman Sachs, Lehman Brothers, Bear Stearns, J. P. Morgan Chase, and UBS Warburg—in other words, the biggest swinging dicks on Wall Street. Only a few of the media reports noted that the size of the settlement was puny compared to the collective balance sheets of these firms, but the fundamental problem was not that these stories weren't critical. The problem was their timing.

The illegal practices that were the basis for the settlement had been brought to light not by the press but by the investigative arm of the New York State attorney general's office. Where were these business reporters back in the go-go years of 1999 and 2000? Writing glowing stories about Enron's business model?

Today, in light of yesterday's financial services scandals, we should be asking our reporters to look at the bigger picture of how those scandals occurred—how, for instance, might deregulation of the financial services sector have contributed to this and other scandals?—but also to look ahead: where should we consumers be looking next? It's on stories like those where good reporters should make their bones.

But don't hold your breath. Many in the press today have become what one *Mother Jones* editor called "sheep in wolves' clothing." Their image is ferocious enough: we've all seen the packs of press "wolves" assaulting grieving families with microphones and a fusillade of questions. Could this be the same breed that meekly participated in a sham press conference with President Bush, complicit in the staging even while knowing that the administration had picked questions and questioners in advance?

The level of meekness today suggests to me that, three years into the Bush administration, bottom-line preoccupations have been fused with something much darker: blatant political censorship. Intimidation tactics and clamp downs on information by the administration have been met in the corporate media by acquiescence and willfully blind allegiance.

In no period was it worse than in the run up to the Iraq War. Between January 30 and February 12, 2003 (encompassing the time of Colin Powell's presentation to the UN of the administration's case for an Iraq invasion), the media watchdog group FAIR conducted a study of who the networks used to comment on the administration's case for preemptive war.

Of on-camera network news sources quoted, 76 percent were current or former government officials. Further, according to FAIR, "at a time when 61 percent of US respondents were telling pollsters that more time was needed for diplomacy and inspections, only 6 percent of US sources on the four networks were skeptics regarding the need for war." Only three of 393 sources—less than 1 percent—were identified as being affiliated with anti-war activism.[9]

Phil Donahue, once and briefly a liberal voice on MSNBC, seems to have been a victim of network cowardice. In the weeks before the shooting started in Iraq, there was an internal report within NBC that argued that Donahue would be "a difficult public face for NBC in a time of war. . . . He seems to delight in presenting guests who are antiwar, anti-Bush and skeptical of the administration's motives." At the time his show was canceled, Donahue had the highest ratings on MSNBC.

Arianna Huffington, the independent California crusader and columnist, had her feisty column bounced from an Oregon newspaper because, the editor said, when she wrote about SUVs and the connection between our addiction to oil and national ambitions in the Persian Gulf, she crossed the line from journalist to advocate.

Peter Arnett, a Pulitzer Prize–winning reporter, was reporting "unembedded" for NBC from hostile territory, but he granted a prewar interview to Iraqi TV in which he said, probably accurately but certainly controversially, that his reports from Baghdad were being used by the US and European antiwar movements. The National Geographic Society, his employer, and NBC, for whom he was freelancing, initially defended him. But in the twenty-four hours before he was fired, *National Geographic* received thirty thousand subscription cancellations, and it didn't take long before the companies caved to the pressure.

And in what I believe should be considered one of the most scandalous media embarrassments in a shameful time, the story of the staging of Pvt. Jessica Lynch's "rescue" from her Iraqi captors was brought to light, not by American reporters, but by the BBC and Canadian television. Though our coalition partner, the British government, was spinning, too, *their* media stayed appropriately skeptical of the official line. Ours did not. Why?

First, we're seeing a level of political hardball that is simply unprecedented. This is the most locked-down, secretive White House since the dawn of broadcast, and they will punish news organizations that, in their opinion, step out of line. The White House's leak of CIA operative Valerie Plame's cover in apparent reprisal for her husband's, Joseph Wilson, criticism of Bush's pretext for war is a particularly vicious, but hardly unique, example.

Christiane Amanpour, the CNN reporter, recently acknowledged the previously unspeakable about CNN's prewar coverage: "Perhaps, to a certain extent, my station was intimidated by the administration and its foot soldiers at Fox News."[10]

As I write this, in the spring of 2004, a controversy is brewing about the still-enduring censorship of war coverage. ABC's *Nightline* has announced that it will devote an entire show to a reading of the names of the soldiers who have died in the Iraq War, while a photograph of each shows on the screen. But, according to MoveOn.org, dozens of ABC affiliate stations around the country will be blocked from airing the special. The Sinclair

Broadcasting Group, the company that owns those affiliates, has said that the *Nightline* plans are political and "contrary to the public interest."

But it isn't just war coverage affected by these tactics. In the spring of 2003, *Washington Post* reporter Jonathan Weisman recounted his own story of "playing ball" with the White House, allowing them to manipulate a quote from a White House source in a story about Bush economic advisor R. Glenn Hubbard.

When Weisman's story ran with only a part of the concocted quote, Weisman was, he writes, treated to "an angry denunciation by the White House press official, telling me I had broken my word and violated journalistic ethics." Using measured words that, if anything, understate the problem, Weisman writes: "the notion that reporters are routinely submitting quotations for approval, and allowing those quotes to be manipulated to get that approval, strikes me as a step beyond business as usual."[11]

Careful, measured words from the mainstream. Angry denunciations from the White House and their allies. There's a window here onto a second aspect of the war of intimidation and information control. In a War is Peace turn worthy of an Orwell novel, the press and the public have been subjected to a tidal wave of allegations of "liberal media," charges that would be laughable if they didn't have the effect of making careful, measured media types even more wimpy. Bernard Goldberg's *Bias* and Ann Coulter's *Slander* sat prominently on best-seller lists for months, and their arguments, defensible or not, continue to echo through the political system. Louisiana congressman Billy Tauzin has, for instance, announced an investigation of PBS for allowing Bill Moyers's "liberal crusade" on the air. Those of us who have felt all along that these protests were little more than political mischief making were vindicated recently when Matt Labash, a senior writer at the conservative *Weekly Standard*, was quoted on the nature of the game being played: "Criticize other people for not being objective. Be as subjective as you want. It's a great little racket."[12]

Second, the administration knows what makes news today and, when they're up to something sneaky and want to stay *out* of the news, they're very good at exploiting the weaknesses of the press to do so.

Recently *Mother Jones*'s editors produced a package of stories on the administration's "stealth" campaign against the environment. The central strategy, clearly aimed at the dismantling of thirty years of environmental protection, has been to wreak havoc with environmental law not through the legislative process but quietly, within the "sleep-inducing realm" of bureaucrats and regulation. So that when, for instance, they appoint Mark Rey, for twenty years a preeminent lobbyist for the timber and paper industries, to be our top forestry official, it goes missing from the news.

Fourth, to feed the content needs of a 24/7 news world, the right has created a formidable and prolific spin machine.

Sure, you know about Rush Limbaugh. His numbers are impressive—some 20 million people listen to Rush every week compared to 11.8 million people who tune in every week to NPR's *Morning Edition*. But Limbaugh is only the delivery guy. The apparatus feeding him material is as extensive as it is extreme.

Check out, for instance, the Web site "NGOWatch.org." The conservative American Enterprise Institute (AEI), along with the Federalist Society, has created a site where one can learn about the threats posed by, yes, nongovernmental organizations (NGOs)—a category that includes CARE, Doctors without Borders, and Amnesty International. According to the AEI, NGOs are undermining democracy by waging "network warfare on corporations." The AEI is advocating the use of private contractors in international relief work if the NGOs don't respond to their call to "publicize the US brand" when they deliver aid.

The Heritage Foundation, with a 2002 budget of $23.5 million, proudly calls itself the "megaphone of conservatism." Heritage runs a think tank and a research institute, publishes 440,000 copies of more than 230 research papers and studies, maintains two Web sites frequented by 22 million people, and regularly sends its top policy analysts to brief the cabinet and congressional leaders. Their biannual is attended by both Republicans and Democrats. And they make it their business to meet with, inform, and train in data analysis members of the media in order to help them to "better understand the facts, so their stories are more accurate."

Let's hand it to 'em. They work hard at perfuming their pigs. In an article in the *American Prospect* the linguist George Lakoff discusses how conservatives have become very adept at using frameworks of words that make their ideas sound palatable to a broad swath of Americans. For instance, on the day that George W. Bush took office, he began to speak of "tax relief." Those words, says Lakoff, bring to mind a whole set of associations: 1) the affliction of taxes, 2) the victims of taxes (that would be you), 3) the villains who inflict taxes, and 4) the heroes who relieve us of them.[13]

If you go to the Web site of the Environmental Working Group, you can see a doozy of an example of Compassionate Conservative–speak: Republican political strategist Frank Luntz's memo to Republican Party leaders in which he urges them to use a form of enviro-speak in their public utterances so as to mask the true impact of environmental deregulation. Advising leaders to redefine labels by choosing terms like "climate change" rather than "global warming" or "conservationists" rather than "preservationists," he evokes positive, commonsense connotations that avoid extremist associations.

So as conservatives work to reduce environmental safeguards, advocating changes which, if they were fully understood, would be unpopular, Luntz provides tips for rhetorical cover, the palatable language that obscures the threat. This isn't Madison's "popular information"—it is sophistry, *dis*information, and whether the end result is confusion or a false sense of security, the loser is our democracy.

Cynical? Absolutely.

Transparent? Yeah, if you're paying attention.

Effective? Well, if the lead sound bite on the evening news is a focus-group tested, green-washed platitude from the president about Clear Skies or Healthy Forests, and the reporters covering the White House are too lazy or too scared to point out the gap between the administration's words and its actions, it seems quite possible that the average Joe or Jill, with not a lot of time, not a lot of money, who may listen to Rush Limbaugh, who may only read the magazines you can buy at Wal-Mart, who quite possibly may still hold, with a lot of the rest of us, a deeply felt desire to believe our leaders, may swallow the party line. For a while. Perhaps for many months.

But what happens when they find out the truth? If you think there was an earthquake when the voters of California took the measure of Gray Davis, just imagine what's possible if we can get the truth out about the Bush-Cheney mob.

There is already plenty of evidence that, in the face of ideological drivel on the one hand (e.g., Fox "News") and bland homogeneity on the other (e.g., the networks), many people are simply choosing not to spend their time with the traditional news channels.

According to surveys from the Pew Center for the People and the Press, the audience for traditional news sources is plummeting. Between 1993 and 2002, the percentage of Americans watching local TV news nightly fell from 77 to 57 percent. The percentage watching nightly network news fell from 60 to 32 percent. Daily newspaper readership declined from 58 to 41 percent.[14]

These are huge audience losses in only nine years. And to the extent that the news has turned into an entertainment, you could argue that it shows, once again, that the people may be smarter than the news folks give them credit for. But for the people simply to abandon the news is problematic. We're in a dangerous time and ignorance is not a solution.

James Madison went on to say that "a people who mean to be their own governors must arm themselves with the power which knowledge gives." The stakes in the information war couldn't be higher. The choice between popular information and disinformation is the choice between democracy and fascism.

I believe that it is up to thinking people from across the political spectrum to turn this situation to the benefit of our democracy, to the health of our body politic. So let's go to work. What do we have to work with?

By abandoning mass news in droves, the American people have shown they aren't masochists—that's a start.

Further, most of us were born with fairly well-developed "shit detectors," to borrow a phrase from Hemingway. Sure, schools and jobs and social norms can throw sand in the gears, but they're there, ready to be tuned up and switched on.

Further still, there is an amazing, often awe-inspiring independent press that is getting their stories straight and keeping them bubbling until they can burst into view on Main Street. With your help, the independents can be a much more powerful network for getting the word out.

I don't say this lightly. There have been dark times in our country's history when the independent press was absolutely central to fundamental, even radical, change. Have you ever heard of the *Liberator*? According to journalist Bob Ostertag, this tiny abolitionist newspaper, first published in 1831 by William Lloyd Garrison,

> had only 3,000 subscribers at its peak. Even by the standards of its time this was a tiny operation, yet . . . its demand for an immediate, as opposed to gradual, end to slavery moved from the outer fringe to the core of the emancipation movement and finally to Lincoln's Emancipation Proclamation.

Such boldness leaves a legacy: the *Liberator*'s uncompromising style spread beyond the abolitionists to inspire and inform the early women's rights activists. If one crusading publisher can effect that kind of change, think what is possible today, when the independent choices are greater and collectively more powerful than ever.

At the end of the 1960s, at that peak of social ferment, the Alternative Press Index included seventy-two active periodicals on the "alternative" end of the spectrum. Today, the Independent Press Association represents over five hundred member publications. Independent weekly newspapers have filled the void left by the chaining of metropolitan dailies and crusade effectively within their hometowns. Pacifica Radio has center-of-the-dial FM licenses in five of America's biggest cities and hundreds of affiliate community radio stations across the country. Free Speech TV and Link TV are 24/7 satellite stations dedicated to independent news and community values. Newsletters like Jim Hightower's *Lowdown* bundle facts with attitude in the spirit and form of the Revolutionary-era pamphleteers. Alternet, Salon.com, and TomPaine.com offer daily news, commentary, and thoughtful analysis to anyone who has an Internet connection.

Reality check: there are some significant, uh, structural problems within the independent media world.

Distribution, for one. Consolidation has reduced the number of mainline magazine distribution companies to four majors, and big retailers from Safeway to Walgreen's to Wal-Mart allocate precious rack space to only high-margin titles.

Money for another. There may be a rich tradition of independent publishing in this country, but we're talking rich in thought as opposed to rolling in dough. Two of my favorite publications, *Harper's* and the *Nation*, have together been publishing for more than three hundred years—and together they've mustered just one year in the black. The lack of financial prospects for many independent media endeavors severely limits access to traditional investment capital and, because of that, the availability of money for marketing, for promoting both products and ideas to new audiences is scarce to nonexistent. We need, through a combination of smarter business practices and a deeper appreciation among capitalists and philanthropists of how ideas are spread, to channel money to the functions that increase our reach and impact.

Then there are self-inflicted wounds. The good guys can be weighty and whiney and, though righteous, tedious and depressing. Shortly after I began working at *Mother Jones*, my wife offered me a new tagline for the magazine—"*Mother Jones*: Things Are Even Worse Than You Thought." But we've worked, and we keep working, on tone, on the narrative pull of the writing, on art direction and photography that invites readers into even challenging subjects, and, yes, even on humor. Jim Hightower reminds us, "Mr. Humor is our friend."

For all those chronic lacks, there is great power—enormous, often underrated power—in the network of the independent media. And our greatest allies in the work that lies ahead are people who take pride in keeping themselves informed.

If you're one of those (hint: you're reading this book), you probably have more influence than you know. Your braniac tendencies, the ones that may have caused you social problems in high school, will serve us all well if we can harness them and get them pointed in the right direction. You are, or could be, looked up to by the people with whose lives you intersect, respected for your engagement in the world. It is my deeply held belief that if we can combine the best work of the independent press with the clout our readers have in their own communities, if together we break out of our comfort zones and stand up for better media, we can effect great change in the quality of the news and, through that, in our politics.

Should we spend our time trying to legislate the broadcast news toward some kind of public interest ideal? Probably not. Sure, we should fight back against further consolidation, fight to roll back the worst of the FCC changes, use our clout to return the use of our broadcast frequencies to a public interest standard. But the greatest force for change in the mass channels will be the market.

Those numbers that I quoted to you about the decline in news viewership? They scare the bejesus out of the media moguls. It's possible that some will panic and that television news will become even more sensational. (If the news norm of today is "if it bleeds, it leads," just imagine what might tomorrow bring? Others may try to compete with quality. Just by tuning in to watch the good stuff, we might get more Jon Stewarts, more *Daily Shows*.)

But for you people of action out there, I have some modest suggestions about what you can do to grease the wheels of the market and put them on more of a "popular information" track.

First, if you haven't already done so, put yourself on a media diet. Read, watch, listen to and support independent media. As too much fat or sugar clogs your arteries, a diet too rich in sweet stuff of commercial broadcast news narrows your mind. Yes, I do believe that all of us who have the means and want to know what's what should read a national daily newspaper. (If you don't have the means but have access to a computer, read one online for free.) But if the daily paper is your fiber, think of independent media as the fruits and vegetables of a healthy media diet: strive for five—at least five servings of independent thought every day. The media diet doesn't have to be boring. For a hoot sometime go window-shopping on the Web site of the Independent Press Association: there are over five hundred righteously independent member publications from Bitch and Bust to Adbusters, Clamor, and Fader.

My second charge to you is to invite your neighbors over for dinner and organize a media watch squad for your town. Help keep your local media honest. Write to, or meet with, local editors and broadcasters—praise what they do well and take them to task for the gaps in their coverage. Remind them of those popular information ideals that first called them into journalism.

Meanwhile, broaden your circle. Clip, physically or digitally, your favorite stories and pass them on to others, share insights and information. If you have kids, go to their school and agitate for media literacy to be part of the curriculum—get those BS detectors switched on at an early age.

Finally, as Bay Area media guru Scoop Nisker says, "if you don't like the news, go out and make some of your own." You can, of course, make news by agitating for the things you care about. Ten million people in the streets in February 2003 forced the mainstream news to cover the peace movement and, in so doing, touched millions more who had their doubts about "pre-emptive" war. And you can "make news" by making media. Become a part of the all-important connective tissue that will get more of us informed, engaged, and networked independent of the networks—whether or not Big Media wakes up.

NOTES

1. Letter to W. T. Barry, August 4, 1822, http://press-pubs.uchicago.edu/founders/documents/v1ch18s35.html.

2. "Letter to America," *Financial Times*, May 29, 2004, p. 44.

3. Barry Lynn, "Hydrogen's Dirty Secret," *Mother Jones* (May/June 2004): 15.

4. Michael Scherer, "The Making of the Corporate Judiciary," *Mother Jones* (November/December 2003): 72.

5. Ibid.

6. Stephanie Mencimer, "Death by a Thousand Cuts," *Mother Jones* (November/December 2004): 48.

7. Ted Turner, "Monopoly or Democracy?" *Washington Post*, May 30, 2003, p. A23.

8. Although this was told to the *Mother Jones* editor, it was never published.

9. See http://www.fair.org/reports/iraq-sources.html.

10. CNBC transcript of *Topic A with Tina Brown* interview, September 10, 2003.

11. First posted at http://www.poynter.org/forum/default.asp?id=32246.

12. Interview at http://www.journalismjobs.com/matt_labash.cfm.

13. See http://www.alternet.org/mediaculture/19811/.

14. See graphs at http://people-press.org/reports/display.php3?PageID=834.

II

MASS DECEPTION

How Corporate Media Are
Systematically Misleading Americans

4

MONOPOLY MEDIA MANIPULATION

MICHAEL PARENTI
POLITICAL ANALYST

MICHAEL PARENTI *is an internationally known, award-winning political analyst. Nominated for a Pulitzer Prize in 2003, he has won awards from Project Censored, the Caucus for a New Political Science, New Jersey Peace Action, the city of Santa Cruz, and various academic and political organizations. Receiving his PhD in political science from Yale University, he has taught at a number of colleges and universities in the United States and abroad. Dr. Parenti is the author of seventeen books and some 250 articles appearing in scholarly journals, political periodicals, and various magazines and newspapers. Among his recent books are* The Assassination of Julius Caesar *(New Press, 2003),* The Terrorism Trap *(City Lights Books, 2002), and* Democracy for the Few *(Wadsworth, seventh edition, 2002). Dr. Parenti appears widely on radio and television talk shows to discuss current issues, and his lectures and commentaries are aired on radio stations and cable community access stations in the United States, Canada, and abroad.*

An earlier version of this paper appeared in Michael Parenti, *America Besieged*. Copyright © 1998 by Michael Parenti. Reprinted by permission of City Lights Books.

In a capitalist society like the United States, the corporate news media more or less reflect the dominant class ideology of their owners in both their reportage and commentary. At the same time, these media leave the impression that they are free and independent, capable of balanced coverage and objective commentary. How they achieve these seemingly contradictory but legitimating goals is a matter worthy of study. Notables in the media industry claim that occasional inaccuracies do occur in news coverage because of innocent errors and everyday production problems such as deadline pressures, budgetary restraints, and the difficulty of reducing a complex story into a concise report. Furthermore, no communication system can hope to report everything, hence selectivity is needed.

To be sure, such pressures and problems do exist and honest mistakes are made, but do they really explain the media's overall performance? True the press must be selective, but what principle of selectivity is involved? I would argue that media bias usually does not occur in random fashion; rather, it moves in more or less consistent directions, favoring management over labor, corporations over corporate critics, affluent whites over low-income minorities, officialdom over protestors, the two-party monopoly over leftist third parties, privatization and free-market "reforms" over public sector development, US dominance of the third world over revolutionary or populist social change, and conservative commentators and columnists over progressive or radical ones.

SUPPRESSION BY OMISSION

Some critics complain that the press is sensationalistic and invasive. In fact, it is more often muted and evasive. More insidious than the sensationalistic hype is the artful avoidance. Truly *sensational* stories (as opposed to sensationalistic) are downplayed or avoided outright. Sometimes the suppression includes not just vital details but the entire story itself, even ones of major import. Reports that might reflect poorly upon the national security state are least likely to see the light of day. Thus we hear about political repression perpetrated by officially designated "rogue" governments, but information about the brutal murder and torture practiced by US-sponsored surrogate forces in the third world and other crimes committed by the US national security state are denied public airing, being suppressed with a consistency that would be called "totalitarian" were it to occur in some other countries.

The media downplay stories of momentous magnitude. In 1965 the Indonesian military—advised, equipped, trained, and financed by the US military and the CIA—overthrew President Achmed Sukarno and eradicated the Indonesian Communist Party and its allies, killing half a million people (some estimates are as high as a million) in what was the greatest act of political mass murder since the Nazi Holocaust. The generals also destroyed hundreds of clinics, libraries, schools, and community centers that had been established by the Communists. Here was a sensational story if ever there was one, but it took three months before it received passing mention in *Time* magazine and yet another month before it was reported in the *New York Times* (April 5, 1966), accompanied by an editorial that actually praised the Indonesian military for "rightly playing its part with utmost caution."

Over the course of forty years, the CIA involved itself with drug traffickers in Italy, France, Corsica, Indochina, Afghanistan, and Central and South America. Much of this activity was the object of extended congressional investigation—by Senator Frank Church's committee and Congressman Otis Pike's committee in the 1970s, and Senator John Kerry's committee in the late 1980s. But the corporate capitalist media seem not to have heard about it.

ATTACK AND DESTROY THE TARGET

When omission proves to be an insufficient mode of censorship and a story somehow begins to reach larger publics, the press moves from artful avoidance to frontal assault in order to discredit the story. In August 1996, the *San Jose Mercury News,* drawing from a year-long investigation, ran an in-depth series about the CIA-contra crack shipments that were flooding East Los Angeles. Holding true to form, the major media mostly ignored the issue. But the *Mercury News* series was picked up by some local and regional newspapers, and was flashed across the world on the Internet copiously supplemented with pertinent documents and depositions supporting the charges against the CIA. African American urban communities, afflicted by the crack epidemic, were up in arms and wanted to know more. The story became difficult to ignore. So the major media began an all-out assault. A barrage of hit pieces in the *Washington Post* and *New York Times* and on network television and PBS assured us that there was no evidence of CIA involvement, that the *Mercury News* series was "bad journalism," and that its investigative reporter Gary Webb was irresponsibly playing on the public's gullibility and conspiracy mania. By a process of relentless attack and shameless mendacity, the major media exonerated the CIA from any involvement in drug trafficking.

LABELING

Like all propagandists, mainstream media people seek to prefigure our perception of a subject with a positive or negative label. Some positive ones are "stability," "the president's firm leadership," "a strong defense," and "a healthy economy." Indeed, not many Americans would want instability, wobbly presidential leadership, a weak defense, and a sick economy. The label defines the subject without having to deal with actual particulars that might lead us to a different conclusion.

Some common negative labels are "leftist guerrillas," "Islamic terrorists," "conspiracy theories," "inner-city gangs," and "civil disturbances." These, too, are seldom treated within a larger context of social relations and issues. The press itself is facilely and falsely labeled "the liberal media" by the hundreds of conservative columnists, commentators, and talk-shows hosts who crowd the communication universe while claiming to be shut out from it. Some labels we will never be exposed to are "class power," "class struggle," and "US imperialism."

A new favorite among deceptive labels is "reforms," whose meaning is inverted, being applied to any policy dedicated to *undoing* the reforms that have been achieved after decades of popular struggle. So the destruction of family assistance programs is labeled "welfare reform." "Reforms" in eastern Europe, and most recently in Yugoslavia, have meant the heartless impoverishment of former Communist countries, the dismantling of what remained of the public economy, its deindustrialization and expropriation at fire-sale prices by a corporate investor class, complete with massive layoffs, drastic cutbacks in public assistance and human services, and a dramatic increase in unemployment and human suffering. "IMF reforms" is a euphemism for the same kind of bruising cutbacks throughout the third world. As economist and media analyst Edward Herman once noted, "reforms" are not the solution, they are the problem.

In April 2001, the newly elected prime minister of Japan, Junichiro Koisumi, was widely identified in the US media as a "reformer." His free-market "reforms" include the privatization of Japan's postal saving system. Millions of Japanese citizens have their life savings in the postal system and the "reformer" Koisumi wants private investors to be able to get their hands on these funds.

"Free market" has long been a pet label, evoking images of economic plenitude and democracy. In reality, free-market policies undermine the markets of local producers, provide state subsidies to multinational corporations, destroy public sector services, and create greater gaps between the wealthy few and the underprivileged many.

Another favorite media label is "hard-line." Anyone who resists free-market "reforms," be it in Belarus, Italy, Peru, or Yugoslavia, is labeled a "hard-liner." An article in the *New York Times* (October 21, 1997) used "hard-line" and "hard-liner" eleven times to describe Bosnian Serb leaders who opposed attempts by NATO forces to close down the "hard-line Bosnian Serb broadcast network." The radio station in question was the only one in all of Bosnia that offered a perspective critical of Western intervention in Yugoslavia. The forceful closing of this one remaining dissenting media voice was described by the *Times* as "a step toward bringing about responsible news coverage in Bosnia." The story did note "the apparent irony" of using foreign soldiers for "silencing broadcasts in order to encourage free speech." The NATO troops who carried out this repressive task were identified with the positive label of "peacekeepers."

It is no accident that labels like "hard-line" are never subjected to precise definition. The efficacy of a label is that it not have a specific content which can be held up to a test of evidence. Better that it be self-referential, propagating an undefined but evocative image.

PREEMPTIVE ASSUMPTION

Frequently the media accept as given the very policy position that needs to be critically examined. Whenever the White House proposes an increase in military spending, press discussion is limited to how much more spending is needed, how much updating of weaponry; are we doing enough or need we do still more? No media exposure is given to those who hotly contest the already gargantuan arms budget in its totality. It is assumed that US forces must be deployed around the world and that hundreds of billions must be spent each year on this global military system.

Likewise with media discussion of Social Security "reform," a euphemism for the privatization and eventual abolition of a program that is working well. The media preemptively assume the very dubious position that needs to be debated: that the program is in danger of insolvency (in thirty-five years) and therefore in need of drastic overhauling today. Social Security operates as a three-pronged human service: in addition to retirement pensions, it provides survivors' insurance (up until the age of eighteen) to children in families that have lost their breadwinner, and it offers disability assistance to persons of preretirement age who have sustained serious injury or illness. But from existing press coverage you would not know this—and most Americans do not.

FACE-VALUE TRANSMISSION

Many labels are fabricated not by news media but by officialdom. US governmental and corporate leaders talk about "our global leadership," "national security," "free markets," and "globalization" when what they mean is "All Power to the Transnationals." The media uncritically and dutifully accept these official views, transmitting them to wider publics without any noticeable critical comment regarding the actual content of the policy. Face-value transmission has characterized the press's performance in almost every area of domestic and foreign policy.

When challenged on this, reporters respond that they cannot inject their own personal views into their reports. Actually, no one is asking them to. My criticism is that they already do, and seldom realize it. Their conventional ideological perceptions usually coincide with those of their bosses and with officialdom in general, making them face-value purveyors of the prevailing orthodoxy. This uniformity of bias is perceived as "objectivity."

The alternative to challenging face-value transmission is not to editorialize about the news but to question the assertions made by officialdom, to consider critical data that might give credence to an alternative view. Such an effort is not an editorial or ideological pursuit but an empirical and investigative one, albeit one that is not usually tolerated in the capitalist press beyond certain safely limited parameters.

REPETITION AND NORMALIZATION

In keeping with their propaganda function, the media often rush into areas that politicians might at first avoid. Before the attack on Yugoslavia, various news stories ran unsubstantiated reports about mass killings. Because of the scarcity of evidence and unreliability of reports, the word "genocide" at first appeared in these stories in quotation marks, indicating that such a sweeping and sensationalized term was being used tentatively. But then once the word was in the air, and after repeated use, the quotation marks soon disappeared, and *genocide* it was, almost always blamed on the Serbs and established as a firm fact impervious to contrary evidence. Indeed, evidence became quite irrelevant.

The September 11, 2001, terrorist attacks on the World Trade Center and the Pentagon, resulting in the loss of some three thousand lives, were labeled several times on that very day by NBC anchorman Tom Brokaw as "a war." Brokaw said what no politician yet dared to say: "This is *war!*" Other commentators and pundits also quickly announced that Americans are going to have to surrender a good amount of their freedom in order to have more security. Thus did media spokespersons, like the good propagandists they are, clear away new ground for political leaders to venture upon, in this instance providing us with war against Afghanistan and repressive measures such as the PATRIOT Act. Here was normalization: making the unthinkable acceptable by saying it again and again.

For several months the press was consumed by September 11 and its aftermath. Every panel of pundits, every hosted TV show, newspaper editorial, letter to the editor, syndicated column, guest column, and just about every news story dwelled on the terrorist attacks, offering a seemingly infinite constellation of spin-off stories. One favorite was the interviews with various individuals who would say something like: "I was a peacenik during the Vietnam era but this time I am all for bombing the hell out of those terrorists in Afghanistan." Another instance of normalization.

Throughout the autumn of 2002, a controversy raged within the United States and across the entire globe as to whether the United States had the right to invade Iraq. While many US news outlets took no vigorous editorial stand on the issue, the media did play a crucial role in making the war acceptable by repeatedly running reports on the military preparedness that was taking place. "If we *do* go to war," newscasters would intone, "these are the kinds of missiles that will be used with deadly accuracy" (accompanied by footage of a missile hitting its target). So day after day, the public was treated to reports about reservists being called up, fleets taking to the seas, air attack squadrons put at the ready, troops running through desert maneuvers in Kuwait, and US supply lines being set up in the Middle East. Through a seemingly neutral face-value exposure and repetition, the matter-of-fact coverage of preparedness for war made military intervention in Iraq seem likely, urgent, inevitable, needed, and quite acceptable.

SLIGHTING OF CONTENT

One has to marvel at how the corporate news media can give so much emphasis to surface happenings, to style and process, and so little to the substantive issues at stake. A glaring example is the way elections are covered. The political campaign is reduced to a horse race: who will run? Who will get the nomination? Who will win the election? News commentators sound like theater critics as they hold forth on how this or that candidate projected a positive image, came across effectively, and had a good rapport with the audience. The actual issues are accorded scant attention, and the democratic dialogue that is supposed to accompany a contest for public office rarely is heard through the surface din.

Accounts of major strikes—on those rare occasions the press attends to labor struggles—offer a similar slighting of content while focusing heavily on process. We are told how many days the strike has lasted, the inconvenience and cost to the public and the economy, and how negotiations threaten to break down. Missing is any reference to the substance of the conflict, the grievances that drive workers reluctantly to the extreme expediency of a strike, such as cutbacks in wages and benefits, loss of seniority, safety issues, or the unwillingness of management to negotiate a contract.

Media pundits often talk about the "larger picture." In fact, their ability or willingness to link immediate events and issues to larger social relations is almost nonexistent, nor would a broader analysis be tolerated by their bosses. Instead, they regularly give us the *smaller* picture, this being a way of slighting content and remaining within politically safe boundaries. Thus the many demonstrations against international free-trade agreements beginning with NAFTA and GATT are reported, if at all, as contests between protestors and police with little reference to the issues of democratic sovereignty and unaccountable corporate power that impel the protestors.

Consider the press treatment of the suppression of the vote in Florida during the 2000 presidential campaign. After a count of ballots by the *Miami Herald* and *USA Today*, which took a limited view of what was open to challenge, major media across the country announced that Bush in fact won in Florida. Other investigations indicate that such was not the case at all, but these remain largely unpublicized. Furthermore, press treatment has focused almost exclusively on problems relating to questionable counts, with much discussion of ballot "dimples" and "chads." But in the aftermath, hardly a word was uttered about the ballots that were never collected and the thousands of people who were disfranchised by the repressive ploys of Florida officials and state troopers. Again, what we got was the smaller (safer) picture, one that does not challenge the legitimacy of the electoral process and the authorities who preside over it.

FALSE BALANCING

In accordance with the canons of good journalism, the press is supposed to tap competing sources to get both sides of an issue. In fact, both sides are seldom accorded equal prominence. One study found that on NPR, supposedly the most liberal of the mainstream media, right-wing spokespeople are often interviewed alone, while liberals—on the less frequent occasions they appear—are almost always offset by conservatives. Furthermore, both sides of a story are not usually *all* sides. The whole Left-progressive and radical portion of the opinion spectrum is amputated from the visible body politic.

False balancing was evident in a BBC World Service report (December 11, 1997) that spoke of "a history of violence between Indonesian forces and Timorese guerrillas"—with not a hint that the guerrillas were struggling for their lives against an Indonesian invasion force that had slaughtered some two hundred thousand Timorese. Instead, the genocidal invasion of East Timor was made to sound like a grudge fight, with "killings on both sides." By imposing a neutralizing gloss, the BBC announcer was introducing a serious distortion.

The US-supported wars in Guatemala and El Salvador during the 1980s were often treated with that same kind of false balancing. Both those who burned villages and those who were having their villages burned were depicted as equally involved in a contentious bloodletting. While giving the appearance of being objective and neutral, one actually neutralizes the subject matter and thereby drastically warps it.

FOLLOW-UP AVOIDANCE

When confronted with an unexpectedly dissident response, media hosts quickly change the subject, or break for a commercial, or inject an identifying announcement: "We are talking with [whomever]." The purpose is to avoid going any further into a politically forbidden topic no matter how much the unexpected response might seem to need a follow-up query. An anchorperson for the BBC World Service (December 26, 1997) enthused, "Christmas in Cuba: For the first time in almost forty years Cubans were able to celebrate

Christmas and go to church!" She then linked up with the BBC correspondent in Havana, who observed, "A crowd of two thousand have gathered in the cathedral for midnight mass. The whole thing is rather low key, very much like last year." Very much like last year? Here was something that craved clarification. Instead, the anchorperson quickly switched to another question: "Can we expect a growth of freedom with the pope's visit?"

On a PBS talk show (January 22, 1998), host Charlie Rose asked a guest, whose name I did not get, whether Castro was bitter about "the historic failure of communism." No, the guest replied, Castro is proud of what he believes communism has done for Cuba: advances in health care and education, full employment, and the elimination of the worst aspects of poverty. Rose fixed him with a ferocious glare, then turned to another guest to ask: "What impact will the pope's visit have in Cuba?" Rose ignored the errant guest for the rest of the program.

FRAMING

The most effective propaganda relies on framing rather than on falsehood. By bending the truth rather than breaking it, using emphasis and other auxiliary embellishments, communicators can create a desired impression without resorting to explicit advocacy and without departing too far from the appearance of objectivity. Framing is achieved in the way the news is packaged, the amount of exposure, the placement (front page or buried within, lead story or last), the tone of presentation (sympathetic or slighting), the headlines and photographs, and, in the case of broadcast media, the accompanying visual and auditory effects.

Newscasters use themselves as auxiliary embellishments. They cultivate a smooth delivery and try to convey an impression of detachment that places them above the rough and tumble of their subject matter. Television commentators and newspaper editorialists and columnists affect a knowing tone designed to foster credibility and an aura of certitude, or what might be called "authoritative ignorance," as expressed in remarks like, "How will this situation end? Only time will tell." Or, "No one can say for sure." Trite truisms are palmed off as penetrating truths. Newscasters learn to fashion sentences like, "Unless the strike is settled soon, the two sides will be in for a long and bitter struggle." And, "The space launching will take place as scheduled if no unexpected problems arise." And, "Unless Congress acts soon, this bill is not likely to go anywhere."

STUFF JUST HAPPENS

Many things are reported in the news but few are explained. Little is said about how the social order is organized and for what purposes. Instead we are left to see the world as do mainstream pundits, as a scatter of events and personalities propelled by happenstance, circumstance, confused intentions, bungled operations, and individual ambition—rarely by powerful class interests. Passive voice and impersonal subject are essential rhetorical constructs for this mode of evasion. So we read or hear that "fighting broke out in the region," or "many people were killed in the disturbances," or "famine is on the increase." Recessions apparently just happen like some natural phenomenon ("our economy is in a slump"), having little to do with the constant war of capital against labor and the contradictions between productive power and earning power.

If we are to believe the media, stuff just happens. Consider "globalization," a pet label that the press presents as a natural and inevitable development. In fact, globalization is a deliberate contrivance of multinational interests to undermine democratic sovereignty throughout the world. International "free trade" agreements set up international trade councils that are elected by no one, are accountable to no one, operate in secrecy without conflict-of-interest restrictions, and with the power to overrule just about all labor, consumer, and environmental laws, and all public services and regulations in all signatory nations. What we actually are experiencing with GATT, NAFTA, FTAA, GATS, and the WTO is *de*globalization, an ever-greater concentration of politico-economic power in the hands of an international investor class, a global coup d'etat that divests the peoples of the world of any trace of protective democratic input.

In keeping with the liberal paradigm, the media never asks *why* things happen the way they do. Social problems are rarely associated with the politico-economic forces that create them. So we are taught to truncate our own critical thinking. Imagine if we attempted something different. Suppose we report, as is seldom reported, that the harshly exploitative labor conditions existing in so many countries generally have the backing of their respective military forces. Suppose further that we cross another line and note that these right-wing military forces are fully supported by the US national security state. Then suppose we cross that most serious line of all and instead of just deploring this fact we also ask *why* successive US administrations have involved themselves in such unsavory pursuits throughout the world. Suppose we conclude that the whole phenomenon is consistent with a dedication to making the world safe for free-market corporate capitalism, as measured by the kinds of countries that are helped and the kinds that are attacked. Such an analysis almost certainly would not be printed anywhere except in a few select radical publications. We crossed too many lines. Because we tried to explain the particular situation (bad labor conditions) in terms of a larger set of social relations (corporate class power), our presentation would be rejected out of hand as Marxist—which indeed it is, as is much of reality itself.

In sum, the news media's daily performance under what is called "democratic capitalism" is not a failure but a skillfully evasive success. We often hear that the press "got it wrong" or "dropped the ball" on this or that story. In fact, the media do their job remarkably well. Media people have a trained incapacity for the whole truth. Their job is not to inform but—in regard to some ideologically sensitive issues—to disinform, not to advance democratic discourse but to dilute and mute it. Their task is to give every appearance of being conscientiously concerned about events of the day, saying so much while meaning so little, offering so many calories with so few nutrients. When we understand this, we move from a liberal complaint about the press's sloppy performance to a radical analysis of how the media maintain the dominant paradigm with much craft and craftiness.

5

THE MYTH OF THE LIBERAL MEDIA

ERIC ALTERMAN
ALTERCATION, MSNBC

ERIC ALTERMAN, *renowned author and journalist, is the "Altercation" weblogger for MSNBC.com, media columnist for the* Nation, *and a fellow at the Center for American Progress, where he writes and edits the "Think Again" column. Author of* What Liberal Media? The Truth about Bias and the News *(2003, 2004), his most recent books are* The Book on Bush: How George W. (Mis)leads America *(with Mark Green, February 2004) and* When Presidents Lie: Deception and Its Consequences *(October 2004). He has been a contributing editor to or columnist for numerous publications in the United States and abroad, including* Worth, Rolling Stone, Elle, Mother Jones, World Policy Journal, *and the* Sunday Express *(London). Alterman is also a senior fellow of the World Policy Institute at New School University and adjunct professor of journalism at Columbia University. He received his BA in history and government from Cornell, his MA in international relations from Yale, and his PhD in US history from Stanford.*

This chapter is a version of chapter 2 of Eric Alterman, *What Liberal Media? The Truth about Bias and the News* (New York: Perseus Books, 2003), pp. 14–27. Reprinted by permission of the publisher.

"Repeat something often enough and people will believe it," goes the old adage, and this is nowhere truer than in American political journalism. As four scholars writing in the *Journal of Communication* observed in a study of the past three elections, "claiming the media are liberally biased perhaps has become a core rhetorical strategy by conservative elites in recent years." As a result, these unsupported claims have become a "necessary mechanism for moving (or keeping) analytical coverage in line with their interests."[1] Another way of saying this is that conservatives have successfully cowed journalists into repeating their baseless accusations about a liberal bias by virtue of their willingness to repeat them endlessly. . . . It does not matter that the evidence for liberal bias often disintegrates upon careful scrutiny. It works anyway! . . .

"LIBERAL" ON WHOSE STANDARDS?

The Right's ideological offensive of the past few decades has succeeded so thoroughly that the very idea of a genuinely philosophically "liberal" politics has come to mean something quite alien to American politics. Contemporary intellectual definitions of liberalism derive by common accord from the work of the political theorist John Rawls. The key concept upon which Rawls bases his definition is what he terms the "veil of ignorance"—the kind of social compact based on a structure that would be drawn up by a person who has no idea where he or she fits into it. In other words, such a structure would be equally fair if judged by the person at the bottom as well as the top—the CEO as well as the guy who cleans his toilets.[2] In real-world American politics, this proposition would be considered so utopian as to be laughable. In 2001 the average CEO of a major company received $15.5 million in total compensation, or 245 times, on average, what the company paid its employees.[3] The steps that would need to be taken to reach a Rawlsian state in such a situation are politically unthinkable, beginning (and ending) with a steeply progressive income tax, to say nothing of making universally available, high-quality health care, education, housing, public parks, beaches, and last but not least, political power. Ethicist Peter Singer notes, moreover, in his study of the morals of globalization that even Rawls's demanding standards do not take into account our responsibilities as citizens to those who live beyond our borders, in places where starvation, disease, and child mortality are rampant. These, too, are fundamental liberal causes, almost entirely unmentionable in a society that offers the world's poor barely one-tenth of 1 percent of its gross domestic product in development aid.[4] Judged by this standard, even to begin to argue on behalf of a genuinely liberal political program is to invite amused condescension . . . at best.

Some researchers seeking to demonstrate the liberal bias of the elite press corps have tried to prove that reporters are liberals who vote Democratic and look down their noses at people who don't. The Right's Rosetta Stone in this regard is the now famous poll of "Washington bureau chiefs and congressional correspondents" released in 1996 by the Freedom Forum. "Ever since a now-legendary poll from the Media Studies Center showed that 89 percent of Washington journalists voted for Clinton in 1992, it has been hard to deny that the press is 'liberal,'" writes *Weekly Standard* writer Christopher Caldwell for the *Atlantic Monthly*, in one typical rendering, that, while mistaken about its source, could stand for thousands more such assertions.[5]

The conservative pundit James Glassman employed these results to declare in the *Washington Post*: "The people who report the stories are liberal Democrats. This is the shameful open secret of American journalism. That the press itself . . . chooses to gloss over it is conclusive evidence of how pernicious the bias it."[6] Here Glassman makes a groundless claim, insisting that the denial of crime is evidence of guilt. In addition, he equates Clinton voters with "liberal Democrats," again positing no evidence. The intellectual indefensibility of the latter claim should be evident to anyone who takes a moment to consider it. Bill Clinton ran in 1992 quite self-consciously as a "new Democrat," heavily supported by the centrist Democratic Leadership Council. He hailed from a conservative southern state. He supported the death penalty, "free trade," and "an end to welfare as we know it." In foreign policy, his hawkish views won him the support of right-wingers like William Safire and many hard-line neoconservatives. The only way to conclude that a Clinton voter is de facto a "liberal Democrat" is by refusing to make any distinctions between the words "liberal" and "Democrat"—a distinction that keeps the party in office in much of the southern and western parts of the nation.[7]

Outside the context of US politics, the insistence that "Democrat" equals "liberal" grows even more problematic. The entire context of American politics exists on a spectrum that is itself well to the Right of that in most industrialized democracies. During the 1990s, Bill Clinton was probably further to the Right than most ruling western European conservatives, such as Germany's Helmut Kohl and France's Jacques Chirac. Indeed, virtually the entire axis of political conversation in the United States takes place on ideological ground that would be considered conservative in just about every nation in democratic western Europe. . . .

Then again, let's not kid ourselves. The percentage of elite journalists who voted for Bill Clinton in 1992 was probably consistent with those he received among all well-educated urban elites, which was pretty high. Most people who fit this profile do indeed hold socially "liberal" views on issues like gun control, abortion, school prayer, and so on, and I have no doubts that most journalists do, too. The journalists whose alleged biases concern conservatives live, according to the current parlance, in "red" states and, when it comes to social issues, carry with them typical "red state" values. The vast majority are pro-choice, pro–gun control, pro–separation of church and state, pro-feminism, pro–affirmative action, and supportive of gay rights.

But if we put the question of ideology aside for a moment, it is not hard to see that in 1992 journalists had strong, *self-interested* reasons to prefer Bill Clinton to George H. W. Bush. A second Bush administration, peopled with many of the same figures who served in the three administrations that preceded it, would have meant a full sixteen years without a break in which journalists were forced to cover the same old guys saying the same old things about the same old issues. What could possibly be the fun in that? More than enough careers had already been made during the Reagan/Bush years, and it was time now to give a new bunch of people a chance to show their stuff.

I would not deny that I sensed a great deal of excitement among the press corps in Little Rock on Election Day 1992, but it had little to do with ideology. Part of the thrill was generational. Bush was part of Reagan's generation; Clinton was, like most reporters, a baby boomer. Part of the exhilaration was substantive. Clinton was king of the political policy wonks, armed and ready with blueprints for a decade's worth of ambitious programs ready to go. He and his advisers would make politics fun again in a way that Republicans, who acted like the button-down CEOs so many of them happen to be, could not. Moreover, Democrats generally admit to liking journalists and enjoy both leaking to and socializing with them. They are also not terribly good about disciplining themselves when they disagree with one another—which is most of the time—and, hence, prove to be far richer sources for reporters as well. In addition, lest we forget, Clinton's reputation as the world's biggest horndog was by this time well known to all of us. Careers could be made in scandal reporting—just look at David Brock. Paul Gigot, the fiercely conservative columnist, now editor of the *Wall Street Journal* editorial pages, has quipped, "Clinton was a gold mine. I often joke that if I had known back in 1992 what he would do for my career, I probably would have voted for him."[8] . . .

Most journalists, as sociologist Herbert Gans explains, are also congenitally "reformist." They believe in the possibility of improving things or they would not have chosen the profession in the first place.[9] But both reformist sympathy and the "elite" association can cut more than one way, in political terms. Beginning with the 1980 election of Ronald Reagan and accelerating in 1994, conservatives began to capture the language of reformism, in opposition to what Newt Gingrich termed "reactionary liberalism." Much of the media bought into this etymological transformation and, hence, a bias toward "reform" gives little clue about a person's ideology anymore. Journalists were naturally in sympathy with liberal (and in the case of John McCain, conservative) efforts to reform our campaign finance laws. But they also appeared quite well disposed to efforts to "reform" the nation's Social Security system so as to introduce private stock market accounts—at least before the Nasdaq crashed.

Also, lest we forget, journalists are not entirely immune to the seduction affluence can offer. While they are not nearly as well paid as the nation's corporate, legal, or medical elite, high-level Washington and New York journalists do make considerably more money than most Americans. They have spouses who do, too, and, hence, live pretty well. According to a study conducted by the sociologist David Croteau, 95 percent of elite journalists' households earned more than $50,000 a year and 31 percent earned more than $150,000. He points out, "High levels of income tend to be associated with conservative views on economic issues such as tax policy and federal spending."[10] And journalists are no different. The journalists' views on economic matters are generally consistent with their privileged position on the socioeconomic ladder, and, hence, well to the Right of most Americans. They are more sympathetic to corporations, less sympathetic to government-mandated social programs, and far more ideologically committed to free trade than to the protection of jobs than are their fellow citizens.[11] Polls, of course, are always of limited value, and comparing ones taken at different moments in history, based on differently worded questions, invites rhetorical abuse. I would not take any of these individual statistics to the bank. Nevertheless, the overall pattern is undeniably consistent, and it is not "liberal." . . .

AND WHAT WOULD IT MATTER ANYWAY?

When it comes to news content, the journalist is often the low person on the totem pole. He is "labor," or if he is lucky, "talent." He is not "management."

He does not get to decide by himself how a story should be cast by himself. As *Washington Post* columnist Gene Weingarten put it in a column he wrote about an editorial disagreement with his bosses:

> My company is a large, liberal-minded institution that thrives on convivial collegial consensus among persons who—as human people professionally partnered in common goal-oriented pursuits—are complete coequals right up to the time an actual disagreement occurs. At this point, the rules of the game change slightly. We go from Candy Land to rock-paper-scissors. Editors are rock. Writers are those gaily colored wussy plastic paper clips. In short, I was given a choice: I could see the lucent wisdom of my editors' point of view and alter the column as directed, or I could elect to write a different column altogether, or (in an organization this large and diverse, there are always a multitude of options) I could be escorted to the front door by Security.[12]

Weingarten is a much-beloved columnist and so is given quite a bit of freedom. Moreover, he does not cover politics—this column was published in the Style section, which affords him even more latitude. But even so, print journalists have editors who have editors above them who have publishers above them and who, in most cases, have corporate executives above them. Television journalists have producers and executive producers and network executives who worry primarily about ratings, advertising profits, and the sensibilities of their audience, their advertisers, and their corporate owners. When it comes to content, it is these folks who matter, perhaps more than anyone.

Examine, for a moment, the corporate structure of the industry for which the average top-level journalist labors. Ben Bagdikian, former dean of the journalism schools at the University of California at Berkeley, has been chronicling the concentration of media ownership in five separate editions of his book, *The Media Monopoly*, which was first published in 1983 when the number of companies that controlled the information flow to the rest of us—the potential employment pool for journalists—was fifty. Today we are down to six.[13]

Consider the following: when AOL took over Time Warner, it also took over Warner Brothers Pictures, Morgan Creek, New Regency, Warner Brothers Animation, and a partial stake in Savoy Pictures, Little Brown & Co., Bullfinch, Back Bay, Time-Life Books, Oxmoor House, Sunset Books, Warner Books, the Book-of-the-Month Club, Warner/Chappell Music, Atlantic Records, Warner Audio Books, Elektra, Warner Brothers Records, Time-Life Music, Columbia House, a 40 percent stake in Seattle's Sub Pop records, *Time* magazine, *Fortune*, *Life*, *Sports Illustrated*, *Vibe*, *People*, *Entertainment Weekly*, *Money*, *In Style*, *Martha Stewart Living*, *Sunset*, *Asia*

Week, Parenting, Weight Watchers, Cooking Light, DC Comics, 49 percent of the Six Flags theme parks, Movie World and Warner Brothers parks, HBO, Cinemax, Warner Brothers Television, partial ownership of Comedy Central, E!, Black Entertainment Television, Court TV, the Sega channel, the Home Shopping Network, Turner Broadcasting, the Atlanta Braves and Atlanta Hawks World Championship Wrestling, Hanna-Barbera Cartoons, New Line Cinema, Fine Line Cinema, Turner Classic Movies, Turner Pictures, Castlerock productions, CNN, CNN Headline News, CNN International, CNN/SI, CNN Airport Network, CNNfi, CNN radio, TNT, WTBS, Turner Classic Movies, and the Cartoon Network. The situation is not substantially different at Disney, Viacom, General Electric, News Corporation, or Bertelsmann.[14]

The point of the above is to illustrate the degree of potential conflict of interest for a journalist who seeks to tell the truth, according to the old *New York Times* slogan, "without fear or favor," about not only any one of the companies its parent corporation may own, but also those with whom one of the companies may compete, or perhaps a public official or regulatory body that one of them may lobby, or even an employee at one of them with whom one of his superiors may be sleeping, or divorcing or remarrying, or one of *their* competitors, or competitors' lovers, ex-lovers, and so on. While the consumer is generally unaware of these conflicts, the possibilities are almost endless—unless one is going to restrict one's journalism to nothing but preachy pabulum and celebrity gossip. The natural fear for journalists in this context is direct censorship on behalf of the parent's corporate interests. However, the number of incidents of even remotely documented corporate censorship are actually pretty rare. But focusing on examples of direct censorship in the US media misses the point. Rarely does some story that is likely to arouse concern ever go far enough to actually need to be censored at the corporate level. The reporter, the editor, the producer, the executive producer, and so on, all understand implicitly that their jobs depend in part on keeping their corporate parents happy.

Television viewers received a rare education on the corporate attitude toward even the slightest hint of criticism of the big cheese when, on the morning after Disney took over ABC, *Good Morning America* host Charles Gibson interviewed Thomas S. Murphy, chairman of Capital Cities/ABC and Disney's Michael D. Eisner. "Where's the little guy in the business anymore?" Gibson asked. "Is this just a giant that forces everybody else out?" Murphy, now Gibson's boss, replied, "Charlie, let me ask you a question. Wouldn't you be proud to be associated with Disney? . . . I'm quite serious about this."[15]

While some editors and producers profess to be able to offer the same scrutiny to properties associated with their own companies that they offer to the rest of the world, in most cases, it taxes one's credulity to believe them. Journalists, myself included, are usually inclined to give their friends a break. If you work for a company that owns a lot of other companies, then you automatically have many such friends in journalism, in business, and in government. Michael Kinsley, the founding editor of Slate.com, which is funded entirely by the Microsoft Corporation, did the world a favor when he admitted, "Slate will never give Microsoft the skeptical scrutiny it requires as a powerful institution in American society—any more than *Time* will sufficiently scrutinize Time Warner. No institution can reasonably be expected to audit itself. . . . The standard to insist on is that the sins be of omission, not distortion. There will be no major investigations of Microsoft in Slate."[16] Eisner said much the same thing, perhaps inadvertently, when he admitted (or one might say, "instructed"), "I would prefer ABC not to cover Disney. . . . I think it's inappropriate."[17]

Media magnates have always sought to reign in their reporters, albeit with mixed success. In 1905, Standard Oil baron John D. Rockefeller predicted of the *New York World*, "The owner of the *World* is also a large owner of property, and I presume that, in common with other newspaper owners who are possessed of wealth, his eyes are beginning to be opened to the fact that he is like Samson, taking the initiative to pull the building down upon his head."[18] Similarly, advertisers have always attempted to exert pressure on the news and occasionally succeeded. What has changed is the scale of these pressures, given the size and the scope of the new media conglomerates and the willingness of news executives to interfere with the news-gathering process up and down the line. One-third of the local TV news directors surveyed by the Project on Excellence in Journalism in 2000 indicated that they had been pressured to avoid negative stories about advertisers, or to do positive ones.[19] Again, by the time you get to actual pressure on an editor or writer, a great many steps have already been taken. A 2000 Pew Research Center study found that more than 40 percent of journalists felt a need to self-censor their work, either by avoiding certain stories or softening the ones they wrote, to benefit the interests of the organizations for which they work.[20] As the editors of the *Columbia Journalism Review* put it: "The truth about self-censorship is that it is widespread, as common in newsrooms as deadline pressure, a virus that eats away at the journalistic mission."[21] And it doesn't leave much room for liberalism.

Conservative critics of the so-called liberal media (SCLM) often neglect the power not only of owners and advertisers, but also the profit motive to determine the content of the news. Any remotely attentive consumer of news has noticed, in recent years, a turn away from what journalists like to term "spinach," or the kind of news that citizens require to carry out their duties as intelligent, informed members of a political democracy, toward pudding—the sweet, nutritionally vacant fare that is the stock in trade of news outlets. The sense of a news division acting as a "public trust"—the characterization of the major networks throughout the cold war—has given way to one that views them strictly as profit centers, which must carry the weight of shareholder demands the same way a TV sitcom or children's theme park must.

The net result has been the expansive growth of a form of "news" that owes more to sitcoms and theme parks than to old-fashioned ideas of public and civic life. Instead of John Kennedy and Nikita Khrushchev as the iconic images of the world of "news," we are presented the comings and goings of Madonna, O. J. Simpson, Princess Diana, Gary Condit, and Chandra Levy. Again, this tabloid contagion, which afflicts almost all commercial news programs and newspapers, has many unhappy implications, but one obvious one is that the less actual "news" one covers, the less opportunity alleged liberals have to slant it.

Moreover, the deeply intensified demand for profit places renewed pressure on all media to appeal to the wealthiest possible consumer base, which pretty much rules out the poor and the oppressed as the topic of investigative entrepreneurship. As *New York* magazine's Michael Wolff observed of the creation of two new "leisure" sections in the *New York Times* and the *Wall Street Journal*, "They don't want to be old-fashioned newspapers at all, but information brands, sensibility vehicles, targeted upscale-consumer media outlets. . . . The battle that has been joined is for the hearts and minds of the 2 million or 3 million wealthiest and best-educated people in the nation." In the not-so-distant past, Wolff notes, this kind of market-driven, consumerist definition of news would have inspired journalistic purists into principled opposition. But, "there's very little of that now: Any journalist with any career prospects is also a marketer, and packager, and all-around design- and demographic-conscious media professional. Every journalist is also a worried journalist, united with the business side in concerns about 'being viable.'"[22] Even in a tough year like 2001, media companies were demanding—and receiving—profit margins in the 20 percent range.[23] There is not much room for an overriding liberal bias on the great issues of the day between that particular rock and hard place, I'm afraid, even with the best (or worst) of intentions. Reporters could be the most liberal people on earth. But for all the reasons discussed above, it would hardly matter. They simply do not "make" the news.

The intensified emphasis on profits of recent years has resulted in a few high-profile scandals in the business. The *LA Times* sold its journalistic soul to the Staples Center in exchange for a pittance in paid advertising, offering to share advertising revenue in a phony magazine supplement designed to look like a genuine news report. Meanwhile, ABC News almost gave Ted Koppel, its most distinguished journalist, his walking papers for a comedy program with lower ratings but higher advertising profits. *San Jose Mercury News* publisher Jay Harris resigned in a loud and eloquent protest against Knight Ridder's adherence to the "tyranny of the markets" that he said was destroying his newspaper.[24] But no less important than the scandals are the nonscandals—the ones that are perhaps even more egregious in terms of the news values but, for whatever reason, are never brought before the public.

These priorities were never more evident than in the winter of 2002 during the long, drawn-out debate over campaign finance reform. The dramatic events in question dominated domestic coverage for weeks if not months—a fact that many conservatives attributed to liberal media bias, since Americans, while supportive of reform, did not appear to be passionately interested in the story. But even within this avalanche of coverage, virtually no one in the media thought it worthwhile to mention that media industry lobbyists had managed to murder a key provision of the bill that would have forced the networks to offer candidates their least expensive advertising rates.[25] True it was a hard story for which to create snappy visuals—"Dead behind the eyes" in Dan Rather's parlance.[26] But why is that not viewed as a challenge rather than a cause for capitulation? Political campaigns have become a get-rich-quick scheme for local television station owners, whose profit margins reflect the high rates they charge for them. This is no small factor in the mad pursuit of money that characterizes virtually every US political campaign, and which makes a mockery of our claims to be a "one person, one vote" democracy.

Estimates of the income derived from these advertisements are up to $750 million per election cycle and continue to rise.[27] The provision in question, originally passed by the Senate by a 69 to 31 margin, died in the House of Representatives following a furious lobbying campaign by the National Association of Broadcasters and the cable television industry. After the House vote, *Broadcasting & Cable* magazine reported, "Back in their headquarters, the National Association of Broadcasters popped the champagne, deeply appreciative of the strong bipartisan vote [stripping the advertising provision]." The broadcasters' victory left the United States alone among the 146 countries, according to one study, in refusing to provide free television time to political candidates.[28]

The silent treatment given the advertising amendment was, in many ways, a repeat of the noncoverage of an even more significant story: the 1996 Telecommunications Act. When the Republicans took over Congress in 1994, the party leadership invited telecommunications corporate heads to Washington, sat down with them, and asked, "What do you want?"[29] This result, after many millions of dollars' worth of lobbying bills, was a milestone of deregulation that vastly increased the ability of the big media conglomerates to increase (and combine) their market share in almost every medium. This expansion came, virtually without exception, at the expense of the smaller voices in those markets. The net result turned out to be a significant diminution in the opportunities for citizens to experience, and participate in, democratic debate.[30] Based on a quick perusal of TV listings for 1995, apparently not one of the major TV news magazines of Westinghouse/CBS (*48 hours, 60 Minutes*), Disney/Cap Cities/ABC (*PrimeTime Live, 20/20*), or General Electric/NBC (*Dateline NBC*) devoted even a minute of their three hundred or so hours of airtime to the bill or the issues that lay beneath it.[31] Where, one might ask, were the SCLM when their corporate owners were rewriting the rules of democratic debate to increase their own profits?

Ultimately, as Tom Johnson, former publisher of the *LA Times* and later president of CNN, would observe, "It is not reporters or editors, but the owners of the media who decide the quality of the news . . . produced by or televised by their news departments. It is they who most often select, hire, fire, and promote the editors and publishers, top general managers, news directors, and managing editors—the journalists—who run the newsrooms. . . . Owners determine newsroom budgets, and the tiny amount of time and space allotted to news versus advertising. They set the standard of quality by the quality of the people they choose and the news policy they embrace. Owners decide how much profit should be produced from their media properties. Owners decide what quality levels they are willing to support by how well or how poorly they pay their journalists."[32]

To ignore the power of the money at stake to determine the content of news in the decisions of these executives—given the role money seems to play in every other aspect of our society—is indefensibly childish and naive. The two heads of AOL Time Warner, Gerald Levin and Steve Case, took home a combined $241 million in 2001. Michael Eisner of Disney pulled down nearly $73 million.[33] Leave aside that stocks of each of these companies performed miserably in the same years, something you will probably not find discussed much in the myriad media properties they control. Ask yourself if the men and women who earn numbers like these are really sending forth aggressive investigators of financial and political malfeasance, charged, as the saying goes, to "afflict the comfortable and comfort the afflicted?" As longtime editor and executive Harold Evans points out, in a situation like the current one, "the problem that many media organizations face is not to stay in business, but to stay in journalism."[34]

As a result of all of the above, it is both misleading and ultimately dishonest to focus on what may or may not be the (unproven) liberal biases of journalists to demonstrate that "the news" is also biased. Between the journalist and what he or she reports sits a whole host of factors—not least of which is an increasingly concentrated corporate structure—that make such biases beside the point. Conservatives, not liberals, own the media. And as everyone in America knows, you get what you pay for.

NOTES

1. See David Domke et al., "The Politics of Conservative Elites and the 'Liberal Media' Argument," *Journal of Communication* (Autumn 1999): 35–58.

2. See John Rawls, *A Theory of Justice*, rev. ed. (Cambridge, MA: Harvard University Press, 1999) and *Political Liberalism* (Cambridge, MA: Harvard University Press, 1995).

3. Lawrence Mishel, Jared Bernstein, and Heather Boushey, *The State of Working America, 2001–2002* (Ithaca, NY: ILR Press, 2003), p. 213.

4. See Peter Singer, *One World: The Ethics of Globalization* (New Haven: Yale University Press, 2002), pp. 150–76.

5. Eric Alterman, *The Liberal Media, RIP*, quoted in *Nation*, March 13, 2000, http://past.thenation.com/cgi-bin/framizer.cgi?url=http://past.thenation.com/issue/000313/0313alterman.shtml; see also Eric Alterman, *What Liberal Media? The Truth about Bias and the News* (New York: Perseus Books, 2003), p. 124

6. Alterman, *Bias*, p. 124.

7. The Freedom Forum poll itself turns out to be based on only 139 respondents out of 323 questionnaires mailed—a response rate so low that most social scientists would reject it as inadequately representative. What's more, they were not the right 139. Independent investigative journalist Robert Parry contacted the Roper Center in Connecticut, where the results were tabulated, and was given a list of the company affiliations of the original recipients. This, too, proved problematic. Fewer than 20 percent of the questionnaires were sent to the major elite media outlets such as the *New York Times*, *Washington Post*, CBS, NBC, ABC, *Time*, *Newsweek*, and so

on. See Robert Parry, "Media Mythology: Is the Press Liberal," 1997, http://www
.consortiumnews.com/archive/story21.html.

8. Paul Gigot, "Green Bay to Wall Street, a Long Road," *Milwaukee Journal
Sentinal*, May 8, 2002, http://www.jsonline.com/news/metro/may02/41911.asp.

9. Herbert Gans, "Are American Journalists Dangerously Liberal," *Columbia
Journalism Review* (November/December 1985): 32–35. See also Gans, *Deciding
What's News: A Study of CBS Evening News, NBC Nightly News, Newsweek, and
Time* (New York: Pantheon, 1979).

10. See David Croteau, "Examining the 'Liberal Media' Claim: Journalists'
Views on Politics, Economic Policy, and Media Coverage," *International Journal of
Health Services* 29, no. 3 (1999): 627–55.

11. Croteau notes that 44 percent of regular people put NAFTA at the bottom of
the list of its priorities while fewer than one-fifth as many journalists—just 8 percent
—did. Twenty-four percent of journalists thought NAFTA expansion in the rest of
Latin America to be among the "top few" priorities to "expand the NAFTA trade
agreement to include other countries in Latin America," compared with just 7 percent
of the general public. More than twice as many journalists (71 percent) told pollsters
they support giving the president "fast-track" authority to negotiate trade agreements
without interference from Congress, while, according to an October 1997 Hart-
Teeter/NBC News/*Wall Street Journal* poll, the number for the public was only 35
percent, and the number opposing it was five times as high. This conservative jour-
nalist/liberal public dichotomy carries over to the larger philosophical question of the
proper role of corporate power in society. Just 57 percent of the journalists agreed
that "too much power is concentrated in the hands of a few large companies." However, when the Times Mirror Center asked the same question of the general public in
October 1995, the number who agreed was 77 percent. The number disagreeing
reached 43 percent for the journalistic survey, but only 18 percent for the public. A
repeat of this pattern is discernible with regard to tax fairness. Seventy-two percent
of the general public, when questioned in 1992, told pollsters that Bill Clinton's tax
plan did not go far enough in raising taxes on the wealthy. Fewer than half the journalists questioned agreed. See Croteau, "Examining the 'Liberal Media' Claim."

12. Gene Weingarten, *Washington Post*, May 12, 2002, p. W3.

13. Author's interview with Ben Bagdikian, April 22, 2002.

14. See www.whatliberalmedia.com, appendix 3, Nation Media Ownership
chart.

15. Transcript, *Good Morning America*, July 31, 1995.

16. *Slate*, December 26, 1997, http://slate.msn.com/?id=2217.

17. Trudy Lieberman, *Slanting the Story: The Forces That Shape the News*
(New York: New Press, 2000), p. 146.

18. Rockefeller is quoted in Miles Maguire, "Business as Usual," *American
Journalism Review* (October 2002), http://www.ajr.org/Article.asp?id=2648.

19. Andrew Kohut et al., "The Truth about Self-Censorship," *Columbia Journalism Review* (May/June 2000), http://www.cjr.org/year/00/2/2/may-juneindex.asp.

20. Pew Research Center for the People and the Press, "Self Censorship: How Often and Why—Journalists Avoiding the News," April 30, 2000, http://www.peoplepress.org/reports/display.php3?ReportID=39.

21. "The Truth about Self-Censorship."

22. Michael Wolff, "The New Old News," *New York*, April 29, 2002.

23. As David Shaw noted in the *LA Times*, "Gannett earns profit margins of 25 percent. Knight Ridder newspapers, like most newspapers, continue to be very profitable—a profit margin of 20.8 percent last year and, despite this year's sour economy, 18.5 percent in the first quarter of 2001, slightly better than the industry average. That is more than double the profitability of the average Fortune 500 company." *Los Angeles Times*, July 3, 2001, p. A1.

24. Quoted in Howard Gardner, Mihaly Csikszentmihalyi, William Damon, *Good Work: When Excellence and Ethics Meet* (New York: Basic Books, 2001), p. 133. See also *Los Angeles Times*, March 21, 2001, p. A15.

25. Among the exceptions were the *Wall Street Journal*, NPR, and *Variety*.

26. Rather is quoted by Frank Rich in "The Weight of an Anchor," *New York Times Magazine*, May 19, 2002, http://www.nytimes.com/2002/05/19/magazine/19ANCHOR.html?pagewanted=print&position=top.

27. *Washington Post*, February 25, 2002, p. C1.

28. *Washington Post*, February 24, 2002, p. B7.

29. Ben Bagdikian, *The Media Monopoly*, 5th ed. (Boston: Beacon Press, 1997), p. xiv.

30. *Congressional Quarterly* Web site, cited April 29, 1997.

31. Carl Jenson, *Censored: The News That Didn't Make the News and Why: The 1996 Project Censored Yearbook* (New York: Seven Stories Press, April 1996), pp. 50–51.

32. Tom Johnson, "Excellence in the News: Who Really Decides," speech delivered at Paul White Award Dinner, October 2, 1999. Quoted in Bill Kovach and Tom Rosenstiel, *The Elements of Journalism* (New York: Three Rivers Press, 2001), p. 63.

33. "Top Executive Salaries for Major Media Companies," *Advertising Age* (2001).

34. Gardner, Csikszentmihalyi, and Damon, *Good Work*, p. 131.

III

BREACH OF PROFESSIONAL STANDARDS

Why Corporate Media Need to Investigate Themselves

6

UNDERSTANDING MEDIA ETHICS IS IMPORTANT, CHANGING MEDIA IS ESSENTIAL

DANNY SCHECHTER

MEDIACHANNEL.ORG

DANNY SCHECHTER, *known as the "News Dissector," edits Media-channel.org, the world's largest online media issues network. His latest books are* Media Wars *(Rowman and Littlefield) and* Embedded: Weapons of Mass Deception *(Prometheus Books). He is making a film about the media coverage of the war, called* WMD. *As a media maker, Schechter has made award-winning films and newsmagazine series on human rights for Globalvision, an independent media company. He has also produced for ABC News 20/20, CNN, and local TV outlets in Boston; has spent ten years as the news director/news dissector at WBCN-FM in radio; and has been an investigative journalist for* Ramparts *magazine. His career in journalism began on the* Clinton News, *the student newspaper at De Witt Clinton High School in the Bronx. His media adventures are chronicled in the book* The More You Watch, the Less You Know *(Seven Stories Press).*

W hy bother to learn about the media? What's the point of analyzing its power or measuring its impact? Is there a deeper rationale for doing the studies many of us take on to show how broadcasting and the press limit the discourse, muddle our understanding, and set the political agenda?

Media ethics have traditionally been offered up as a way to insure high standards in the media and to elevate the quality of our media discourse. There are books on the subjects, guidelines for individuals, and debates about what should or does constitute ethical conduct. Most of this is directed at individuals. Media scandals tend to occur when these standards, especially bars on plagiarism and "making it up," are violated. Always concerned with its credibility and appearance, the media industry is vigilant about enforcing ethical codes, especially after high-profile incidents such as the ones that occurred at the *New York Times* and *USA Today* involving individual reporters.

The problem is that ethics cannot just be reduced to individual malpractice. They have to be situated in institutional settings in which the role and performance of the institution has to be assessed, not only in terms of the accuracy or balance in individual stories but also the larger social impact of media outlets. We need an ethical media—not just lip service paid to ethics in the media.

As a journalist who has worked in print, radio, TV, network news, cable programming, and Web sites, my approach is broader, raising deeper questions about the function and performance of the media itself. Bear in mind the admonition of the writer Thomas Pynchon in his book *Gravity's Rainbow*: "If they can get you asking the wrong questions, they don't have to worry about the answers."[1]

TOWARD AN ETHICAL MEDIA

In an age in which media bashing seems second in popularity only to media watching, we need to consider what it will take to make an ethical advocacy media more of a priority for those who despair at our political environment and cringe at the incompleteness and spin of so much of the news we see and hear.

I write during a political year when campaigning and political debates have aroused public interest as never before. And never before has the role of media companies been more omnipresent in our politics. Debates which were once held by ostensibly nonpartisan political groups are now sponsored by networks and newspapers that appear disinterested and above the fray but often have undisclosed interests or agendas. Seldom is there any scrutiny of their own political agendas, lobbying efforts, or political donations.

At the same time, critics of the media tend to focus only on the worst excesses of those they oppose—and not the system itself. The Left denounces the Fox News Channel often with self-righteous putdowns that do not ask how *and why* Fox has becomes as successful as it has. At the sane time, many on the Right continue to campaign as if by rote against so-called liberal media bias.

THE MYTH OF THE FOURTH ESTATE

The myth of the media as fourth estate is still with us despite the fact that our political system remains compromised by a campaign finance scandal in which the media is totally complicit. All political candidates spend most of their time raising money for political ads, and that money goes directly into the coffers of media companies.

The Pentagon's plan for fighting the Iraq War spoke of the media as "The fourth front," not an autonomous fourth estate. Military planners used information warfare techniques to control its spin. David Miller, editor of an important new book called *Tell Me Lies* (Pluto), explains:

> As Col. Kenneth Allard has written, the 2003 attack on Iraq "will be remembered as a conflict in which information fully took its place as a weapon of war." The interoperability of the various types of "weaponized information" has far reaching, if little noticed, implications for the integration of propaganda and media institutions into the war machine.[2] The experience of Iraq in 2003 shows how the planned integration of the media into instruments of war fighting is developing. It also shows the increased role for the private sector in information dominance, a role which reflects wider changes in the armed services in the US and the UK.
>
> Information dominance provides the underpinning rationale for all information-related work. As applied to traditional media management activities the key to dominance is that "nothing done makes any difference." In practice this means that the US and UK can tolerate dissent in the media and alternative accounts on the Internet. Dissent only matters if it interferes with their plans.
>
> We were held hostage by a multichannel confidence game driven by breaking news, armchair generals, embedded reporters, endless government "briefings, sanitized pictures, murdered journalists, distorted history, inaccurate information, hyped updates—all part of a nonstop flow of fast-paced "mili-tainment."

It signaled for many, in the heart of what was once a profession but is now a business, that we have entered the final days, not of the world—no, the Messiah is not returning—but of TV news, and even journalism itself, in this age of ever-consolidating media merges and purges.

This merger between the military and the media has ushered in a new era of newspeak and perception management. It raised broad ethical questions about the role of the media and its independence. Public relations people used to focus on getting the word out; perception managers *seek* to engineer how it is processed and understood. The correspondent as publicist and lapdog has supplanted the reporter as truth seeker and watchdog. In the old days, we demanded more investigative journalism. Now our demand must become *investigate journalism*.

As a journalist I am doing my own investigation with a new film called *WMD, Weapons of Mass Deception*. I am looking into the relationship of network lobbying of the FCC for beneficial rule changes and the uncritical approach that network news took to covering the invasion of Iraq. Before the war in Iraq began, American media companies began lobbying the FCC for rule changes that would benefit their bottom lines. There was a question raised: did the FCC agree to waive the rules if the media companies agreed to wave the flag? Here are some comments from people I interviewed:

Jihad al-Khazen, Top Arab Journalist

"We've been in this business long enough to be very careful. But I'm sure they were working for a deal and were hoping that being supportive of the war would get them a deal. Remember what Rupert Murdoch did when he was in China? He was the only one defending China, despite all the abuses of human rights, because he was working on a TV deal, which he eventually got in China."

Nicholas Johnson, Former FCC Commissioner

"Power, not just media power, power tends to go with power. Primarily they want to support whoever is in the White House, they want to support government, they want to support other large corporate interests. They don't want to rock the boat, generally."

Maurice Hinche, NY Congressman

"This is not something that happened yesterday or overnight. It has been going on here in the United States for about two decades at least. It has been an organized, concerted, thought out, well-planned, and well-executed process, going on back to the Reagan administration, flowing through the first Bush administration and now being picked up successfully so far by the second Bush administration. . . . This is a plan, its not serendipitous, it doesn't happen accidentally, it's what they want. They want to be able to control the political discussion."

John Stauber, PR Watch

"Who was the FCC commissioner with whom they were trying to curry favor, who was acting on their behalf during this period, it was Michael Powell, the son of Colin Powell. . . . It becomes sort of a, you scratch my back, I scratch your back."

Ralph Nader

"Chairman Michael Powell justifies media consolidation on the grounds that 1) it can bail out some failing newspapers or 2) it takes a lot of expenses to send those crews over to Iraq and cover the war. That is the most specious rationalization I have heard by an FCC commissioner."

Michael Wolff, Media Analyst

"I think it's very clear that the major media companies in this country had business before the government. Boom, it's a conflict of interest."

MEDIAOCRACY

We live in an age of media politics, governed not just by politicians but by what is in effect a "mediaocracy," a mutually dependent *and interactive* relationship between major media and politics, a nexus of power in which political leaders use media exposure to shape opinions and drive policy while media outlets use politicians to confer legitimization and offer what *Time* magazine called "Electotainment." Political candidates increasingly rely on

their media advisors and spend small fortunes to buy airtime to broadcast ads
to get poll-tested messages across. Governments don't have to buy time, but
their media operations have even bigger budgets to hire small armies of strategists and speechwriters, spin doctors and PR specialists. This mediaocracy
then sets the agenda and frames what issues get the focus, and which do not.

Media has become the fulcrum of political life throughout the West and
the driver of economic life as well. Commercials excite demand. TV celebri-
ties become commodities. Marketing strategies sell products, and programs
focused on markets also sell ideology. The ups and downs of share prices get
more attention than the rate of unemployment or indices of social misery.
Young people spend more time in the living room than in the classroom.
Many scholars believe that television has become their principal teacher.
Some critics call TV a "plug-in drug."

US media, given constitutional sanction by the US Constitution under
the First Amendment, now often degrades democracy, promoting the business system over the culture of civil society. The biggest businesses it boosts
is itself, as media companies become billion-dollar businesses thanks to
mergers and acquisitions. This has led to unprecedented consolidation and
concentration of ownership in fewer and fewer hands.

As commercial media expands, infiltrating into every corner of life,
public service media clones its formulas for survival, joining in the dumbing
down of content and loosening of public interest standards. Bottom-line pressures impact on every side as competition leads to splintering of the audience
into smaller and smaller, demographically designed niches. At the same time,
larger economic problems limit state subsidies and advertising revenues.

One problem is that many prominent political leaders don't recognize that
the media problem is at the heart of the political crisis in America. The Democratic leader Al Gore had avoided discussing the role of the media during his
failed bid for the presidency in 2000. Two years later and just before he
decided to drop out of politics, he finally spoke out. It was as if he had finally
seen the power of a media system that Marshall McLuhan once called "trans-
parently invisible." In an interview with the *New York Observer*, Gore pointed
to an institutional imbalance in the media system that tilts in favor of conservatives and conservative values. According to writer Josh Benson:

> Mr. Gore has a bone to pick with his critics: namely, he says, that a sys-
> tematically orchestrated bias in the media makes it impossible for him and
> his fellow Democrats to get a fair shake. "Something will start at the Re-
> publican National Committee, inside the building, and it will explode the
> next day on the right-wing talk-show network and on Fox News and in the

newspapers that play this game, the *Washington Times* and the others. And then they'll create a little echo chamber, and pretty soon they'll start baiting the mainstream media for allegedly ignoring the story they've pushed into the *zeitgeist*. And then pretty soon the mainstream media goes out and disingenuously takes a so-called objective sampling, and lo and behold, these R.N.C. talking points are woven into the fabric of the *zeitgeist*."

And during a lengthy discourse on the history of political journalism in America, Mr. Gore said he believed that evolving technologies such as cable television and the Internet have combined with market forces to lower the media's standards of objectivity.[3]

"The established news organizations became the high-cost producers of a low-cost commodity," said Mr. Gore. "They're selling a hybrid product now that's news plus news-helper; whether it's entertainment or attitude or news that's marbled with opinion, it's different. Now, especially in the cable-TV market, it has become good economics once again to go back to a party-oriented approach to attract a hard-core following that appreciates the predictability of a right-wing point of view, but then to make aggressive and constant efforts to deny that's what they're doing in order to avoid offending the broader audience that mass advertisers want. Thus the Fox slogan 'We Report, You Decide,' or whatever the current version of their ritual denial is."

IS THE MEDIA THE SOLUTION OR THE PROBLEM?

In 2000, the bipartisan Alliance for Better Campaigns (Jimmy Carter and Jerry Ford, chairs) issued a detailed report showing how local TV stations violated federal law by overcharging candidates and then packaging their ads into blocks that made them unwatchable. This media profiteering was never even reported or, much less, investigated and prosecuted.

Back in the turbulent sixties, activists used to say "you're either part of the problem or part of the solution." To many, the expectation remains that our media system is part of the solution, a watchdog on power, a check on corrupt government practices and corporate abuses. Politicians scramble to get on the media, while activists crave their ten seconds of fame as a sound bite in some news story. As the media tilts Right in an atmosphere of intensifying media concentration, little focus is paid to how media has become a giant problem, rather than just a constant complaint.

Complaints tend to be ventilated about while some problems demand to be addressed. This is not to say that no one has or is addressing them. Media historian Robert McChesney's latest book is called *The Problem of the*

Media.[4] He is one of the few academics who promotes and organizes a media reform movement. In his view, "The symptoms of the crisis of the US media are well-known—a decline in hard news, the growth of infotainment and advertorials, staff cuts and concentration of ownership, increasing conformity of viewpoint and suppression of genuine debate." His book deals with issues such as the declining quality of journalism, the question of bias, the weakness of the public broadcasting sector, the state of media studies as an academic discipline, and the limits and possibilities of antitrust legislation in regulating the media. "It points out the ways in which the existing media system has become a threat to democracy, and shows how it could be made to serve the interests of the majority."

There is no question that the public is open to, if not totally supportive of, media reform. A Pew poll some years back found that 70 percent of the American public was dissatisfied with the media, for a range of reasons, and that 70 percent of people who work in the media shared that dissatisfaction. When Lou Dobbs asked his CNN audience in late 2003 if "big media companies should be broken up," five thousand people responded and a whopping 96 percent agreed.

Nearly three million Americans wrote to Congress and the FCC to protest new rule changes that would place media ownership in fewer hands. Several political candidates also addressed the issue. Media coverage of the Dean campaign turned negative after Governor Dean took up the issue. "Who woulda thunk that it would become a hot political issue?" commented the *Washington Post*'s media watcher Howard Kurtz, who showed a stunning personal disconnect about public attitudes on one of the key issues he writes about. "Not me," he added.[5] He characterized the public outrage as a revolution. Media had suddenly gone from being a complaint to being an issue.

The problem was that the FCC campaign was reactive and single-issue oriented. The public had the power to raise the issue, even put it on the agenda, but not to mobilize enough political clout to win more than a compromise and a victory for the status quo. Ultimately, media owners prevailed with incremental gains, and the larger issues of who will control broadband and cable were not even raised. The rage and discontent that fueled the massive letter-writing campaigns soon moved back onto the safer and more familiar ground of personality-dominated electoral politics.

Some candidates did raise it. Ohio congressman Dennis Kucinich made it central to his campaign but soon his campaign itself was no longer being covered. When Vermont governor Howard Dean lashed out at media companies, media criticism of his campaign, which had been touted as the front runner, sharpened. Dean quickly went from being a political wonder boy to a wannabe. Was it his media stance? Not surprisingly, the media never discussed the possibility. Media as an issue moved into the background.

MEDIA MANAGEMENT

On the Right the focus of the administration remains on using the media with an artfully calculated, well-focused, and audience-tested approach. No detail on how to shape and present a message goes unattended to. Public relations firms like Luntz Research specialize in how to tailor issues for media and political consumption. Owner Frank Luntz takes credit for coming up with buzzwords like "Contract with America," "Partial Birth Abortion," "The Marriage Tax," and "The Death Tax." They have a way with words because they understand the importance of words in *framing* the way the media covers stories and the way people understand them. They say they "revolutionized" political research and communication in America because they "specialize in language." "We alone," they boast, while differentiating themselves from other PR firms, "offer numbers strategic direction and the actual words and phrases that have literally changed history . . . others may have more clients. But (we) are counseling a movement."[6]

The administration puts its own media research to practical use in preparing its officials for media appearances. Thanks to a document released by former treasury secretary Paul O'Neill to journalist Ron Susskind in the course of preparing the book *The Price of Loyalty*, the public learned just how the public can be manipulated on popular TV interview programs.[7] Susskind's Web site posted a document by O'Neill's press secretary, Michele Davis. The memo advised the treasury secretary on how to spin and avoid hostile questions. Here's part of what is said, which shows us how politicians are prepped to use the media to advantage:[8]

Message

First answer. No matter what the question: We must act to ensure our economy recovers and put people back to work.

Key lines to deliver. An economic security package to make the recession shorter and put people back to work faster. Creating jobs is the key to success.

Word choices. Economic security, not stimulus. Talk about people and their jobs, not growth and surplus.

There follows a reference to what O'Neill's *tone* should be as well as an admonition. "You need to interject the president's message," Davis coached O'Neill, "even if the question has nothing to do with that."

If conservatives are adept at using media to selling their ideas, liberal politicians tend to be vaguer and more responsive to questioners, as if their interrogators are sincere in wanting responses. The whole Q&A format tends to simplify issues and results in incomplete responses. The truth is that show biz has merged with news biz *allowing less air time for* real scrutiny of the issues and their formulations.

THE LEFT DISTRUSTS BUT RARELY COMPETES

On the Left, there is more distrust and dislike of the media but not necessarily any agreement on what can be done to challenge and confront it. Many on the Left look at Rupert Murdoch's Fox News channel as if its coverage is totally unique and much worse than the channels it competes with. They focus on the excesses of commentators like Bill O'Reilly but not the packaging and attitude that resonate with many viewers because it appears to be more independent and outspoken. Activist groups like MoveOn.org and others focus on challenging government power as if elected officials have more power than the corporate sector whose interests it serves. They do not promote campaigns to challenge the media, perhaps because they fear that criticizing the media may lead to less access to the media.

MEDIA FOR DEMOCRACY

The Mediachannel.org that I created believes we can do both—lobby on electoral issues and media issues at the same time. We are trying to galvanize public interest on media coverage of elections because the coverage is so crucial to their outcomes. We set up Media for Democracy 2004, a nonpartisan citizens' initiative to monitor mainstream news coverage of the 2004 elections and advocate standards of reporting that are more democratic and issues-oriented. Media for Democracy educates and activates a growing base of concerned citizens by delivering alerts—breaking news and analysis of mainstream media election coverage. Our goal is to build a constituency of people across the political spectrum that can put news executives on notice when their reporting strays from best practices for fair media coverage of elections.

In just a few months we attracted fourteen hundred members—citizens ready to lobby companies, challenge distorted news, and call for more coverage. We realize that private media companies are there to serve shareholders before viewers or listeners. We recognize that many are sensitive to perceived interference in their editorial process, as if the constitutional protections of a free press outlaw efforts to insist on high standards or accountability to the journalistic canons they claim to uphold.

Journalists and media companies often operate in bubbles of their own making, detached and cut off from the communities they claim to serve. Elitism and class prejudice is common. Many identify more with the interests of business than labor, with the needs of the powerful more than the demands of the powerless. They see themselves as mediators while many critics see them more like servants of the status quo.

So it is difficult for outsiders to press, the press which too often looks at critics as irresponsible advocates of ideological agendas. They can see the agendas of others more clearly than their own. At the same time, many calls to politicians are ignored or dismissed. You never know how and if your e-mail or call will be heard.

Clearly more is needed, but this is a good first step. It turns complaints into issues and helps put media issues on the larger agenda where they belong.

Media for Democracy also monitors campaign coverage, reporting on work by groups like Fairness and Accuracy in Reporting and the Tyndall Report, which monitors US network coverage. Media Tenor, an international organization, does a weekly summary for us on media coverage of campaigns.

Members of the campaign are encouraged to write to media outlets. Here is an example of one of our initiatives. Media for Democracy members have asked executives at several of America's largest news organizations to provide us with a better understanding of the ways they respond to a smear campaign when it comes across their news desks.

We refer not only to the most recent allegation of an affair between Senator John Kerry and an intern, which appeared in mid-February on Matt Drudge's Web site, but also to other rumors, photographs, and "gotcha" news items that originate from politically biased sources. Media for Democracy members are concerned over the apparent ease with which rumors migrate up the media food chain and spread into mainstream news coverage.

This request has been taken seriously by news executives. Here are the responses we received as of March 2004:

USA Today *Executive Editor Brian Gallagher*

"We have no plans to report rumors now [or] in the future. We have no more enthusiasm for another sex scandal than the public does. On the other hand, we also will not censor political news or facts, and we would like to help people separate fact from rumor when we can do so responsibly."

Washington Post *Editor Leonard Downie*

"We do not publish an allegation of this kind unless our own reporting determines that it is both true and relevant to the public actions of a public figure. We have not published many, many similar rumors and allegations made in past campaigns, mostly because our reporting determined that they were not true, even though some of them were published or broadcast elsewhere."

Boston Globe *Editor Martin Baron*

"The *Boston Globe* withholds publication of rumors about public figures, including political candidates and public officials, unless it can verify them and determine that they are relevant. If a public figure chooses to publicly address rumors, we may report on those statements, giving them the level of prominence that seems appropriate to the circumstances. If the rumors remain unverified, such statements by a public figure are not likely to receive much prominence. The *Globe* frequently refrains from publishing rumors because our standards are not met."

Lexington Herald-Leader *Managing Editor W. Thomas Eblen*

"The *Lexington Herald-Leader* does not publish rumors. In fact, our standards for attribution are higher than at most newspapers. All information and quotes in staff-written stories must be attributed to named sources. . . . While this practice occasionally costs us a scoop we can't get on the record, I'm sure it saves us from errors at least as often. We do sometimes publish wire stories containing unnamed sources; because of the way Washington works, that's often unavoidable. Even then, we are judicious. We are especially wary of stories like the Kerry rumor that are likely to be politically motivated. . . . We didn't publish anything about the Kerry rumor until the young woman went public to deny it. Then, it was a short item inside the paper."

Austin American-Statesman *Managing Editor Fred Zipp*

"We publish facts or, occasionally, credible allegations that get to the heart of a candidate's or officeholder's ability to do the job and maintain the public's trust. We don't publish rumors, and we're reluctant to delve into a public figure's private life."

Palm Beach Post *Managing Editor John Bartosek*

"The Internet circulates a thousand rumors, with more every day, about the famous, near-famous, and infamous. The *Post* rarely reports any of them. We publish stories that have facts in them, based on statements and records. One good example: When the White House released records of Bush's military service and discussed his time in the National Guard, then we had statements and records. That's when it reached the front page, and not before."

Toledo Blade *Executive Editor Ron Royhab*

"We do not print rumors, period, whether they are sourced or not. We are in the news business, not the rumor business. We would not and did not pick up the rumor on Matt Drudge's Web site alleging that Senator Kerry had an affair with an intern. However, when Kerry was asked publicly about the allegation, we used a brief quoting Kerry as saying it wasn't true."

Responses from other news organizations are posted as they come in.

ZAPATISTA MEDIA THINKING

Media for Democracy represents a reformist approach to media change. Others favor more radical efforts. Subcommandante Marcos, the charismatic Zapatista rebel leader, taped a message in the mountains of Mexico's impoverished Chiapas region for screening at a January 1997 *Freeing the Media* teach-in in New York. No networks covered it. He said in part:

> The world of contemporary news is a world that exists for the VIPs—the very important people. Their everyday lives are what is important; if they get married, if they divorce, if they eat, what clothes they wear or what clothes they take off—these major movie stars and big politicians. But common people

only appear for a moment—when they kill someone or when they die. For the communications giants, the others, the excluded, only exist when they are dead, when they are in jail or in court. This cannot go on.

It will lead, Marcos warns, to more confrontation. "Sooner or later this virtual world clashes with the real world." Significantly, Marcos and his guerrillas use modern media to transmit their messages, which tend to get stripped of their substance on image-driven TV programs, but do, nevertheless, find a supportive global audience via lengthy communiqués relayed over the Internet. So what were the choices he saw? We can ignore mass media was the first option he considered:

> We can have a cynical attitude in the face of the media, to say that nothing can be done about the dollar power that creates itself in images, words, digital communication, and computer systems that invades not just with an invasion of power, but with a way of seeing that world, of how they think the world should look. We could say, well, "that's the way it is" and do nothing.

His second option was to just denounce the media: "We can simply assume incredulity: we can say that any communication by the media monopolies is a total lie. We can ignore it and go about our lives."

His recommendation was to become the media—to create independent media to take on the big guns.

> There is a third option that is neither conformity, nor skepticism, nor distrust: that is to construct a different way—to show the world what is really happening—to have a critical worldview and to become interested in the truth of what happens to the people who inhabit every corner of this world.

> The problem is not only to know what is occurring in the world, but to understand it and to derive lessons from it— just as if we were studying history—a history not of the past, but a history of what is happening at any given moment in whatever part of the world. This is the way to learn who we are, what it is we want, who we can be, and what we can do or not do.

> By not having to answer to the monster media monopolies, the independent media has a life work, a political project and purpose: to let the truth be known.[9]

Yet even this approach doesn't recognize yet another option—to engage big media and make its power and irresponsibility an issue. That involves more than protest or resignation. Not everyone has the inclination, skills, or interest to become a media maker. Many are attracted/addicted to mainstream media as a principal source of information. They need to be reached and involved in campaigns for honest coverage and more diverse perspectives. At the same time, they need to be introduced to independent and alternative sources and media outlets critical of the media. This media war has yet to produce an effective opposition, an antiwar movement or cultural resistance that can challenge its trajectory and impact.

CHALLENGING MEDIA

Such a movement, however, is bubbling up from below, with parents calling for a more informative way of rating TV shows to safeguard their children, teachers promoting media literacy, activists asking for corporate account-ability, consumers demanding enforcement of antitrust laws, media watchers critiquing news coverage, critics seeking more meaningful program content, producers creating alternative work, and independent producers like me agitating for better and fairer journalism.

Media institutions that report on the corporate irresponsibility of others, like the endless stream of indicted Wall Street operators, need to turn the cameras on themselves. How socially responsible and accountable are they? How transparent? Had activists been paying attention, there would have been a protest against revelations in 2000 by the Alliance for Better Campaigns that showed how many local TV stations violated federal laws by over-charging candidates while reducing their electoral coverage.

What this points to is the need for media students to become media activists not only to become better informed about the way big media works —and the way the government works with it. We are all living in the crosshairs of powerful media institutions. Their fire is "incoming," into our living rooms—and then into our brains. We need more than self-defense. We need to take collective action to challenge those "crosshairs" and push back. We need to support independent media, with our eyeballs, our dollars, and our marketing know-how. We need to encourage media literacy education in our schools. We need to challenge candidates to speak out on these issues, and media outlets to cover them.

And yet many progressive activists didn't get it—and still don't. They give out leaflets and try to buy antiwar ads on TV—many of which are rejected. They have no media strategy beyond reacting to right-wing campaigns.

During the 1980s and 1990s, the Right invented a bugaboo called the lib-eral media and went after it with a vengeance. They complained, criticized, bullied, and created their own media outlets. They didn't want to take on media; they were determined to take it over.

And they seem to be on the way to succeeding.

First there were opinion magazines, then talk radio, then bloggers like Matt Drudge, who soon had his own radio show on Rush Limbaugh's network. Then there was the FCC overruling its own staff recommendations not to let Murdoch buy Fox, then there was Republican Guard media guru Roger Ailes financed to launch the Fox News Network, and then, and then—what's next?

On the other side are underfunded, undermarketed, and underpromoted independent media outlets, which include a scattering of magazines, weekly newspapers, Pacifica radio, public access TV, two satellite channels, many Web sites, and various Indy Media Centers. This can hardly be considered a counterweight to the combined power of mainstream media outlets.

That's where Web sites like Mediachannel.org and Mediareform.net, and the research of groups like Fairness and Accuracy in Reporting (FAIR) and Media Tenor, come in. They aim to broaden media education and connect to the need to change media, not just understand it.

NOTES

1. Thomas Pynchon, *Gravity's Rainbow* (New York: Penguin, 1995).

2. David Miller, *Tell Me Lies: Propaganda and Media Distortion in the Attack on Iraq* (London: Pluto, 2003).

3. Josh Benson, "Gore's TV War: He Lobs Salvo at Fox News," *New York Observer*, December 2, 2002, http://www.findarticles.com/cf_dls/m0ICQ/2002_Dec_2/95643874/p1/article.jhtml (accessed May 10, 2004).

4. Robert McChesney, *The Problem of the Media: U. S. Communication Politics in the Twenty-First Century* (New York: Monthly Review Press, 2004).

5. Howard Kurtz, "A Slap at the Media," *Washington Post*, July 24, 2003, http://www.politicalposts.com/news/index.asp?id=182303 (accessed May 10, 2004).

6. Danny Schechter, "Media Word Play—The Right's Mastery of the Echo Chamber," *Mediachannel.org*, March 15, 2004, http://www.mediachannel.org/views/dissector/affalert155.shtml (accessed May 10, 2004).

7. Ron Susskind, *The Price of Loyalty: George W. Bush, the White House, and the Education of Paul O'Neill* (New York: Simon & Schuster, 2004).

8. Schechter, "Media Word Play."

9. "Statement by Subcommandante Marcos Concerning *The Freeing the Media Teach-In*," Organized by the Learning Alliance, Paper Tiger TV, and FAIR in cooperation with the Media and Democracy Congress, January 31 and February 31, 1997, http://www.geocities.com/Athens/Acropolis/1232/Marcos.html (accessed May 10, 2004).

7

WHAT WOULD CRONKITE DO?

Journalistic Virtue, Corporate News,
and the Demise of the Fourth Estate

ELLIOT D. COHEN
INSTITUTE OF CRITICAL THINKING

ELLIOT D. COHEN, *PhD Brown University, is a writer and editor world renowned for his contributions in applied and professional ethics and philosophical counseling. He is director of his own research facility, the Institute of Critical Thinking, and editor in chief and founder of the* International Journal of Applied Philosophy, *the world's first comprehensive journal of applied philosophy. A principle founder of the philosophical counseling movement in the United States, he is cofounder and executive codirector of the American Society for Philosophy, Counseling, and Psychotherapy, the nation's premier academic association of philosophical counseling. He has appeared as a guest on National Public Radio and has been interviewed in the* New York Times Magazine. *The author of eleven books and numerous articles, his books include* What Would Aristotle Do? Self-Control through the Power of Reason *(Prometheus Books, 2003);* Philosophers at Work: Issues and Practice of Philosophy *(Wadsworth, 2000);* The Virtuous Therapist: Ethical Practice in Counseling and Psychotherapy *(Wadsworth, 1999);* Journalism Ethics *(ABC-CLIO, 1997); and* Philosophical Issues in Journalism *(Oxford University Press, 1994).*

A version of this paper also appears in the *Journal of Mass Media Ethics* 19, nos. 3 and 4 (2004). Reprinted by permission of the publisher.

T he current climate of American journalism is fraught with incestuous relations between government and Fortune 500 corporations. The end product is an environment in which the watchdog of American democracy, the press, has become a docile representative of governmental authority. It is in this context that the concept of journalistic virtue should be defined, for it is in this context that the *very purpose* of the press has been called into question.

While it is not news that the press, especially the broadcast media, have been largely influenced by their sponsors, the form of censorship and control examined in this chapter is that in which the corporations in question own the media and are in business with government.[1] The problem here lies in the incompatibility of corporate logic with the American media mission of holding the government accountable.

As John Ladd has argued, the expectation that corporations act as morally responsible agents is a "category mistake,"[2] one that now threatens the survival of a free press. Inasmuch as the central goal of a corporation is to maximize its bottom line, whatever is most cost-effective in achieving this goal is predictably the path that a corporation will follow. Legal regulations that constrain profit are therefore obstacles to be eliminated if this can be done cost-effectively. The quid pro quo of deregulation of media by government, procurement of defense contracts, and other financial arrangements in exchange for the media's adjusting the news to suit the purposes of government is thus a foreseeable corollary of the logic of corporate media decision making.

HOW GOVERNMENT USES CORPORATE LOGIC
TO CONTROL NEWS MEDIA

The American news media today is owned and operated by a relatively few major corporations.[3] There is also an intricate web of corporate relationships that bind news corporations to government. For example, General Electric supplies jet engines to Lockheed Martin, which is a major weapons contractor for nuclear weapons and ballistic missile defenses including components of the strategic defenses (Star Wars), which was scrapped during the Clinton administration but revived by the Bush administration.

In 2000, Microsoft, which co-owns the cable news channel MSNBC with General Electric (GE), created its government division, which has as its main purpose the procurement of government contracts, especially lucrative ones such as those afforded by the US Department of Defense. And it has a history of government defense contract partnerships with such major defense contractors as General Dynamics.[4] So it is easy to see how corporate logic might dictate reporting the case for war with Iraq in a favorable light or upgrading the threat posed by Saddam Hussein to US security where this portends a government contract.

In June 1999, shortly after George W. Bush declared his candidacy for the presidency, GE CEO Jack Welch was contacted by Bush's political adviser, Karl Rove, who guaranteed media deregulation in a manner that would mean large profits for GE and other corporate media giants if Bush was elected. Welch reciprocated by making it well known throughout NBC News that the standard for promotion of journalists would be "outstanding contribution to the financial well-being of General Electric," which included favorable coverage of George W. Bush. Under these new administrative pressures, journalists like Tim Russert and Chris Matthews became model GE employees.[5]

In December 2003, when MSNBC's Chris Matthews played *Hardball* with then Democratic presidential candidate Howard Dean, Matthews asked Dean the *leading* question, "If we elect you, when will the geyser go off?" implying that Dean had a bad temper.[6] In even attempting to answer this question, Dean would have effectively admitted that he had a bad temper. While such a tactic might be dismissed as merely a journalistic device to uncover the truth, this explanation becomes exceedingly less credible when it is realized that the interlocutor works for a company that is already "playing ball" with a Bush administration which was seeking a second term in the White House. Whether or not Matthews would have thrown the same "curve ball" had Dean been a member of Bush's team is far from clear, but the appearance of conflict even if not the reality still poisons the waters.

This appearance is not improved when it is learned that Matthews's younger brother, Jim Matthews, is a Republican Party activist and chairman of the Montgomery County, Pennsylvania, commission.[7] Of course, this does not mean that Chris Matthews can't be objective with a Democratic hopeful. He, in fact, used to write speeches for Democratic House Speaker Tip O'Neill. In itself, the fact that his brother may have aspirations within the Republican Party proves nothing. Nor is it, in itself, significant that Chris Matthews voted for Bush in 2000 against his longtime friend Al Gore and that this was the first time he had ever voted Republican in a presidential race.[8] On the other hand, taken in the context of colossal, revenue-driven corporations like GE, in which Matthews is "embedded," such facts, collectively, are consistent with the appearance if not the reality of ideological conformity and loss of independence of judgment among successful, main-stream journalists such as he.

As I have emphasized in the introduction to this book, media codes of ethics typically instruct journalists to avoid conflict of interest, real or perceived.[9] Yet, if the companies by whom individual journalists are employed ignore such fundamental ethics, then there is an obvious strain placed upon individual journalists to practice within the strictures of professional ethics. It is presently this challenge that is likely to separate virtuous journalists from those who become conduits to unethical corporate media practices that undermine the essential purpose or end of a democratic press.

VIRTUOUS JOURNALISM AND THE PURPOSE OF A DEMOCRATIC PRESS

When the First Amendment of the United States Constitution states that Congress shall make no law abridging freedom of speech, or of the press, it aims at a separation of the press from governmental control. It is no accident that such a separation was placed foremost in the minds of the Founding Fathers, for it is a fundamental condition of a democratic nation. Democracy implies autonomous rule by the people. People cannot decide autonomously if they are not adequately informed. They cannot decide freely if government controls the flow of information they receive.

One central purpose of news organizations in a democratic state, as distinct from a dictatorship, is thus that of providing an independent source of information by which the governed can exert autonomous control over their own lives. That the end of a *democratic* press is dissemination of information necessary for self-government is a tautology. It is like saying that the purpose of a watchdog is to guard against trespass (a popular metaphor used to characterize the function of the press). This is just what it *means* to have a democratic press.[10]

In this context, the term "democratic" has sometimes been confused with a partisan view according to which the press embraces, or should embrace, a liberal party politic. On this confusion, Republican critics of the press sometimes speak of "the liberal press," which they perceive as the embodiment of a given party politic, that of Democrats.[11] This is to equivocate on "democratic," however. The purpose of a democratic press is not to advance or to supplant a given party politic but instead to serve as a precondition of continuing the free and unfettered debate between competing political ideologies. Toward this end, the press functions like a fourth branch of government that checks for and exposes abuses in the judicial, legislative, and executive branches. To the extent that the press satisfactorily serves this function, it is democratic; to the extent that this function is impaired, it is *un*democratic.[12]

Within a democracy, the virtues of journalists include character traits that are conducive to the stated end of journalistic practice, just as the virtues of lawyers in an adversary system in a democracy are defined according to the promotion of substantive and procedural justice, or in medicine, according to the promotion of patient health. Following Aristotle, these character traits can be defined as *habits* or *dispositions* to act in manners that advance the end of a democratic press.[13] These habits involve dedication to principles of conduct that follow from the journalistic end of serving democracy. Insofar as this end is a moral end, these virtues and their corresponding principles are also moral. Even a cursory look at the variety of journalistic codes of ethics can give insight into what some of these virtues are. Thus, according to Article 1 of the *Statement of Principles* of the American Society of Newspaper Editors, entitled "Responsibility,"

> The primary purpose of gathering and distributing news and opinion is to serve the general welfare by informing the people and enabling them to make judgments on the issues of the time. The newspapermen and women who abuse the power of their professional role for selfish motives or unworthy purposes are faithless to that public trust. The American press was made free not just to inform or just to serve as a forum for debate but also to bring an independent scrutiny to bear on the forces of power in the society, including the conduct of official power at all levels of government.[14]

According to the *Code of Ethics* of the Society of Professional Journalists, under "Seek Truth and Report It," "Journalists should be honest, fair, and courageous in gathering, reporting, and interpreting information."[15] And they "should be free of obligation to any interest other than the public's right to know."

According to the *Code of Ethics* of the Radio Television News Directors Association, radio and television journalists should not "accept gifts, favors, or compensation from those who might seek to influence coverage"; and they should "present the news fairly and impartially, placing primary value on significance and relevance."

Journalists should cultivate habits of being responsible, loyal, fair, impartial, honest, and courageous in reporting the news. These virtues are also part of what it means to be a *competent* journalist. Journalistic competence cannot easily be severed from the moral routes of its ultimate mission. As Stephen Beauchamp and Tom Klaidman suggest, "Tape can be edited accurately, fairly, and objectively, or it can fail to meet these criteria. The editing cannot justifiably be called competent unless they are satisfied, which suggests that moral criteria are embedded in our very conception of competent journalistic practice."[16]

It has sometimes been argued that the journalistic virtues highlighted in professional codes of ethics such as those mentioned above are intended as guidelines to be followed under ordinary circumstances. However, it is contended that journalists do not usually work under ordinary circumstances. Therefore, these guidelines are often not realistic. As Stephen Daniel argues, "it comes as little surprise that many journalists place little weight in philosophical arguments for respecting the privacy of individuals or for avoiding conflicts of interest." For example, in the world inhabited by journalists, he argues, even eavesdropping may be in line with "standards of excellence" in journalism.[17] The concept of journalistic virtue Daniel depicts would therefore drive a wedge between journalistic competence and ordinary morality. There is, in this view, a tension between the realistic demands of journalism and those of ordinary life. Virtues such as honesty and loyalty may be conditions of the morality of everyday life but not of journalism.

Such a view might seem to make it easier to stretch the lines of acceptable journalistic practice to include disregard for conflicts of interest with government and corporate authority. However, such an extension would be misguided, even on the concept of journalistic practice Daniel describes. This is true because even this concept tolerates disregarding conflicts of interest and engaging in violations of privacy and trust only when such conduct helps to keep lines of information flowing to the public. Keeping the public informed is still perceived to be the ultimate goal of the news media.

The concept of journalistic practice Daniel describes suffers from its failure to reconcile deceitful and untrustworthy tactics with the democratic spirit of the news media. In a democracy, the press exists primarily to promote democracy. This logic—which says that journalists can, and should, engage in conduct that is ordinarily considered unethical in order to achieve the common good—is not compatible with democracy. The idea that anything—or almost anything—goes in the interest of "national security" is an example of the same sort of reasoning, which has not infrequently been proffered by very *un*democratic governments for purposes of achieving secret, self-aggrandizing ends having little or nothing to do with the common good. If individual journalists use such suspect logic to rationalize their cooperation in deals struck between government and their corporate bosses, then they are betraying their primary role as guardians of democracy.

Insofar as democracy supports justice, it does not seek to violate the serious rights of individuals in order to achieve the greater good of others. As the late John Rawls writes:

> Each member of society is thought to have an inviolability founded on justice or, as some say, on natural right, which even the welfare of everyone else cannot override. Justice denies that the loss of freedom for some is made right by a greater good shared by others. The reasoning which balances the gains and losses of different persons as if they were one person is excluded. Therefore, in a just society the basic liberties are taken for granted and the rights secured by justice are not subject to political bargaining or to the calculus of social interests.[18]

From behind a Rawlsian "veil of ignorance,"[19] no rational person would wish to be traded off for the good of others. Because the democratic media seek to ensure the rational self-determination of the populace by keeping it informed, it is unacceptable—and self-defeating—to violate individual rights in the process. This includes saying nothing in order to increase the bottom line or to appease governmental authorities, where reporting the news accurately could prevent the violation of individual rights.

It is doubtful that journalistic practice can promote the common good, at least in the long run, if journalists generally disregard the moral standards prescribed by journalistic codes of ethics. If journalists disregard these standards, the institution of journalism will suffer. A press that continually violates individual rights to obtain the news and involves itself in conflicts of interest will chill public trust—not to mention its news sources. Such a press will lose its ability to fulfill its democratic function. Journalism that does not "treat sources, subjects, and colleagues as human beings deserving of respect"[20] will not work.

Unfortunately, in the present environment in which the news is being influenced by deals struck between government and corporate media, competence has been severed from its moral roots, and journalistic virtue has become an empty aspiration to which journalists have been paying lip service. Under the direction of its corporate and government masters, the press's silent acquiescence in the façade that it still honors its democratic charter may be among its greatest breaches of public trust. As Norman Solomon remarked, "deceptive propaganda can only succeed to the extent that journalists are gullible—or believe that they must pretend to be—while encouraging the public to go along with the charade."[21] Putting on the façade of conducting business as usual, while delivering half the news or disseminating government propaganda, like fiddling while Rome burns, is neither honest, courageous, responsible, nor fair. Nor, in the end, is it likely to conduce to the common good.

Aristotle remarked that the courageous or brave person "feels and acts according to the merits of the case and in whatever way the rule directs," even if this involves great personal sacrifice.[22] The professional standards of ethical conduct of journalists clearly direct journalists to avoid conflicts of interest and to remain steadfast to their primary democratic end. Under the present circumstances, this involves speaking out loudly against those powers surreptitiously working to undermine the public trust. This is what being a journalist in a democratic society means. This is nonnegotiable and comes with the territory. It is not only cowardly to remain silent; it is journalistically incompetent.

The French existentialist philosopher Jean-Paul Sartre said that "to choose to be this or that, is to affirm at the same time the value of what we choose."[23] When a journalist chooses to work for a newspaper or a news corporation that is violating the public trust, he or she cannot avoid responsibility for whatever evils that are worked by that network. In choosing the network he or she is responsible for the violation and all that it entails. That "I only work here" is not an adequate defense, because the journalist can choose not to work here. For Sartre, the journalist who acquiesces in news deception without admission of his complicity is a coward.[24]

When CBS news anchor Dan Rather appeared on the David Letterman show six days after the September 11 attack, he stated, "George Bush is the president, he makes the decisions," and "wherever he wants me to line up, just tell me where. And he'll make the call." Eight months after the 9/11 tragedy, in a BBC television interview, Dan Rather of CBS admitted that he and other journalists had been intimidated about "asking the toughest of the tough questions" for fear of being branded unpatriotic.[25]

On CNN's *Reliable Sources*, in an interview about whether the media have provided just coverage of protests against war in Iraq, Dan Rather guardedly stated,

> We've tried on the *CBS Evening News*, for which I'm responsible . . . to give the coverage we think is merited, but I'm open to the criticism. The White House and the administration power is able to control the images to a very large degree. It has been growing over the years. And that's the context in which we talk about, well, how much coverage does the antiwar movement merit? And I think it's a valid criticism it's been underreported.[26]

It is unfortunate that Rather's admissions were not voiced consistently and unequivocally before the American public. His willingness to continue as an anchor for CBS, despite these admissions, speaks more to his willingness to "line up" wherever he is told. To this extent, Rather betrayed the public trust he, as a journalist, was supposed to uphold. Courage here would have meant standing on principles—those of honesty, responsibility, fairness, and loyalty to the journalistic faith—instead of allowing himself to be intimidated, even if this meant personal sacrifice.

In contrast is a journalist like NPR's Daniel Schorr, who, in 1976, was fired by CBS News for sending a secret congressional intelligence report to the *Village Voice* when CBS refused to cover the story. According to Schorr, the network had struck a deal with the White House to go easy on the administration.[27]

Schorr placed the democratic mission of the press on a higher plane than his career. In the words of the Society of Professional Journalists, a journalist should be "vigilant and courageous about holding those with power accountable."[28] This appears to be what Schorr attempted to accomplish, and he was fired for the undertaking.

Arthur Kent, who earned the name "Scud Stud" for his coverage of the first Gulf War, effectively ended his career with NBC when he publicly derided *Dateline* for its manipulation and reediting of stories.[29] On January 30, 2003, and again on January 31, 2003, Paul Begala, the Democratic proponent of CNN's *Crossfire*, boldly denounced the news media for its politically biased and shoddy coverage of news surrounding the Bush administration.[30]

In 2000, Walter Cronkite, world renowned for his forthrightness and unwavering commitment to a democratic press, helped to launch Mediachannel .org, an online news organization devoted to the exploration of media concerns. He stated:

> As you know, I've been increasingly and publicly critical of the direction that journalism has taken of late, and of the impact on democratic discourse and principles. Like you, I'm deeply concerned about the merger mania that has swept our industry, diluting standards, dumbing down the news, and making the bottom line sometimes seem like the only line. It isn't and it shouldn't be.
>
> . . . Pressure to go along, to get along, or to place the needs of advertisers or companies above the public's need for reliable information distorts a free press and threaten democracy itself. . . .
>
> We're always ready to speak out when journalists are at risk. But today we must speak out because journalism *itself* is at risk.[31]

Daniel Schorr, Arthur Kent, Walter Cronkite, and other journalists of their ilk, who have taken the journalistic high road of *speaking out* about political concerns despite personal risk and sacrifice, are more appropriate models of journalistic excellence than those, like Dan Rather or Chris Matthews, who have earned their fame by being good corporate employees. If the watchdog of democracy is to have teeth, then those who carry the torch must proceed without fear of intimidation from those who would distract them from their primary mission. If the press is to be restored to its rightful democratic throne, then a clear media voice must stand for separation of government and press. Virtuous journalists who care more for this journalistic faith than they do about their own reputations must carry the torch.

DEMOCRATIZING THE PRESS: THE CHALLENGE TO VIRTUOUS JOURNALISTS

The road to a democratic press in the rough wilderness of corporate oligopoly is not likely to be short and straight. As the history of those who have stood upon principle reveals, there are likely to be roadblocks and resistance offered by corporate and government benefactors of current media conditions. Journalists who have become allies, accomplices, and servants of these benefactors are likely to stand against journalists who resist. Complacency with the status quo is likely to be rewarded by the powerful, and courage and patriotism made to look like cowardice and sedition. In this relentlessly duplicitous environment where fair is foul and foul is fair, change may be gradual and fraught with peril. So what can be done?

Schools of journalism can help by teaching the prospective purveyors of democracy the importance of their role in a free society. Emphasis on teaching the technical skills of editing, reporting, copyediting, and the like are empty without seeing these in their *moral* context. Ethics should not be an adjunct to instruction since this artificially bifurcates morality from competence. Instead, the moral quality of technical competence should be flaunted and the skills viewed as empty corpses until the democratic spirit of the press breathes life into them.

Journalistic associations should be vigilantly vocal about the current state of American journalism. For example, the Society of Professional Journalists has recognized "a special obligation to ensure that the public's business is conducted in the open and that government records are open to inspection."[32] In this regard, it publishes a list of "red flags" on its Web site

that indicates when such freedom of information is in danger of being violated (for example, "government files, which had been available, suddenly
become unavailable").[33] But it should also be emphasized that the very news
institutions entrusted with delivering the news may *themselves* be active participants in concealing the news from the public. This requires the generation
of a new set of red flags that should send signals to individual journalists that
the usurpation of freedom of information may, like an insidious Trojan horse,
be coming from within the news organization.

The issue of how to stop corporate media from devouring democracy is
one treated extensively throughout this book. One important safeguard
against the demise of democracy is the emergence of nonprofit, noncommercial news organizations (national as well as community based)[34] whose executive boards are free from conflict of interest and affiliation with government
agencies, special interest groups, and powerful corporations, and which are
not dependent upon corporate advertising funds for their survival.[35] Although such organizations would require substantial government ("public")
funding, the clear absence of the self-interested, bottom-line logic that
presently drives corporate media and undermines public trust would greatly
diminish opportunity for quid pro quo between government and media.

Another safeguard is an open-access Internet, protected by government
regulation against encroachment by commercial, revenue-driven corporate
interests and conflicts.[36] A third safeguard is the legal control of the corporate
media by Congress and the FCC through judicious maintenance and application of media-specific ownership rules created to serve the public interest
and not the private interests of politicians and corporate media moguls.[37]

But such needed media reform is not likely to proceed if journalists
themselves are complicit in the antidemocratic journalistic practices of their
corporate media bosses. Journalists who are disposed to cooperate through
intimidation and fear of being branded "unpatriotic" should think twice about
their public charge in the defense of democracy, and what "patriotism" really
means in the context of journalistic practice.

In the seventeenth century, Thomas Hobbes wrote,

> It is annexed to the sovereignty [government] to judge of what opinions and
> doctrines are averse, and what conducing to peace; and consequently, on
> what occasions, how far, and what men are to be trusted withal in speaking
> to multitudes of people; and who shall examine the doctrines of all books
> before they be published. For the actions of men proceed from their opin-
> ions, and in the well governing of opinions consists of the well governing
> of men's actions in order to their peace and concord. And though in matter

of doctrine nothing ought to be regarded but the truth, yet this is not repugnant to regulating of the same by peace.[38]

It is instructive to note that, in this passage, Hobbes was discussing the way a successful *dictator* should deal with the media. His argument that truth should be "regulated" for the sake of "peace" is an old dictatorial saw, more commonly these days coached in terms of "national security." This is not the language of democracy or of a free society. Dictatorships have always sought to silence or control the press, and it is one of the first things they do when they come to power. A red flag that we may have budding dictatorship is that we have a press intimidated to speak out. Recall the confessional of Dan Rather. There is much need now for virtuous journalists to come forth and speak out. This is not optional. It is urgent and of the essence of what it means to be a journalist in a democracy.

NOTES

1. By "business" I also include the quid pro quo of agreements for mutual advantage without any formal contract or monetary transaction. This form of mutuality between government and media is not new. For example, during Richard Nixon's 1972 reelection campaign, major newspapers promised Nixon editorial support in exchange for his support of the Newspaper Preservation Act. As a result, newspaper corporations were able to attain monopolies in many American cities. See Robert W. McChesney, *Rich Media, Poor Democracy: Communication Politics in Dubious Times* (New York: New Press, 2000), p. xvi. As I suggest below, such quid pro quo between corporate media and government now appears to be widespread in the broadcast media.

2. John Ladd, "Morality and the Ideal of Rationality in Formal Organizations," *Monist* 54, no. 4 (October 1970).

3. See Mark Crispin Miller, "The Big Ten Media Giants," in *Censored 2003: Media Democracy in Action*, ed. Peter Phillips (New York: Sevens Stories Press, 2002), pp. 231–40.

4. Pat Kearney, "Microsoft Does Business with the Department of Defense," *TheStranger.com* 10 (September 27, 2000), http://www.thestranger.com/2000-09-21/city5.html.

5. David Podvin and Carolyn Kay, "Democracy, General Electric Style," *Midwest Today*, Web exclusive, October 2001, http://www.midtod.com/exclusives/jack-welch.phtml (accessed May 11, 2004).

6. Miranda Daniloff Mancusi, "Hardball with Chris Matthews and Former Vermont Governor Howard Dean," *New Stories*, the Kennedy School of Govern-

ment, Harvard University, http://www.ksg.harvard.edu/news/news/2003/hardball_dean_120103.htm (accessed April 29, 2004).

7. Richard Leihy, "Chris Mathews, Not Smarting from Bush's Dumb Brother Joke," Washingtonpost.com, March 23, 2004, http://www.washingtonpost.com/wp-dyn/articles/A16282-2004Mar22.html (accessed April 29, 2004).

8. Ibid.

9. See Deni Elliott, "Conflicts of Interest," in *Journalism Ethics*, ed. Elliot D. Cohen and Deni Elliott (Santa Barbara, CA: ABC-CLIO, 1997), pp. 91–96.

10. John Dewey, *The Public and Its Problems* (New York: Henry Holt & Co., 1927).

11. See, for example, Bernard Goldberg, *Bias* (Washington, DC: Regnery Publishing, 2001).

12. "I would go so far as to say that media reform is not an issue that is best cast along left-right lines. It is better thought of as elementary to democracy. . . . It is a cannon of liberal democracy, not socialist theory . . . that a democracy cannot exist without a press system that provides a rigorous accounting of people in power and the presentation of a wide range of informed opinions on the important issues of the day and age. Without such a media system, the promise of democracy becomes very hollow very quickly." McChesney, *Rich Media, Poor Democracy*, p. xxviii.

13. Aristotle, *Nichomachean Ethics* (Amherst, NY: Prometheus Books, 1987).

14. American Society of Newspaper Editors, *Statement of Principles*, http://www.asne.org/kiosk/archive/principl.htm.

15. Society of Professional Journalists, *Code of Ethics*, http://www.spj.org/ethics_code.asp.

16. Stephen Klaidman and Tom L. Beauchamp, "The Virtuous Journalist: Morality in Journalism," in *Philosophical Issues in Journalism*, ed. Elliot D. Cohen (New York: Oxford University Press, 1992), p. 45.

17. Stephen H. Daniel, "Some Conflicting Assumptions of Journalistic Ethics," in Cohen, *Philosophical Issues in Journalism*, p. 51.

18. John Rawls, *A Theory of Justice* (Cambridge, MA: Harvard University Press, 1971), p. 28.

19. Ibid., pp. 136–41.

20. Society of Professional Journalists, *Code of Ethics*.

21. Norman Solomon, "Media War and the Rigors of Self-Censorship," in Phillips, *Censored 2003*, p. 248.

22. Aristotle, *Nicomachean Ethics*, Book 3, Ch. 7.

23. Jean-Paul Sartre, "Existentialism," in *Philosophers at Work: Issues and Practice of Philosophy*, ed. Elliot D. Cohen (Fort Worth: Harcourt, 2000), p. 246.

24. "Those who hide their complete freedom from themselves out of a spirit of seriousness or by means of deterministic excuses, I shall call cowards." Sartre, "Existentialism."

25. Solomon, "Media War and the Rigors of Self-Censorship," pp. 241–42.

26. CNN, *Reliable Sources*, March 9, 2003.

27. Podvin and Kay, "Democracy, General Electric Style."

28. Society of Professional Journalists, *Code of Ethics*.

29. Ibid.

30. In particular, on January 31, he said the following: "Last night I reported to you on the breath-taking hypocrisy of President Bush, praising the work of the Boys and Girls Clubs, calling them 'little beacons of light,' then cutting off their electricity by reducing their budget $10 million. I suggested that none of the major media would have the guts to report President Bush's brazen bad faith. I was wrong a little. One reporter, Mike Allen, at one newspaper, 'The Washington Post,' wrote one sentence about it. Nothing in 'The New York Times,' nothing on the AP, nothing on CNN, except here on CROSSFIRE, or any of the other so-called news networks. The lesson, you can bask in the glow of a wonderful group even if you've cut its budget, because the press corps is so cowed by the Bush White House, you can almost hear them moo. President Bush, of course, could not be reached for comment. He was too busy laughing his ass off." CNN, *Crossfire*, Transcripts, January, 31, 2003, http://www.cnn.com/TRANSCRIPTS/0301/31/cf.00.html.

31. Walter Cronkite, MediaChannel.org, February 2000, http://www.mediachannel.org/originals/cronkite.shtml.

32. Society of Professional Journalists, *Code of Ethics*.

33. Society of Professional Journalists, "'Red Flags' to violation of Freedom of Information (FOI)," http://www.spj.org/foia_opendoors_flags.asp.

34. See Mark Cooper, "Building a Progressive Democratic Media and Communications Sector," this volume, p. 157.

35. While public media such as NPR exist today, such media are largely dependent upon corporate advertisers and receive insufficient public funding. This is in comparison to other nations such as England and Japan, which maintain a more robust and autonomous nonprofit media. See, for example, Robert McChesney, "Making Media Democratic," *Boston Review* 23 (1998): 4–10, http://www.uiowa.edu/~c036088/mcchesney.html (accessed May 10, 2004).

36. See Barry Steinhardt and Jay Stanley, "Protecting the Future of the Free Internet," this volume, p. 237.

37. See Harold Feld and Cheryl Leanza, "How Can Government Constitutionally Compel Mass Media to Provide News and How Can Citizens Make It Happen?" this volume, p. 185.

38. Hobbes, "Dictatorship," in Cohen, *Philosophers at Work*.

IV

ABRIDGMENT OF THE FIRST AMENDMENT

How Corporate Media Have Sold Out
Freedom of Speech and Artistic Expression
in America and How to Reclaim Them

8

BUILDING A PROGRESSIVE, DEMOCRATIC MEDIA AND COMMUNICATIONS SECTOR

MARK COOPER
CONSUMER FEDERATION OF AMERICA

MARK COOPER *is director of research at the Consumer Federation of America where he has responsibility for energy, telecommunications, and economic policy analysis. With a PhD from Yale University and a former Yale University and Fulbright Fellow, Dr. Cooper is a fellow at the Stanford Law School Center for Internet and Society and an associated fellow at the Columbia University Institute on Tele-Information. He is the author of numerous articles in trade and scholarly journals, as well as several books, including* Media Ownership and Democracy in the Digital Information Age: Promoting Diversity with First Amendment Principles and Market Structure Analysis *(Center for Internet and Society, 2003) and* Cable Mergers and Monopolies: Market Power in Digital Media and Communications Networks *(Economic Policy Institute, 2002). Dr. Cooper has provided expert testimony in over 250 cases for public interest clients, including attorneys general, people's counsels, and citizen interveners, before state and federal agencies, courts, and legislators in almost four dozen jurisdictions in the United States and Canada.*

America experienced a conservative shift during the last two decades of the twentieth century that emphasized the economic aspects of the media and communication sectors at the expense of public interest obligations, but the recent efforts of the Federal Communications Commission (FCC) to dramatically relax media ownership limits caused such a backlash that even senior politicians were caught off guard.[1] Deep concern about the impact of the commercial mass media on American democracy long antedated the proposed change in the rules.[2] However, the "Copernican Revolution"[3] that FCC chairman Michael Powell declared may actually mark the start of a vigorous movement for media reform that shifts policy in the opposite direction, toward progressive mass media and open communications networks. For the average citizen, rule makings in Washington are usually distant and arcane, but there are indications that the omnibus assault on democratic discourse and open communications by the FCC may not pass with the public indifference that greets most FCC decisions. Hundreds of thousands of ordinary citizens took the time to voice their opposition to relaxation of ownership limits.

In this chapter I suggest that there is a grassroots rebellion because the narrow view of the First Amendment and the acceptance of discriminatory behavior in access to the means of communication adopted by the commission is offensive to the traditions of vibrant civic discourse and an open society that the American people and the Supreme Court have always embraced. The groups on the Left and the Right that banded together to oppose the new media rules did so because they are minorities who feel that their "social, political, aesthetic, moral, and other ideas" should have an equal opportunity to be aired. There is growing consensus that the current media system is not nurturing informed democratic discourse. The members of this movement may not believe that all ideas are of equal value, but they do believe that they should have a fair chance to be heard. They certainly do not want the outcome of democratic discourse to be determined by who owns the media and the means of communications.

The public recognizes the fundamental problem of media concentration and that the commercial mass media is failing them,[4] a view that is fully supported by the social scientific evidence.[5] They believe that media markets are far too concentrated and that public policy should make it harder, not easier, for mergers to take place in this industry. They believe that the media is unresponsive to their local and diverse needs and that mergers reduce diversity and undermine the public interest.

This chapter outlines principles for progressive democratic media and communications in the American capitalist, digital economy. It presents a normative framework for progressive media and communications policy in the sense that it assumes that the goal of communications policy is to create an uninhibited forum for democratic discourse that stimulates citizens to participate actively in the political process and uncover truth through robust debate.[6] In so doing, it integrates First Amendment principles in the mass media with Communications Act principles of open communications networks. While media and telecommunications policy have been separate for most of the twentieth century, the convergence of all media into a single, digital information platform in the new millennium compels rethinking and integration of the two.

A positive case for this view has been made elsewhere and will briefly be reviewed here.[7] A demonstrable empirical link exists between the specific goals for the forum for democratic discourse and the institutional arrangements. If media and communications institutions are configured in specific ways, they are more likely to produce the stated goals. By demonstrating that progressive policies are well grounded in American jurisprudence and supported by social scientific evidence, my goal is to help give coherence to the political sentiment that is leaning in that direction.

THE BOLD ASPIRATION FOR THE FIRST AMENDMENT

In the middle half of the twentieth century, from roughly 1927 to 1978, the Supreme Court articulated what I call a *bold aspiration* for the First Amendment in the age of electronic media. The unique characteristics of broadcast media were recognized by Congress early in the century, and the airwaves (radio spectrum) were defined as a public resource.[8] Public policies to ensure that the immense power of the new media promote democratic debate and the free flow of information were repeatedly upheld by the Court.

Because the "widest possible dissemination of information from diverse and antagonistic sources is essential to the welfare of the public,"[9] the Court has found that Congress has the right to ensure that the electronic media serve the public interest. Consequently, limits and obligations on media owners—limitations on ownership and owner rights, and on programming aired, as well as obligations to air specific types of programming—do not violate the First Amendment.

The objective of discourse is to draw citizens into participation in civic affairs. "The greatest menace to freedom is an inert people; that public discussion is a political duty; and that this should be a fundamental principle of American government."[10] In *Red Lion Broadcasting v. FCC*, the seminal television case, the Court expressed a similar sentiment, noting that "speech concerning public affairs is more than self-expression; it is the essence of self-government."[11] The discourse must be full and open because "[i]t is the right of the viewers and listeners, not the right of the broadcasters, which is paramount . . . the right of the public to receive suitable access to social, political, aesthetic, moral, and other ideas and experiences which is crucial here. [T]he 'public interest' in broadcasting clearly encompasses the presentation of vigorous debate of controversial issues of importance and concern to the public."[12]

Moreover, the First Amendment is not limited to preventing government from impeding the free flow of ideas.[13] The decisions in the cases spawned by the Telecommunications Act of 1996, *Fox v. FCC* and *Sinclair Broadcast Group v. FCC*, reiterate the principle that restraints on the economic interests of licensees are legitimate in the effort to promote the public's interest in diversity.[14]

In order to ensure that discourse is balanced, it is permissible for policy to prevent undue concentration of economic power and excessive influence. In *FCC v. National Citizens Committee for Broadcasting*,[15] a 1978 case, the Court upheld limitations on ownership "on the theory that diversification of mass media ownership serves the public interest by promoting diversity of program and service viewpoints, as well as by preventing undue concentration of economic power."[16] In 2002, the DC Circuit Court in *Sinclair* restated the broad purpose in promoting the public interest when it stated, "the greater the diversity of ownership in a particular area, the less chance there is that a single person or group can have an inordinate effect, in a political, editorial, or similar programming sense, on public opinion at the regional level."[17]

Having established this broad base for public policies that created an environment in which vigorous debate would thrive, I turn to the issue of scarcity. The need to license spectrum is one of the bases on which public obligations can be imposed on the holders of licenses. Starting with a 1943 radio case, *National Broadcasting Co. v. United States*[18] and continuing through the most recent cases, the Supreme Court found that "where there are substantially more individuals who want to broadcast than there are frequencies to allocate, it is idle to posit an unabridgeable First Amendment right to broadcast comparable to the right of every individual to speak, write, or publish."[19]

Opponents of a bold aspiration for the First Amendment would like to see this scarcity as the sole basis for public policy so that they can declare an abundance of cable and satellite channels available and escape their public interest obligations. The claim is wrong because it is a listener/viewer analysis, not a speaker analysis. Even if hundreds of channels are available to citizens as listeners, this does not empower them as speakers. In fact, cable and satellite owners control all of the channels, so they are a single powerful voice. It is not the scarcity of spectrum that matters, but the scarcity of voices. In a nation of almost three hundred million people, the number of channels is still far exceeded by the number of persons wishing to broadcast to the public.

KEEPING THE LINES OF COMMUNICATION OPEN IN DEMOCRACY AND CAPITALISM

Throughout American history communications policy was equally progressive. As codified in Title II of the Communications Act of 1934, telecommunications carriers were subject to common carrier obligations. In providing service:

> All charges, practices, classifications, and regulation for and in conjunction with such service, shall be just and reasonable. . . .
>
> It shall be unlawful for any common carrier to make any unjust or unreasonable discrimination in charges, practices, classifications, regulations, facilities, or services for or in connection with like communications service, directly or indirectly, by any means or device, or to make or give any undue or unreasonable preference or advantage to any particular person, class of persons, or locality or to subject any particular person, class of persons, or locality to any undue or unreasonable prejudice or disadvantage.[20]

This principle of open communications networks culminated half a century of evolution in the communications arena. It is deeply embedded in the fabric of capitalism and has played a critical role in producing the dynamic information networks in which communications and commerce converge. Physical and social mobility were anathema to feudalism but essential to capitalism and democracy. Providing for open and adequate highways of commerce and means of communications was critical to allow commerce to flow to support a more complex division of labor, to weave small distant places into a national and later global economy, and to promote democratic discourse.

Common carriage and nondiscrimination were the solutions. Under common law, innkeepers were obligated to serve all travelers, thereby supporting the movement of people, goods, and services. Turnpike trusts were created to build and maintain roads in the seventeenth and eighteenth centuries as private undertakings with a public franchise to collect tolls in a nondiscriminatory manner on the section of a road whose upkeep was the responsibility of the trustee. By the nineteenth century, however, direct public responsibility for roads became the norm and nondiscriminatory access provided without direct fees. Maintaining a network of transcontinental roads became a governmental responsibility.

Later, the principles of nondiscriminatory access were applied to all national communications and transportation networks. Roads and highways, canals, railroads, the mail, telegraph, and telephone—some owned by public entities, most owned by private corporations—have always been operated as common carriers that are required to interconnect and serve the public on a nondiscriminatory basis.

Some argue that the open architecture of the Internet (known as the end-to-end principle), which ensures complete transparency and neutrality of the communications network and relies on intelligence distributed among the users of the network (rather than centralized in the hands of the network owners), converges with the strong commitment in our society to democratic values.

> Relative anonymity, decentralized distribution, multiple points of access, no necessary tie to geography, no simple system to identify content, tools of encryption—all these features and consequences of the Internet protocol make it difficult to control speech in cyberspace. The architecture of cyberspace is the real protector of speech there; it is the real "First Amendment in cyberspace," and this First Amendment is no local ordinance. . . .
>
> The architecture of the Internet, as it is right now, is perhaps the most important model of free speech since the founding.[21]

NARROWING THE LINES OF COMMUNICATION[22]

In the last two decades of the twentieth century, mass media and communications policy turned away from the bold aspiration for the First Amendment and broad commitment to open communications networks. No single statement symbolizes the shift of focus more than the claim by Mark Fowler, Ronald Reagan's first chairman of the Federal Communications Commission, that "television is just an appliance, a toaster with pictures."[23] The details of Fowler's 1982 vision were fleshed out in a 1984 FCC report that sought to eliminate or dramatically reduce many of the limits the FCC had placed on ownership.[24] He encountered stiff congressional resistance, and a twenty-year guerilla war ensued in which smaller changes were made by the FCC and occasionally by Congress.

In 1984 two major actions signaled a shift in direction. The passage of the Cable Act allowed cable operators to escape common carrier obligations and set in motion a series of events that could lead to the elimination of common carrier obligations on the advanced telecommunications networks of the twenty-first century. Similarly, the 1984 breakup of AT&T ushered in an experiment with competition in telecommunications markets. In the face of this new environment, the FCC labored to preserve obligations of nondiscrimination. In the Telecommunications Act of 1996, Congress declared its hope that local telecommunications markets would be competitive and instructed the FCC to reexamine its media ownership policies. While Clinton administration appointees moved slowly, Fowler's vision came to fruition in a series of party-line votes in 2002 and 2003 that proposed to eviscerate media ownership limits and eliminate common carrier obligations for advanced telecommunications networks.

In order to justify a virtual elimination of limits on ownership, the FCC gave up any notion that public policy should strive to promote a fair democratic discourse. The FCC adopted the narrowest vision of the First Amendment imaginable. Rather than promote vibrant discourse, the FCC declared that it was concerned only with preventing the complete censorship of ideas. "In the context of evaluating viewpoint diversity, this approach reflects a measure of the likelihood that some particular viewpoint might be censored or foreclosed, i.e., blocked from transmission to the public."[25]

The broadcasters advanced this view. "What really matters with ideas from a political point of view is whether they can be suppressed. But given the importance of interpersonal communications, it is extremely difficult to suppress ideas—they can 'leak out' even through small or economically minor media outlets."[26]

The "leak out" view of the First Amendment leads to a discourse that looks nothing like the bold aspiration expressed by the Supreme Court. The ideas of the network owners are likely to be broadcast much more widely than those that leak out. The FCC shrugs this off. If the distribution of media ownership undermines a robust exchange of views, the FCC is unconcerned. "Nor is it particularly troubling that media properties do not always, or even frequently, avail themselves to others who may hold contrary opinions. Nothing requires them to do so, nor is it necessarily healthy for public debate to pretend as though all ideas are of equal value entitled to equal airing. The media are not common carriers of speech."[27]

In this citation, the FCC notes that the electronic mass media have not been defined as common carriers of speech. As private carriers they assert editorial control over the content that flows through the powerful channels of communications to which they hold licenses, and obligations are place upon them to ensure they service the public interest.

Common carriers do not exercise control over content, but the commission narrowed the view of the public interest even further when it proposed to eliminate the principle of common carriage. In a feat of reasoning that the Wisconsin Public Service Commission called legal jujitsu,[28] the Commission concluded that owners of advanced telecommunications facilities would no longer be subject to the obligation to provide interconnection and carriage on nondiscriminatory rates, terms and conditions. The commission argued, "[I]t seems as if a provider offering service over their own facilities does not offer 'telecommunications' to anyone, it merely uses telecommunications to provide end-users with wireline broadband Internet access service."[29] FCC chairman Michael Powell made it clear he would not impose obligations on advanced telecommunications networks under any Title of the Act.[30]

Although the Supreme Court has not yet taken up this issue, the Ninth Circuit Court of Appeals twice rejected the claim that the underlying telecommunications service should not be treated as telecommunications. It articulated a clear vision of the need for open communications networks in the digital age.

> Among its broad reforms, the Telecommunications Act of 1996 enacted a competitive principle embodied by the dual duties of nondiscrimination and interconnection. See 47 U.S.C. s. 201 (a) . . . s. 251 (A) (1) . . . Together, these provisions mandate a network architecture that prioritizes consumer choice, demonstrated by vigorous competition among telecommunications carriers. As applied to the Internet, Portland calls it "open access," while AT&T dysphemizes it as "forced access." Under the Communications Act, this principle of telecommunications common carriage governs cable broadband as it does other means of Internet transmission such as telephone service and DSL, "regardless of the facilities used." The Internet's protocols themselves manifest a related principle called "end-to-end": control lies at the ends of the network where the users are, leaving a simple network that is neutral with respect to the data it transmits, like any common carrier. On this role of the Internet, the codes of the legislator and the programmer agree.[31]

The FCC's narrow view of the First Amendment was paralleled by a monopolistic view of the economy. As the commission wrote in its cable ownership limits proceedings, "Some economists, most notably Schumpeter, suggest that monopoly can be more conducive to innovation than competition, since monopolists can more readily capture the benefits of innovation."[32] The chairman adheres to this view,[33] which made its way into media ownership notice under the guise of promoting innovation where it was wedded to the old theory that media monopolies maximize consumer welfare because they have the incentive and ability to serve a broader market through niche programming.[34]

The twenty-first-century communications landscape the FCC had in mind is one in which access to communications and information would be determined by a handful of private corporations with no obligation to air ideas with which they disagree or to allow information to flow in a nondiscriminatory manner. Both the public interest obligations of the broadcasters and the nondiscrimination obligations of the telecommunications companies would disappear. The ideas of citizens who do not own advanced telecommunications networks or hold broadcast licenses can leak out, while those of the dominant owners can be broadcast loudly and distributed widely.

EMPIRICAL EVIDENCE ON THE RELATIONSHIP BETWEEN MEDIA AND DEMOCRATIC DISCOURSE

The narrow view of the First Amendment adopted by the FCC will not support the vibrant discourse that democracy needs to thrive. Diversity promotes democracy by exposing citizens to a broad range of views.[35] The mass media influence the agenda of public policy issues and the public's perception of those issues, especially during election campaigns.[36] The impact of television is pervasive throughout all elections.[37] The impact of television is not only in news coverage but also, and perhaps even more importantly, in advertising and in the interaction between advertising and news.[38]

It has long been recognized that print and broadcast media have unique economic characteristics.[39] To the extent that economics is a consideration, economic competition in commercial mass media markets cannot assure diversity and antagonism.[40] The dictates of mass audiences create a largest market share/lowest common denominator ethic that undercuts the ability to deliver culturally diverse programming,[41] locally oriented programming,[42] and public interest programming.[43] The tendency to avoid controversy and seek a lowest common denominator is augmented by the presence of advertisers, expressing their preferences in the market.[44] News and public affairs programming is particularly vulnerable to these economic pressures.[45] As market forces grow, this programming is reduced.[46] Concentration drains resources from journalistic endeavors and compromises the quality of the programming.[47]

Given the profit-maximizing incentive to recover high fixed costs from the largest audiences, media target the majority. Minorities are underserved and suffer from a form of tyranny of the majority in media markets.[48] The tyranny of the majority in media markets is linked to the tyranny of the majority in politics because the media are the primary means of political communications.[49]

Greater concentration results in less diversity of ownership,[50] and diversity of ownership across geographic, ethnic, and gender lines is correlated with diversity of programming. To put the matter simply, minority owners are more likely to present minority points of view[51] just as females are more likely to present female points of view[52] in the speakers, formats, and content they put forward.[53]

One of the central benefits of promoting deconcentrated and diverse media markets is to provide a self-checking function for the media. The media needs to be accountable to the public, but that function cannot, as a general matter, be provided by government action in our political system.[54] It can best be provided by the media itself, as long as there is vigorous antagonism between sources of news and information.[55] Concentration of ownership undermines the watchdog function because the market tends to produce too little, from the societal point of view.[56] Left unrestrained, the marketplace will produce fewer watchdog activities conducted by less rigorous institutions. Abuses are less likely to be uncovered and more likely to occur because the deterrent of the threat of exposure will be diminished.[57] Conglomeration reduces institutional diversity, undermining vigorous investigative journalism,[58] and raises a qualitatively new type of problem—the potential for institutional conflicts of interest arises.[59]

The central fact that all of these discussions share is that market forces provide neither adequate incentives to produce high-quality media products nor adequate incentives to distribute enough diverse content to meet citizen needs.[60] The weak competition that results from the economic structure of media markets allows owners to use excess profits to pursue their personal agendas. The claim that ownership of the media does not matter to the selection and presentation of content is not plausible.[61] The empirical evidence on news coverage of events[62] and the ongoing battle between the networks over bias in reporting and the use of political advertising[63] reinforces the long-standing opinion of the courts[64] that ownership matters a great deal[65] and is a good proxy for diversity.[66]

The specific concern with localism in mass media policy also finds support in the research literature. In order for the media to meet the needs of diverse groups, it must inform and mobilize them.[67] That these needs have traditionally been centered in localism is understandable, since the primary referent for identity and community has traditionally been and remains significantly local.[68] Concentration of national and local markets into national chains reinforces the tendencies of media owners to ignore local needs.[69]

There is a final, fundamental way in which the narrow view undervalues civic discourse. It fails to consider whether there is a need for a more effective means of public debate. Counting the number of outlets without reference to the population they serve or the issues they must deal with ignores the information needs of the citizenry. The US population has become increasingly diverse and deeply embedded in an increasingly complex global political economy. If citizen participation in civic discourse is to be effective, a substantial improvement in the means of communication at the disposal of the public—far beyond commercial mass media influences—must be promoted through public policy.

While the demand side of the media market has become much more complex, the supply side has become much more powerful. The new technologies of commercial mass media are extremely capital intensive and therefore restrict who has access to them. The size of media organizations presents a growing mismatch between those in control and average citizens. A small number of giant corporations interconnected by ownership, joint ventures, and preferential deals now straddles broadcast, cable, and the Internet. Access to the means of communication is controlled by a small number of entities in each community; these distribution proprietors determine what information the public receives.

The power of digital communications is being greatly enhanced by improved video images with impact heightened by real-time interactivity and ubiquitous personalization. Dramatic increases in the ability to control and target messages and track media use could result in a greater ability to manipulate and mislead, rather than a greater ability to educate and enlist citizens in a more intelligent debate. Individual members of society need new communication skills and access to technology to express themselves and evaluate the information presented by more powerful messengers; citizens need a new kind of "media literacy."

POLICIES TO PROMOTE PROGRESSIVE MEDIA AND OPEN COMMUNICATION NETWORKS

The agenda for media reform must be broad because the structural conditions of media production in advanced capitalist societies poses a grave threat to democratic discourse. Powerful forces of hypercommercialism—unfettered commercial media allowed to concentrate ownership of local markets, consolidate into national and international chains, and conglomerate across media types—overwhelm journalistic values and civic discourse.

All of the old tools that have fallen into disuse need to be revived—ownership limits, public interest obligations, public broadcasting, and obligations of nondiscrimination. Several new tools also must be unleashed—unlicensed spectrum, municipal ownership of networks, and the expansion of noncommercial media. Progressive policy must address three areas—access to the means of distribution, limitations on commercial media ownership, and promotion of noncommercial production. Policy should start by addressing spectrum because much of the history of broadcast media has been intertwined with the issue of spectrum, while the potential for "revolutionary" change is dependent on the populist use of spectrum.

Revolutionizing Distribution

Unlicensing Spectrum: The origin of license scarcity is in interference—the fear that, left unregulated, many citizens would all try to broadcast on the same frequency at the same time, creating noise that would turn broadcasts into gibberish. Though the likelihood of this occurring was debatable, public policy acted as if it was certain and created exclusive temporary rights to use slices of the spectrum for specific purposes. Since citizens cannot speak at will with electronic voices (they are called pirates if they do and driven off the air by the FCC police), the Supreme Court found it constitutional for Congress to demand that license holders serve the public interest.

Technology has created the possibility for the "unlicensing" of the spectrum and allowing unfettered use subject to a set of noninterference rules. Smart radio and other technologies could allow all citizens to become "broadcasters." The application of computer technology and Internet economics to unlicensed spectrum can create abundance and a much more equitable distribution of the resource, holding the promise for a transformation in the means of communications, an opportunity for consumers to become producers. Reapplying the Internet paradigm to spectrum, decentralized investment would result in a wider, more responsive base of affordable investment, experimentation, and innovation that empowers people.

Once unlicensed citizen use of the spectrum becomes a possibility, it should be the compelling goal of First Amendment communications technology policy. There is no justification to insert two interests (a governmental auctioneer and a private property holder) between me and my right to broadcast. The possibility that every American could have an increasingly powerful electronic voice should be the driving force of the bold aspiration for the First Amendment in the twenty-first century. The prospect of millions of electronic voices *compels* the FCC to maximize the unlicensed use of the spectrum under the public interest standard of the Communications Act as interpreted by the Supreme Court.

Community-Owned Media: A second approach to ending the tyranny of the broadcast license holders and communications facility owners is public ownership of distribution facilities. Municipal and cooperative ownership of infrastructure facilities has its origins in the Progressive and New Deal eras. The convergence of media and communications in broadband networks and the refusal of cable operators to open their networks have made this an increasingly attractive option, particularly when local institutional networks (schools, libraries, government services) are added in.

Limiting Ownership

Powerful broadcast voices will continue to exist. Given their entrenched nature, they are likely to continue to have preferential access to the use of the best spectrum. They also have been the beneficiaries of seventy-five years of exclusive licenses. For the foreseeable future this advantaged position continues to provide the basis for the obligation to serve the public interest.

Restricting the Number and Reach of Licenses: Ownership limits on commercial mass media are important constraints because people still turn to these outlets overwhelmingly as their primary source of news and information. Powerful owners in concentrated markets withdraw resources from the watchdog function. In such markets, the dissemination of news and information can be restricted and distorted by excessive owner influence. Ownership limits can place some constraints on the accumulation of media power by individual media owners. They can disperse viewpoints somewhat and preserve the institutional independence of print and TV media.

The effectiveness of ownership policies is limited because the commercial mass media are so powerful. Therefore, ownership limits are only part of a much broader media reform that is needed.

Institutional Independence: Keeping the various media separate provides another fundamental support to promoting the watchdog function. Institutional diversity reflects the special expertise and culture of certain media, such as the newspaper tradition of in-depth investigative journalism. Institutional diversity is grounded in the watchdog function. The quality of investigative reporting and the accessibility of different types of institutions to leaders and the public are promoted by institutional diversity. Institutional diversity involves different structures of media presentation (different business models, journalistic culture, and tradition), and these institutions often involve different independent owners and viewpoints across media, but must be independently owned to achieve the diversity goal. Institutional diversity is also extremely important for the broader public policy issue of noncommercial sources of news.

Nondiscriminatory Access: Limitations on communications' owners involve the obligation to make their networks available on just, reasonable, and nondiscriminatory terms. The owners' prerogative to discriminate unduly is taken away. The convergence of mass media and communications driven by the digital revolution should not confuse policymakers about the need to have nondiscriminatory access to general means of communications. The core functions of telecommunications service promote such a "society-wide discourse role."

Promoting Noncommercial Production

Public Interest Obligations of Commercial Media: Public interest obligations should also be imposed on the holders of broadcast licenses to ensure that some of the large profits created by these licenses are used for informative and high-quality content. This would ensure wider distribution of this content and capitalize on the powerful and expansive reach of the electronic media. For communications networks, universal service is crucial.

Set-asides, or limits on hours and types of programming, is one approach that has traditionally been taken, but others are possible. Providing incentives through tax breaks for the production and distribution of public interest programming is another approach. Set-asides for independent production within the public interest space helps to ensure an independent point of view and the availability of skills for noncommercial production.

Public Broadcasting: Public broadcasting needs greater resources and support. The role of an independent institution with national reach provides a vital watchdog function. The aspiration can be phrased as a question, "Can

PBS become more like the BBC?" The controversy and debate that frequently surrounds the BBC (the base example) is not an indicator of its failure but a measure of its success. It matters a great deal. At the national and global levels, a major institution that is independent of commercial interests, strives for professional excellence, and has resources to compete with commercial media in production values can play an important role in providing a powerful independent voice.

Community Media: Community media, which provides much greater access for, and is much more responsive to, average citizens, should be developed. At the same time, involvement in community media is participatory, promoting the skills necessary to advance the interests of the members of the community. Accessible community media also helps to develop media leaders.

Noncommercial community outlets need the resources and independence to provide an alternative channel of high-quality, objective content. As community and noncommercial media gain a stronger base, they can take on a key role as a forum for democratic discourse and as a watchdog, checking not only government and corporations but also the commercial mass media. They are more likely to preserve a focus on issues of direct interest to local communities. Past efforts have been inadequately funded or restricted. Low-power radio, public access channels, and publicly owned broadband systems require both the opportunity to broadcast and the commitment of resources necessary to achieve the production values to which the public has become accustomed.

CONCLUSION

The intense debate over ownership of the media and communications networks reflects a fundamental conflict between the narrow view of the First Amendment adopted by the FCC and the broad and bold view taken by the Supreme Court. It reflects a conflict between a view that the economic interests of the owners takes precedence over all other considerations and a view that sees the economic interests required to serve the goal of promoting democratic discourse.

This division is well recognized in political theory. On one side is the elitist view of democracy based on the premise "that meaningful understanding of social forces and structural problems is beyond the populace's capacity and, in any event, is marginal to its interest."[70] On the other side is the participatory view in which, "[p]opular political and electoral participation provides the currency that assures that a group's interest are taken into account" and "people expend considerable effort in formulating, evaluating, and choosing interests and values to which they give allegiance."[71]

While the elitist, economic view was dominant in the last two decades of the twentieth century, the recent strong reaction to the effort to eliminate the limits on media ownership and the obligations of network owners tapped into a strong underlying concern about narrow vision. It now portends a movement for genuinely progressive media reform and justice that recaptures the spirit of the bold aspiration for the First Amendment.

NOTES

1. Opening statement of Senator John McCain, *Media Ownership*, Committee on Commerce, Science, and Transportation, October 2, 2003.

2. For example, Ben Bagdikian, *The Media Monopoly* (Boston: Beacon Press, 2000), which described the concentration of media, was first published in 1983 and Martin Esslin, *The Age of Television* (New Brunswick, NJ: Transaction, 2002), which raised concerns about the impact of television on civic and political functions, was first published in 1982.

3. Chairman Michael Powell used the expression in describing the digital convergence (See "Law in the Internet Age," *D.C. Bar Association Computer and Telecommunications Law Section and the Federal Communications Bar Association*, September 29, 1999). The revolution and its implications for the media are woven through his "Broadband Migration" speeches (see "The Great Digital Broadband Migration," Progress and Freedom Foundation, December 8, 2000; "Digital Broadband Migration: Part II," Press Conference, October 31, 2001).

4. Lou Dobbs's *Moneyline* show on CNN ran an online poll asking whether "too few corporations own too many media outlets." Ninety-eight percent said yes. (See Commissioner Jonathan Adelstein, "Big Macs and Big Media: The Decision to Supersize," *Media Institute*, May 20, 2003.) Substantial majorities believe the media are already too concentrated. See *Seattle Post Intelligencer*, PI-Daily Poll, May 2003; Mark Cooper, *Media Ownership and Democracy in the Digital Information Age* (Stanford: Stanford University Center for Internet and Society, 2003), pp. 29–32.

5. Cooper, *Media Ownership*, pp. 33–63.

6. For brief discussion of normative and positive approaches in public policy analysis see John B. Taylor, *Economics*, 2nd ed. (Boston: Houghton Mifflin, 1998), p. 20, and Alfred Kahn, *The Economics of Regulation: Principles and Institutions* (Cambridge, MA: MIT Press, 1988), p. 14.

7. Cooper, *Media Ownership*.

8. Bagdikian, *The Media*, and Robert McChesney, *Rich Media, Poor Democracy: Communication Politics in Dubious Times* (New York: New Press, 2000), provide history and progressive critiques of the development of this policy.

9. *Associated Press v. United States*, 326 U.S. 1, 20 (1945).

10. *Whitney v. California*, 274 U.S. 357 (1927).

11. *Red Lion Broadcasting v. FCC*, 395 U.S. 367 (1969).

12. *Id.* at 390.

13. As Justice Black wrote in *Associated Press*, "[s]urely a command that the government itself shall not impede the free flow of ideas does not afford nongovernmental combinations a refuge if they impose restraints upon that constitutionally guaranteed freedom."

14. *Fox Television Stations, Inc., v. FCC*, 280 F.3d 1027 (D.C. Cir. 2002); *Sinclair Broadcasting, Inc. v. FCC*, 284 F.3d 148 (D.C. Cir. 2002).

15. *FCC v. National Citizens Committee for Broadcasting*, 436 U.S. (1978).

16. *Id.* at 775, 780–81.

17. *Sinclair Broadcasting, Inc. v. FCC*, 160 F.3d 148 (D.C. Cir. 2002).

18. *National Broadcasting Co. v. United States*, 319 U.S. 190 (1943).

19. *Red Lion*, 395 U.S. at 367.

20. *Communications Act of 1934*, Public Law 416, 73rd Congress (June 19, 1934).

21. Lawrence Lessig, *Code and Other Laws of Cyberspace* (New York: Basic Books, 1999), pp. 166–67.

22. "Narrowing the Lines of Communications?" *Washington Post,* February 4, 2002, p. C2.

23. Cited in C. Edwin Baker, *Media Markets and Democracy* (Cambridge: Cambridge University Press, 2002), p. 3.

24. Federal Communications Commission, "Report and Order," *Amendment of Multiple Ownership Rules*, 100 F.C.C. 2d 17 (1984).

25. Federal Communications Commission, "Report and Order," *In the Matter of 2002 Biennial Regulatory Review—Review of the Commission's Broadcast Ownership Rules and Other Rules Adopted Pursuant to Section 202 of the Telecommunications Act of 1996, Cross Ownership of Broadcast Stations and Newspapers, Rules and Policies Concerning Multiple Ownership of Radio Broadcast Stations in Local Markets, Definition of Radio Markets*, MB Docket No. 02-277, MM Dockets 02-235, 01-317, 00-244 July 2, 2003, para. 420.

26. Bruce N. Owen, "Statement on Media Ownership Rules," attachment to "Comments of Fox Entertainment Group and Fox Television Stations, Inc., National Broadcasting Company, Inc. and Telemundo Group, Inc., and Viacom," *In the Matter of 2002 Biennial Regulatory Review—Review of the Commission's Broadcast Ownership Rules and Other Rules Adopted Pursuant to Section 202 of the Telecommunications Act of 1996, Cross Ownership of Broadcast Stations and Newspapers, Rules and Policies Concerning Multiple Ownership of Radio Broadcast Stations in Local Markets, Definition of Radio Markets*, MB Docket No. 02-277, MM Dockets 02-235, 01-317, 00-244, January 2, 2003.

27. Federal Communications Commission, "Report and Order," 2002 Biennial Regulatory Review, para. 353.

28. "Comments of the Public Service Commission of Wisconsin," *In the Matter of Appropriate Framework for Broadband Access to the Internet over Wireline Facilities, Universal Service Obligations of Broadband Providers, Computer III Further Remand Proceedings: Bell Operating Company Provision of Enhanced Services; 1998 Biennial Regulatory Review of Computer III and ONA Safeguards and Requirements, Federal Communications Commission,* CC Dockets Nos. 02-33, CC Dockets Nos. 95-20, 98-10; "Comments of the Texas Office of Peoples Counsel, Consumer Federation of America, Consumers Union, Media Access Project, and the Center for Digital Democracy, *In the Matter of Appropriate Framework for Broadband Access to the Internet over Wireline Facilities, Universal Service Obligations of Broadband Providers, Computer III Further Remand Proceedings: Bell Operating Company Provision of Enhanced Services; 1998 Biennial Regulatory Review of Computer III and ONA Safeguards and Requirements,* Federal Communications Commission, CC Dockets Nos. 02-33, CC Dockets Nos. 95-20, 98-10, called it legal gymnastics.

29. Federal Communications Commission, "Notice of Proposed Rulemaking," *In the Matter of Appropriate Framework for Broadband Access to the Internet over Wireline Facilities, Universal Service Obligations of Broadband Providers, Computer III Further Remand Proceeding: Bell Operating Company Provision of Enhanced Services; 1998 Biennial Regulatory Review – Review of Computer III and ONA Safeguards and Requirements,* CC Docket No. 02-33; CC Docket Nos. 95-20, 98-10, para. 25. Identical language is used to describe advanced telecommunications services over cable networks. See Federal Communications Commission, "Declaratory Ruling and Notice of Proposed Rulemaking," *In the Matter of Inquiry Concerning High-Speed Access to the Internet over Cable and Other Facilities, Internet over Cable Declaratory Ruling, Appropriate Regulatory Treatment for Broadband Access to the Internet over Cable Facilities,* GN Docket No. 00-185, CS Docket No. 02-52, March 15, 2002, para. 41. The cable operators were officially excused from the obligation for nondiscrimination by the declaratory ruling. The FCC excused telephone companies from many of their obligations in a third order (see "Report and Order on Remand and Further Notice of Proposed Rulemaking," *In the Matter of Review of Section 251 Unbundling Obligations of Incumbent Local Exchange Carriers, Implementation of the Local Competition Provisions of the Telecommunications Act of 1996, Deployment of Wireline Service Offering Advanced Telecommunications Capability,* CC Docket Nos. 01-338, 96-98, 98-147.

30. Michael Powell, "Preserving Internet Freedom: Guiding Principles for the Industry," speech at the Digital Broadband Migration: Toward a Regulatory Regime for the Internet Age conference, University of Colorado Law School, Boulder, CO, February 8, 2004, issued a challenge to the industry to voluntarily adhere to some of the nondiscrimination requirements of the Communications Act, but made it clear there would be no enforcement of obligations of nondiscrimination.

31. *AT&T v. City of Portland,* 2000. No. 99-35609, 2000 U.S. App. Lexis 14383 [9th Cir.] June 22.

32. Federal Communications Commission, "Notice of Proposed Rulemaking,"

Implementation of Section 11 of the Cable Television Consumer Protection and Competition Act of 1992 Implementation of Cable Act Reform Provision of the Telecommunications Act of 1996, The Commission's Cable Horizontal and Vertical Ownership Limits and Attribution Rules, Review of the Commission's Regulations Governing Attribution of Broadcast and Cable/MDS Interests, Review of the Commission's Regulations and Policies Affecting Investment in the Broadcast Industry, Reexamination of the Commission's Cross Interest Policy, CS, Docket Nos. 98-82, 96-85, MM Docket Nos. 92-264, 94-150, 92-51, 87-154, September 13, 2001, para. 36.

33. Powell, "The Great Digital Broadband Migration," made its way into the FCC's draft strategic plan.

34. "Comments of the Information Policy Institute," *In the Matter of 2002 Biennial Regulatory Review—Review of the Commission's Broadcast Ownership Rules and Other Rules Adopted Pursuant to Section 202 of the Telecommunications Act of 1996, Cross Ownership of Broadcast Stations and Newspapers, Rules and Policies Concerning Multiple Ownership of Radio Broadcast Stations in Local Markets, Definition of Radio Markets*, Federal Communications Commission, MB Docket No. 02-277, MM Dockets 02-235, 01-317, 00-244, January 2, 2003, 46-59.

35. Diana C. Mutz, "Cross-Cutting Social Networks: Testing Democratic Theory in Practice," *American Political Science Review* 96 (2002): 111; Cass Sunstein, *Republic.com* (Princeton: Princeton University Press, 2001); Sei-Hill Kim, Dietram A. Scheufele, and James Shanahan, "Think about It This Way: Attribute Agenda Setting Function of the Press and the Public's Evaluation of a Local Issue," *Journalism and Mass Communications Quarterly* 79 (2002): 7; Steven Chaffee and Stacy Frank, "How Americans Get Their Political Information: Print versus Broadcast News," *Annals of the American Academy of Political and Social Science* 546 (1996); Jack M. McLeod, Dietram A. Scheufele, and Patricia Moy, "Community, Communications, and Participation: The Role of Mass Media and Interpersonal Discussion in Local Political Participation," *Political Communication* 16 (1999).

36. Nicholas A. Valentino, Vincent L. Hutchings, and Ismail K. White, "Cues That Matter: How Political Ads Prime Racial Issues During Campaigns," *American Political Science Review* 96 (2002): 75; Thomas B. Edsall and Mary D. Edsall, *Chain Reaction: The Impact of Race, Rights, and Taxes on American Politics* (New York: Norton, 1991); Kathleen Hall Jamieson, *Dirty Politics: Deception, Distraction, and Democracy* (New York: Oxford University Press, 1992); Martin Gillens, "Race Coding and White Opposition to Welfare," *American Political Science Review* 90 (1996); Tali Mendelberg, "Executing Hortons: Racial Crime in the 1988 Presidential Campaign," *Public Opinion Quarterly* 61 (1997); Tali Mendelberg, *The Race Card: Campaign Strategy, Implicit Messages, and the Norms of Equality* (Princeton, NJ: Princeton University Press, 2001); Nicholas A. Valentino, "Crime News and the Priming of Racial Attitudes during the Evaluation of the President," *Public Opinion Quarterly* 63 (1999); Scott Coltrane and Melinda Messineo, "The Perpetuation of Subtle Prejudice: Race and Gender Imagery in the 1990's Television Advertising," *Sex Roles* 42 (1990); Robert M. Entman and Andrew Rojecki, *The Black Image in the White Mind: Media*

and *Race in America* (Chicago: University of Chicago Press, 2000); Herman Gray, *Watching Race Television and the Struggle for Blackness* (Chicago: University of Chicago Press, 1995); Travis L. Dixon and Daniel Linz, "Overrepresentation and Underrepresentation of African Americans and Latinos as Lawbreakers on Television News," *Communications Research* 50, no. 9 (2000); Franklin D. Gilliam Jr. and Shanto Iyengar, "Prime Suspects: The Influence of Local Television News on the Viewing Public," *American Journal of Political Science* 44 (2000); Mark Peffley, Todd Shields, and Bruce Williams, "The Intersection of Race and Television," *Political Communications* 13 (1996); Kim, Sheufele, and Shanahan, "Attribute Agenda," p. 381; Doris Graber, *Mass Media and American Politics* (Washington: Congressional Quarterly, 1997); David L. Paletz, *The Media in American Politics: Contents and Consequences* (New York: Longman, 1999); Marion R. Just et al., *Crosstalk: Citizens, Candidates, and the Media in a Presidential Campaign* (Chicago: University of Chicago Press, 1996); Kim F. Kahn and Patrick J. Kenney, *The Spectacle of U.S. Senate Campaign* (Chicago: University of Chicago Press, 1999); Shanto Iyengar and Donald R. Kinder, *News That Matters* (Chicago: University of Illinois Press, 1987); Maxwell E. McCombs and Donald Shaw, "The Agenda-Setting Function of the Mass Media," *Public Opinion Quarterly* 36 (1972); David Domke, David Perlmutter, and Meg Spratt, "The Primes of Our Times? An Examination of the 'Power' of Visual Images," *Journalism* 3 (2002): 131; Jon A. Krosnick and Donald R. Kinder, "Altering the Foundation of Support for the President through Priming," *American Political Science Review* 84 (1990); Zhongdang Pan and Gerald M. Kosicki, "Priming and Media Impact on the Evaluation the President's Performance," *Communications Research* 24 (1997); Marion R. Just, Ann N. Crigler, and W. Russell Neuman, "Cognitive and Affective Dimensions of Political Conceptualization," in *The Psychology of Political Communications*, ed. Ann N. Crigler (Ann Arbor: University of Michigan Press, 1996).

37. LeAnn M. Brazeal and William L. Benoit, "A Functional Analysis of Congressional Television Spots," *Communications Quarterly* 49 (2001): 346–437; Glenn J. Hansen and William Benoit, "Presidential Television Advertising and Public Policy Priorities, 1952–2002," *Communications Studies* 53 (2002): 285; Craig L. Brians and Martin P. Wattenberg, "Campaign Issue Knowledge and Salience: Comparing Reception for TV Commercials, TV News, and Newspapers," *American Journal of Political Science* 40 (1996); Xinshu Zhao and Glen L. Bleske, "Measurement Effects in Comparing Voter Learning from Television News and Campaign Advertisements," *Journalism and Mass Communications Quarterly* 72 (1995); Xinshu Zhao and Steven H. Chaffee, "Campaign Advertisements versus Television News as Sources of Political Issue Information," *Public Opinion Quarterly* 59 (1995); Jon R. Sinclair, "Reforming Television's Role in American Political Campaigns: Rationale for the Elimination of Paid Political Advertisements," *Communications and the Law* 17 (March 1995); Richard Joslyn, "The Impact of Campaign Spot Advertising Ads, *Journalism Quarterly* 7 (1981); Ronald Mulder, "The Effects of Televised Political Ads in the 1995 Chicago Mayoral Election," *Journalism Quarterly* 56 (1997); Michael W. Pfau and Henry C. Kenski, *Attack Politics* (New York: Praeger, 1990).

38. Gregory W. Gwiasda, "Network News Coverage of Campaign Advertisements: Media's Ability to Reinforce Campaign Messages," *American Politics Research* 29 (2001): 461; Lynda Lee Kaid et al., "Television News and Presidential Campaigns: The Legitimation of Televised Political Advertising," *Social Science Quarterly* 74 (1993); Stephen Ansolabehere and Shanto Iyengar, "Riding the Wave and Claiming Ownership over Issues: The Joint Effect of Advertising and News Coverage in Campaigns," *Public Opinion Quarterly* 58 (1995); William L. Benoit and Glenn Hansen, "Issue Adaptation of Presidential Television Spots and Debates to Primary and General Audiences," *Communications Research Reports* 19 (2002).

39. Yochai Benkler, "Intellectual Property and the Organization of Information Production," *International Review of Law and Economics* 22, no. 1 (2002); Carl Shapiro and Hal R. Varian, *Information Rules: A Strategic Guide to the Network Economy* (Boston: Harvard Business School Press, 1999).

40. Steven T. Berry and Joel Waldfogel, "Public Radio in the United States: Does It Correct Market Failure or Cannibalize Commercial Stations?" *Journal of Public Economics* 71 (1999); Michael O. Wirth and James Wollert, "The Effects of Market Structure on Television News Pricing," *Journal of Broadcasting* (1984); Julian L. Simon, Walter J. Primeaux, and Edward M. Rice, "The Price Effects of Monopoly Ownership in Newspapers," *Antitrust Bulletin* (1986); Robert N. Rubinovitz, *Market Power and Price Increases for Basic Cable Service Since Deregulation* (Washington, DC: Department of Justice, Economic Analysis Regulatory Group, August 6, 1991); Benjamin J. Bates, "Station Trafficking in Radio: The Impact of Deregulation," *Journal of Broadcasting and Electronic Media* 37, no. 1 (1993).

41. Joel Waldfogel, *Who Benefits Whom in Local Television Markets?* (Philadelphia: Wharton School, November 2001). Other papers in the series of studies of "preference externalities" were made a part of the record in conjunction with Joel Waldfogel's appearance at the FCC Roundtable, including *Preference Externalities: An Empirical Study of Who Benefits Whom in Differentiated Product Markets*, NBER Working Paper 7391 (Cambridge: National Bureau of Economic Research, 1999); Peter Siegelman and Joel Waldfogel, "Race and Radio: Preference Externalities, Minority Ownership, and the Provision of Programming to Minorities," *Advances in Applied Microeconomics* 10 (2001); Felix Oberholzer-Gee and Joel Waldfogel, *Electoral Acceleration: The Effect of Minority Population on Minority Voter Turnout*, NBER Working Paper 8252 (Cambridge: National Bureau of Economic Research, 2001); Joel Waldfogel and Lisa George, *Who Benefits Whom in Daily Newspaper Markets?* NBER Working Paper 7944 (Cambridge: National Bureau of Economic Research, 2000); Joel Waldfogel, *Comments on Consolidation and Localism*, Federal Communications Commission, Roundtable on Media Ownership (October 29, 2001); Felix Oberholzer-Gee and Joel Waldfogel, *Electoral Acceleration: The Effect of Minority Population on Minority Voter Turnout* (Cambridge, MA: National Bureau of Economic Research, 2001), working paper no. 8252; C. Edwin Baker, "Giving Up on Democracy: The Legal Regulation of Media Ownership," Attachment C, *Comments of Consumers Union, Consumer Federation of America, Civil Rights Forum,*

Center for Digital Democracy, Leadership Conference on Civil Rights, and Media Access Project (before the Federal Communications Commission, In the Matter of Cross-Ownership of Broadcast Station and Newspaper/Radio Cross-Ownership Waiver Policy, MM Docket No. 01-235, 96-197, 3 December 2001), 43; Vernon A. Stone, "Deregulation Felt Mainly in Large-Market Radio and Independent TV," *Communicator* (April 1987): 12; Patricia Aufderheide, "After the Fairness Doctrine: Controversial Broadcast Programming and the Public Interest," *Journal of Communication* (1990): 50–51; Michael L. McKean and Vernon A. Stone, "Why Stations Don't Do News," *Communicator* (1991): 23–24; Vernon A. Stone, "New Staffs Change Little in Radio, Take Cuts in Major Markets TV," Radio-Television News Directors Association *Communicator* (1988); Karen L. Slattery and Ernest A. Hakanen, "Sensationalism versus Public Affairs Content of Local TV News: Pennsylvania Revisited," *Journal of Broadcasting and Electronic Media* (1994); James M. Bernstein and Stephen Lacy, "Contextual Coverage of Government by Local Television News," *Journalism Quarterly* 67 (1992); Raymond L. Carroll, "Market Size and TV News Values," *Journalism Quarterly* (1989); David K. Scott and Robert H. Gobetz, "Hard News/Soft News Content of the National Broadcast Networks: 1972–1987," *Journalism Quarterly* (1992); V. E. Ferrall, "The Impact of Television Deregulation," *Journal of Communication* (1992).

42. Karen L. Slattery, Ernest A. Hakanen, and Mark Doremus, "The Expression of Localism: Local TV News Coverage in the New Video Marketplace," *Journal of Broadcasting and Electronic Media* 40 (1996); Raymond L. Carroll and C. A. Tuggle, "The World Outside: Local TV News Treatment of Imported News," *Journalism and Mass Communications Quarterly* 74, no. 1 (Spring 1997); Charles Fairchild, "Deterritorializing Radio: Deregulation and the Continuing Triumph of the Corporatist Perspective in the USA," *Media, Culture & Society* 21, no. 4 (1999); Charles Layton and Jennifer Dorroh, "Sad State," *American Journalism Review* (June 2002); Kathryn Olson, "Exploiting the Tension between the New Media's 'Objective' and Adversarial Roles: The Role Imbalance Attach and Its Use of the Implied Audience," *Communications Quarterly* 42, no. 1 (1994): 40–41; Alan G. Stavitsky, "The Changing Conception of Localism in U.S. Public Radio," *Journal of Broadcasting and Electronic Media* (1994).

43. Bagdikian, *The Media*, pp. 182–88; Peter Clarke and Eric Fredin, "Newspapers, Television, and Political Reasoning," *Public Opinion Quarterly* 42, no. 2 (1978); Michael Pfau, "A Channel Approach to Television Influence," *Journal of Broadcasting and Electronic Media* 34, no. 2 (1990); Donald T. Cundy, "Political Commercials and Candidate Image," in *New Perspectives on Political Advertising*, ed. Lynda Lee Kaid, Dan D. Nimmo, and Keith R. Sanders (Carbondale: Southern Illinois University Press, 1986); Garrett J. O'Keefe, "Political Malaise and Reliance on the Media," *Journalism Quarterly* (1980); S. Becker and H. C. Choi, "Media Use, Issue/Image Discrimination," *Communications Research* (1987); J. P. Robinson and D. K. Davis, "Television News and the Informed Public: An Information Process Approach," *Journal of Communication* 40, no. 3 (1990); Paul S. Voakes et al.,

"Diversity in the News: A Conceptual and Methodological Framework," *Journalism and Mass Communications Quarterly* (Autumn 1996); Ronald Bishop and Ernest A. Hakanen, "In the Public Interest? The State of Local Television Programming Fifteen Years after Deregulation," *Journal of Communications Inquiry* 26 (2002).

44. C. Edwin Baker, *Advertising and a Democratic Press* (Princeton, NJ: Princeton University Press, 1994); Ronald J. Krotoszynski Jr. and A. Richard M. Blaiklock, "Enhancing the Spectrum: Media Power, Democracy, and the Marketplace of Ideas," *University of Illinois Law Review* (2000): 831.

45. John H. McManus, "What Kind of a Commodity Is News?" *Communications Research* (1992); Olson, "Exploiting the Tension."

46. Bagdikian, *The Media*, pp. 220–21; David L. Paletz and Robert M. Entmen, *Media, Power, Politics* (New York: Free Press, 1981); Neil Postman, *Amusing Ourselves to Death: Public Discourse in the Age of Show Business* (New York: Penguin, 1985); Stephen Lacy, "The Financial Commitment Approach to News Media Competition," *Journal of Media Economics* 5, no. 2 (1992); Jack Bass, "Newspaper Monopoly," in *Leaving Readers Behind*, ed. Gene Roberts, Thomas Kunkel, and Charles Clayton (Fayetteville: University of Arkansas Press, 2001); Pat Gish and Tom Gish, "We Still Scream: The Perils and Pleasures of Running a Small-Town Newspaper," and E. R. Shipp, "Excuses, Excuses: How Editors and Reporters Justify Ignoring Stories," in *The Business of Journalism*, ed. William Serrin (New York: New Press, 2000). Complaints about the failure to cover larger national and international stories also abound (see Peter Phillips and Project Censored, *Censored 2003* [New York: Seven Stories, 2002]; Kristina Borjesson, *Into the Buzzsaw: Leading Journalists Expose the Myth of a Free Press* [Amherst, NY: Prometheus Books, 2002]).

47. Charles Layton, "What Do Readers Really Want?" *American Journalism Review* (March 1999), reprinted in *Breach of Faith*, ed. Gene Roberts and Thomas Kunkel (Fayetteville: University of Arkansas Press, 2001); Bill McConnell and Susanne Ault, "Fox TV's Strategy: Two by Two, Duopolies Are Key to the Company's Goal of Becoming a Major Local Presence," *Broadcasting and Cable*, July 30, 2001; Dan Trigoboff, "Chri-Craft, Fox Moves In: The Duopoly Marriage in Three Markets Comes with Some Consolidation," *Broadcasting and Cable,* August 6, 2001; Dan Trigoboff, "Rios Heads KCOP News," *Broadcasting and Cable,* October 14, 2002; Randal A. Beam, "What It Means to Be a Market-Oriented Newspaper," *Newspaper Research Journal* 16 (1995); Randal A. Beam, "Size of Corporate Parent Drives Market Orientation," *Newspaper Research Journal* 23 (2002); Sharyn Vane, "Taking Care of Business," *American Journalism Review* (March 2002); Sharyn Vane, *The Business of News, the News about Business,* Neiman Reports (Summer 1999).

48. These finding have been reinforced by recent findings of other scholars. See, for example, Philip Napoli, "Audience Valuation and Minority Media: An Analysis of the Determinants of the Value of Radio Audiences," *Journal of Broadcasting and Electronic Media* 46 (2002): 180–81. The author notes agreement with Kofi A. Ofori, *When Being No. 1 Is Not Enough: The Impact of Advertising Practices on Minority-Owned and Minority-Targeted Broadcast Stations* (Washington, DC:

Civil Rights Forum on Communications Policy, 1999); James G. Webster and Patricia F. Phalen, *The Mass Audience: Rediscovering the Dominant Model* (Mahwah, NJ: Erlbaum, 1997); Bruce Owen and Steven Wildman, *Video Economics* (Cambridge, MA: Harvard University Press, 1992); Baker, *Advertising*; James T. Hamilton, *Channeling Violence: the Economic Market for Violent Television Programming* (Princeton, NJ: Princeton University Press, 1998); Steven Wildman, "One-Way Flows and the Economics of Audience Making," in *Audiencemaking: How the Media Create the Audience,* ed. James S. Ettema and Whitney D. Charles (Thousand Oaks, CA: Sage Publications, 1994); Steven S. Wildman and Theomary Karamanis, "The Economics of Minority Programming," in *Investing in Diversity: Advancing Opportunities for Minorities in Media,* ed. A. Garner (Washington, DC: Aspen Institute, 1998).

49. Oberholzer-Gee and Waldfogel, *Participation,* pp. 36–37; Sunstein, *Republic,* discusses the implications for democracy, pp. 108–109.

50. William D. Bradford, "Discrimination in Capital Markets, Broadcast/Wireless Spectrum Service Providers and Auction Outcomes," paper delivered at the University of Washington, School of Business Administration, December 5, 2000.

51. Empirical studies demonstrating the link between minority presence in the media and minority-oriented programming include Marilyn D. Fife, *The Impact of Minority Ownership on Broadcast Program Content: A Case Study of WGPR-TV's Local News Content* (Washington, DC: National Association of Broadcasters, 1979); Marilyn D. Fife, *The Impact of Minority Ownership on Broadcast Program Content: A Multi-Market Study* (Washington, DC: National Association of Broadcasters, 1986); Congressional Research Service, *Minority Broadcast Station Ownership and Broadcast Programming: Is There a Nexus?* (Washington, DC: Library of Congress, 1988); T. A. Hart Jr., "The Case for Minority Broadcast Ownership," *Gannet Center Journal* (1988); Kurt A. Wimmer, "Deregulation and the Future of Pluralism in the Mass Media: The Prospects for Positive Policy Reform," *Mass Communications Review* (1988); Akousa Barthewell Evans, "Are Minority Preferences Necessary? Another Look at the Radio Broadcasting Industry," *Yale Law and Policy Review* 8 (1990); Jeff Dubin and Matthew L. Spitzer, "Testing Minority Preferences in Broadcasting," *Southern California Law Review* 68 (1995); Christine Bachen et al., "Diversity of Programming in the Broadcast Spectrum: Is There a Link between Owner Race or Ethnicity and News and Public Affairs Programming?" paper delivered at Santa Clara University, December 1999; Laurie Mason, Christine M. Bachen, and Stephanie L. Craft, "Support for FCC Minority Ownership Policy: How Broadcast Station Owner Race or Ethnicity Affects News and Public Affairs Programming Diversity," *Communication Law and Policy* 6 (2001).

52. See Stephen Lacy, Mary Alice Shaver, and Charles St. Cyr, "The Effects of Public Ownership and Newspaper Competition on the Financial Performance of Newspaper Corporation: A Replication and Extension," *Journalism and Mass Communications Quarterly* (Summer 1996); T. G. Gauger, "The Constitutionality of the FCC's Use of Race and Sex in Granting Broadcast Licenses," *Northwestern Law*

Review 83 (1989); Howard Klieman, "Content Diversity and the FCC's Minority and Gender Licensing Policies," *Journal of Broadcasting and Electronic Media* (Fall 1991); Lori A. Collins-Jarvis, "Gender Representation in an Electronic City Hall: Female Adoption of Santa Monica's PEN System," *Journal of Broadcasting and Electronic Media* 37, no. 1 (1993); Martha M. Lauzen and David Dozier, "Making a Difference in Prime Time: Women on Screen and behind the Scenes in 1995–1996 Television Season," *Journal of Broadcasting and Electronic Media* (Winter 1999); Patrick B. O'Sullivan, "The Nexus between Broadcast Licensing Gender Preferences and Programming Diversity: What Does the Social Scientific Evidence Say?" paper delivered at the University of California at Santa Barbara, Department of Communication, 2000.

53. Harvey J. Levin, "Program Duplication, Diversity, and Effective Viewer Choices: Some Empirical Findings," *American Economic Review* 61, no. 2 (1971); Stephen Lacy, "A Model of Demand for News: Impact of Competition on Newspaper Content," *Journalism Quarterly* 66 (1989); Thomas J. Johnson and Wayne Wanta, "Newspaper Circulation and Message Diversity in an Urban Market," *Mass Communications Review* (1993); William R. Davie and Jung-Sook Lee, "Television News Technology: Do More Sources Mean Less Diversity," *Journal of Broadcasting and Electronic Media* 37, no. 4 (1993): 455; Wayne Wanta and Thomas J. Johnson, "Content Changes in the St. Louis Post-Dispatch during Different Market Situations," *Journal of Media Economics* (1994); David C. Coulson, "Impact of Ownership on Newspaper Quality," *Journalism Quarterly* (Summer 1994); David C. Coulson and Anne Hansen, "The *Louisville Courier-Journal's* News Content after Purchase by Gannet," *Journalism and Mass Communications Quarterly* (Spring 1995); Petros Iosifides, "Diversity versus Concentration in the Deregulated Mass Media," *Journalism and Mass Communications Quarterly* (Spring 1999); Stephen Lacy and Todd F. Simon, "Competition in the Newspaper Industry," in *The Economics and Regulation of United States Newspapers* (Norwood, NJ: Ablex, 1999).

54. Baker, *Media Markets*, pp. 297–307; Krotozynski and Blailock, "Enhancing the Spectrum," p. 867.

55. Krotoszynski and Blaiklock, "Enhancing the Spectrum," pp. 867–68, Baker, *Media Markets*, p. 64.

56. Baker, "Democracy," p. 64.

57. Ibid.; Cass Sunstein, "Television and the Public Interest," *California Law Review* 8 (2002): 517; Neil Netanal, "Is the Commercial Mass Media Necessary, or Even Desirable, for Liberal Democracy?" paper presented at Telecommunications Policy Research Conference on Information, Communications, and Internet Policy, October 2001, pp. 20–24.

58. Rajiv Shah and Jay Kesan, "The Role of Institutions in the Design of Communications Technologies," paper presented at Telecommunications Policy Research Conference on Information, Communications, and Internet Policy, October 2001; Baker, *Media Markets*, p. 120.

59. Charles Davis and Stephanie Craft, "New Media Synergy: Emergence of Institutional Conflict of Interest," *Journal of Mass Media Ethics* 15 (2000): 222–23.

60. Sunstein, "Television," p. 517, citing Robert H. Frank and Phillip J. Cook, *The Winner-Take-All Society* (New York: Penguin, 1996), p. 191, as well as Pierre Bourdieu, *On Television* (New York: New Press, 1998), and C. Edwin Baker, "Giving the Audience What It Wants," *Ohio State Law Journal* 58 (1997).

61. Krotozynksi and Blaiklock, "Enhancing the Spectrum," pp. 832–33.

62. Sue Carter, Frederick Fico, and Joycelyn A. McCabe, "Partisan and Structural Balance in Local Television Election Coverage," *Journalism and Mass Communications Quarterly* 79 (2002): 50; Kim Fridkin Kahn and Patrick J. Kenny, "The Slant of News: How Editorial Endorsements Influence Campaign Coverage and Citizens' Views of Candidates," *American Political Science Review* 96 (2002): 381; James H. Snider and Benjamin I. Page, "Does Media Ownership Affect Media Stands? The Case of the Telecommunications Act of 1996," paper delivered at the Annual Meeting of the Midwest Political Science Association, April 1997; Benjamin I. Page, *Who Deliberates* (Chicago: University of Chicago Press, 1996); John H. McManus, "How Objective Is Local Television News?" *Mass Communications Review* 18, no. 3 (1991); Edward Rowse, *Slanted News: A Case Study of the Nixon and Stevenson Fund Stories* (Boston: Beacon, 1957).

63. Eric Alterman, *What Liberal Media: The Truth about Bias and the News* (New York: Basic Books, 2002); Borjesson, *Into the Buzzsaw*; Bernard Goldberg, *Bias* (Washington: Regnery, 2002), p. 190; Bob Woodward, *Bush at War* (New York: Simon & Schuster, 2002), p. 207, Michael Kelly, "Left Everlasting," *Washington Post*, December 11, 2002, p. A33; Paul Klugman, "In Media Res," *New York Times*, November 29, 2002, p. A39, which Ailes disputed (see Lloyd Grove, "The Reliable Source," *Washington Post*, November 19, 2002); Seth Ackerman, *The Most Biased Name in News* (New York: Fairness & Accuracy in Reporting, August 2002); *Cable News Wars: Interviews*, PBS, Online *Newshour*, March 2002, p. 2; S. Robert Lichter, "Depends on How You Define 'Bias,'" *Washington Post*, December 18, 2002, p. A19.

64. Hansen and Benoit, "Presidential Television Advertising," p. 285; Gwiasda, "Network News Coverage," p. 461; Brazeal and Benoit, "A Functional Analysis"; Mulder, "Televised Political Ads"; Baker, "Giving the Audience"; Kent Jenkins Jr., "Learning to Love Those Expensive Campaigns," *U.S. News & World Report* 122, no. 10 (1997); Brians and Wattenberg, "Campaign Issue Knowledge"; Sinclair, "Reforming Television's Role"; Zhao and Bleske, "Measurement Effects"; Baker, "Advertising"; Kaid et al., "Television News"; Ansolabehere and Iyengar, "Riding the Wave."

65. John Soloski, "Economics and Management: The Real Influence of Newspaper Groups," *Newspaper Research Journal* 1 (1979); W. Lance Bennett, *News, The Politics of Illusion* (New York: Longmans, 1988); John C. Busterna, "Television Ownership Effects on Programming and Idea Diversity: Baseline Data," *Journal of Media Economics* 1, no. 2 (1988); Edward S. Edwards and Noam Chomsky, *Manufacturing Consent* (New York: Pantheon, 1988); Theodore L. Glasser, David S. Allen, and S. Elizabeth Banks, "The Influence of Chain Ownership on News Play: A Case Study," *Journalism Quarterly* 66 (1989); Jon Katz, "Memo to Local News Directors," *Columbia Journalism Review* (1990); John H. McManus, "Local News: Not a

Pretty Picture," *Columbia Journalism Review* (1990); Monroe E. Price, "Public Broadcasting and the Crisis of Corporate Governance," *Cardozo Arts & Entertainment* 17 (1999).

66. *Fox Television Stations*, 280 F.3d 1027, at 12–13.

67. Baker, *Media Markets*; Baker, "Democracy," p. 16; Sunstein, *Republic*, pp. 46–47.

68. The connection to grounded in self-definition (see Jeremy Rifkin, *The Age of Access* [New York: J. P. Tarcher, 2001], pp. 7–9; Robert D. Putnam, *Bowling Alone the Collapse and Revival of American Community* [New York: Simon & Schuster, 2000]) and links to political involvement (James G. Gimpel, *Separate Destinations: Migration, Immigration, and the Politics of Places* [Ann Arbor: University of Michigan Press, 1999], Robert Huckfeldt and John Sprague, "Political Parties and Electoral Mobilization: Political Structure, Social Structure, and the Party Canvas," *American Political Science Review* 86 [1992]), which is reinforced by the fact that political units are local for purposes of representation (e.g., single-member districts, see John Mark Hanson, "The Majoritarian Impulse and the Declining Significance of Place, in *The Future of American Democratic Politics*, ed. Gerald M Pomper and Marc D. Weiner [New Brunswick, NJ: Rutgers University Press, 2003]) as well as services (e.g., school districts, fire, police, and so on).

69. Krotoszynski and Blaiklock, "Enhancing the Spectrum," pp. 871, 875–76; Waldfogel, "Local Television Markets"; Waldfogel and George, "Daily Newspaper Markets"; as well as Waldfogel, *Consolidation and Localism*.

70. Baker, *Media Markets*, p. 133.

9

HOW CAN GOVERNMENT CONSTITUTIONALLY COMPEL MASS MEDIA TO PROVIDE NEWS, AND HOW CAN CITIZENS MAKE IT HAPPEN?

CHERYL LEANZA AND HAROLD FELD

MEDIA ACCESS PROJECT

CHERYL A. LEANZA *became the principal legislative counsel to the National League of Cities in December 2004 after six and a half years as deputy director of Media Access Project (MAP), which she joined in 1998 after more than two years at the Federal Communication Commission (FCC). Ms. Leanza is a leader in public interest advocacy, fighting for diversity in ownership and other policies furthering First Amendment principles. She has taken leadership roles in the areas of media ownership, low-power radio, and cable Internet open access; acts as lead counsel before the FCC and in the US appellate courts; and has been widely quoted in the trade and mainstream press on these issues. She graduated cum laude from the University of Michigan Law School and simultaneously earned a masters in Public Policy from Michigan's Institute of Public Policy Studies. Ms. Leanza serves as a trustee of the Federal Communications Bar Association Foundation and is admitted in the District of Columbia and New York, the United States Supreme Court, and the US Court of Appeals for the District of Columbia, Third, Fourth, and Ninth Circuits.*

HAROLD FELD *is associate director of MAP, which he joined in August 1999 after practicing communications, Internet, and energy law at Covington & Burling. Mr. Feld served as cochair of the Federal Communica-*

tions Bar Association's Online Committee and has written numerous articles on Internet law and communications policy for trade publications and legal journals. Mr. Feld won the 2000 Burton Award for excellence in writing by a nonacademic. He graduated magna cum laude from Princeton University in 1989, and magna cum laude from Boston University Law School in 1993. He clerked for the Hon. John M. Ferren of the District of Columbia Court of Appeals.

INTRODUCTION

If democracy depends on an informed electorate and vigorous public debate, can the government constitutionally guarantee a robust marketplace of ideas in the mass media without transgressing the First Amendment command to make no law abridging the freedom of the press? Does the First Amendment act merely as a shield to protect individuals from government censorship, or does it also impose obligations on the government to ensure that a proper level of civic discourse takes place?

The history of communications policy and Supreme Court jurisprudence since the mid-twentieth century has rejected the "strict constructionist" interpretation and found a duty on the government to create opportunities for civic discourse and to protect news markets from private power as well as government censorship. At the same time, the First Amendment is a significant barrier to government action protecting private speech. Congress and the Supreme Court have evolved different approaches to First Amendment questions for different media. These variations rely in part on the physical and economic realities of each medium. As a result, print media, broadcast media, cable, direct broadcast satellite (DBS), and the Internet have different rules and different levels of constitutional protection from regulation. Because the agenda for any advocate must begin with a thorough understanding of these principles and how Congress and the courts have applied them, we review them and their trade-offs in this chapter. In doing so, we hope to alert advocates both to the scope of possible policies and to the limitations imposed by the courts on this scope.

In addition, we examine means the government can constitutionally use to promote the production of news and diversity of viewpoints necessary to sustaining a democracy. We suggest a possible checklist of principles for defining an advocacy agenda designed to promote the exchange of ideas and production of news, based on past experience and current principles of First Amendment law.

THE PURPOSE OF THE FIRST AMENDMENT AND THE GOVERNMENT'S ROLE IN FULFILLING THAT PURPOSE

The government's obligation to protect the marketplace of ideas when threatened by private interests was first articulated by no less a figure than the First Amendment's author, James Madison. He regarded deliberative debate as a necessary element of democracy.[1] Citizens, through exposure to each other and to new ideas, develop new perspectives and a general consensus about important political issues. In this conception, "politics is not supposed merely to protect preexisting private rights or to reflect the outcomes of interest-group pressures. It is not intended to aggregate existing private preferences, or to produce compromises among various affected groups with self-interested stakes in the outcome."[2] The deliberative process produces an exchange of ideas in which the collective wisdom of the whole, not only exceeds the sum of its parts, but exceeds it exponentially. Exposure to, and discussion of, multiple points of view thus becomes the essential ingredient without which democracy cannot function.[3]

This conception of the First Amendment must guide the formulation of media policy. We do not protect speakers so that they can speak inside closed rooms. We protect speakers so that citizens can listen to speakers, make their own evaluations, and make their own decisions. For this concept to work, policy cannot protect speakers at the expense of listeners.

In addition, news and information perform a special role in a democracy. Quality news and information ensure that elected leaders perform as their constituents intend, unearth fraud and corruption, and enhance democratic decision making. Politicians and corporate leaders fear scandal and thus alter their behavior. Some constituents will hold politicians accountable when they break their promises, and some citizens will learn about public issues and evaluate them, thus enabling them to educate others and to vote for high-quality leaders.[4] Benefits therefore accrue to society even if very few individuals actually use the news and information themselves.

As Mark Cooper explains, the Supreme Court has historically drawn on these Madisonian ideas when it considers appropriate regulation of mass media. The Supreme Court upholds congressional action when it has "generally been to secure the public's First Amendment interest in receiving a balanced presentation of views on diverse matters of public concern."[5] Congress explicitly embraces this historic and fundamental theory of democracy when it debates and adopts legislation, and it is the cornerstone of American jurisprudence in the area of mass media regulation.[6] The Supreme Court has confirmed that the Federal Communication Commission's broad legal authority to promote the public interest includes the duty to ensure that the public has access to diverse sources of information.[7]

At the same time, the First Amendment has been interpreted to prohibit the government from favoring any one speaker or form of expression over another or from intervening too much with private affirmative speech obligations. Such favoritism would defeat the very purpose of media policy: to allow free citizens to determine, over time, the critical questions of public policy in an independent and intelligent fashion.

This dual function of the First Amendment is particularly complicated in modern mass communications. Prior to the advent of new technologies—when debate took place in town squares, in leaflets, and in newspapers—serving the positive goals of the First Amendment required little regulation of the private sphere. Public spaces—parks, sidewalks, and the US mail—were the means of distribution. Prohibiting government involvement was closely aligned with promoting free speech. While the Supreme Court required states and the federal government to make public spaces equally available to all, it looked with skepticism on any regulation of the media.[8]

But new technologies have complicated this analysis. For technical reasons, the government licenses radio and television stations, but far fewer licenses exist than those who wish to speak.[9] The government must therefore choose which voices the public hears. Cable systems concentrate the decision on who will speak through a subscriber's television set in the hands of a single entity. To prevent such a concentration of power, the Supreme Court allows broader regulation of cable systems than of newspapers.[10]

THE NEED FOR AGGRESSIVE PUBLIC ADVOCACY TO DEVELOP MEDIA POLICIES THAT FURTHER FIRST AMENDMENT GOALS

Any advocate aware of the current state of today's media knows the government has failed dismally in its duty to promote the First Amendment goals described above. Since 1981, the tide of FCC action has moved in one steady direction: deregulation of the media. The FCC has justified each of its deregulatory proceedings on the grounds that the "free market" provides better service to the public than government regulation.

How has deregulation enjoyed such steady success? No one explanation will suffice, but the decline of grassroots advocacy to press elected politicians with a progressive agenda designed to serve the goals of the First Amendment certainly plays a part. When the public has made its anger heard, as it did in 1992 when Congress reregulated the cable industry, politicians have responded. And when the public rose up again in 2003 after the FCC eviscerated the last meaningful ownership restrictions, Congress took notice.[11]

While judicial review of agency action has an important role in such advocacy, the public cannot rely upon it exclusively. Certainly litigation can create new rights for advocates and force positive change. For example, when television stations in the south refused to air coverage of the civil rights movement and the FCC refused to discipline these broadcasters, the federal courts forced the FCC to take appropriate action. The same decision created a right for citizens to participate in license-renewal cases, a potent tool for community advocates for many years.[12] But such cases are the exception. Generally, courts do not create new rights or policies in the area of administrative law, the venue for most FCC disputes. At best, they reverse agency decisions and require the agency to try again. While litigation is an important remedy when the FCC disregards the public interest, it cannot alone form a sustainable basis for positive change. Just as the United States still needed a Civil Rights Act after *Brown v. Board of Education* declared segregation of schools unconstitutional, advocates must have a regulatory and legislative agenda as well as a litigation strategy.

In addition, courts will only reverse an FCC decision if it clearly ignores the recorded evidence or the law, the so-called arbitrary and capricious standard. As long as the FCC can point to some evidence that its deregulation will serve the public interest, courts will affirm the agency—even if another policy would more clearly serve the public better.[13] The courts defer even more to Congress. If Congress decides, for example, to permit greater consolidation in media markets, the courts will most likely defer to that judgment as reasonable despite the First Amendment principles described above. Courts will therefore rarely serve as organs for affirmative change.

The decision in June 2004 by the US Court of Appeals for the Third Circuit in *Prometheus Radio Project v. FCC* illustrates both the importance and the limitations of the court review. In *Prometheus*, the court reviewed the

FCC's June 2, 2003, Report and Order deregulating media ownership. In examining the case, the court paid heed to the breadth of the opposition to the FCC's deregulatory order and to the extensive record compiled by opponents of deregulation. The *Prometheus* court reaffirmed the First Amendment value in regulating media ownership and rejected the arguments of the industry that the First Amendment or principles of administrative law required the FCC to further deregulate media ownership. The court concluded that the FCC had failed to justify the new, looser ownership rules and therefore remanded the rules back to the FCC for another rule making. The court also ordered that the pre–June 2003 rules remain in place until the FCC completed the reevaluation and new rule making.

On the one hand, this represents a great victory for advocates. At the same time, it demonstrated the limits of using the courts. The *Prometheus* court explicitly found that the FCC *did* have the authority to relax the ownership rules and could reasonably rely on the evidence submitted by interested media companies and the FCC's own research to do so. While the FCC had acted arbitrarily in setting the new limits, it could justify relaxed limits with better reasoning.

Of importance, in administrative court proceedings courts rarely rewrite the rules in question. Instead, as in the *Prometheus* case, the court directed the FCC to try again by issuing a remand. What legal advocates achieved, therefore, was a very important temporary delay and an opportunity to make the case for a second time to the FCC and to Congress. The courts are an important vehicle for reopening an issue and reopening the political process with a new status quo and new momentum in a more favorable direction. The *Prometheus* court decision established some parameters for future FCC action, and the court decision did prevent an ideologically motivated agency from running roughshod over the public interest. The court established that much of the process the FCC followed was flawed and ignored the facts and the public participation. But the court did not establish new rules. Therefore, advocates still retain the responsibility to build a record before the FCC or to seek change through the legislature. It lies with Congress and the FCC itself to establish new, better procedures and rules. When it comes to media reform, the courts are a critical element, but they can only go so far.

It therefore falls to the media activists to craft policies that serve the goals of the First Amendment and to advocate for their adoption. In doing so, however, advocates must appreciate the differences in how the courts treat regulation of the various media. As Cooper has explained, the Supreme Court has found authority to affirm the positive goals of the First Amendment when the FCC chose to act. But the Court has also acted to prevent government regulation that might favor one speaker over another.

COMPETITION, ACCESS, MANDATES, AND SUBSIDIES

That the government has a compelling interest in maintaining an informed citizenry, and a concomitant obligation to create conditions under which this occurs, does not end the inquiry. How can the government achieve these ends? The United States has traditionally taken very different approaches to preserve a free and open debate depending on the media in question.

Congress and the FCC have traditionally relied on three mechanisms to ensure the production of news and coverage of civic affairs. First, Congress and the FCC have relied on rules creating competition between programmers or between providers of video services. This relies on the market to provide news, but seeks to ensure that a sufficient number of competing owners exist to provide different perspectives.

Second, Congress has created rights of access to the media. For example, broadcasters who accept political advertisements from one candidate must accept advertisements from all candidates. Cable companies must provide access to their physical plant to local governments for civic and educational programming. Direct broadcast satellite (DBS) providers must set aside channels for educational programmers. Under this theory, Congress ensures the production of news by permitting those with an interest in producing news access to the limited means of mass distribution.

Third, Congress and the FCC in the past have mandated the production of specific *types* of content—although not the actual content itself. For example, the FCC long required programmers to cover matters of interest to their local communities as part of the obligation of licensees to serve the public interest.

In addition to these modes of regulation, Congress has also relied on direct subsidies. Congress created public broadcasting for the express purpose of providing news and educational programming that commercial broadcasters would not produce.[14] Congress has also funded the production of educational or civic programming through grants from agencies such as the National Science Foundation or the National Endowment for the Arts.

FIRST AMENDMENT STANDARDS

While Congress has a wide range of tools at its disposal, it does not have an entirely free hand. Requiring parties to allow others to have access to their facilities or preventing certain business combinations may promote diversity of views, but it also arguably intrudes on the right of the regulated party to speak. As a consequence of technology differences among the media, the courts review such challenges from terrestrial and satellite broadcasters very differently from those of cable operators, and both are treated differently from newspaper publishers.[15]

The Supreme Court has developed a three-tiered system for analyzing regulation under the First Amendment. Under *rational basis*, the Supreme Court will only look to see if some rational connection exists between the law and its intended consequence. The Supreme Court generally reviews federal laws under the rational basis test. As discussed in detail below, the government regulates broadcasting and satellite television (DBS) under this most lenient standard, permitting the most government intervention.

Under *intermediate scrutiny*, also referred to as the *O'Brien Test* for the case which defined the standard,[16] a regulation that burdens speech survives a challenge under the First Amendment if the regulation (a) advances a compelling government purpose (other than the suppression of speech) and (b) burdens speech no more than necessary. For example, in *O'Brien*, the Supreme Court acknowledged that publicly burning a draft card was an expressive act and therefore "speech" under the First Amendment. Congress, however, had a compelling interest in tracking men subject to the draft, and prohibiting people from destroying draft cards advanced that purpose and did not curtail antiwar protest more than necessary. The law therefore passed constitutional muster. The Supreme Court evaluates the regulation of cable television under the intermediate scrutiny standard.

Finally, the Supreme Court uses *strict scrutiny* to examine laws that either compel speech or prohibit speech based on content. Strict scrutiny requires a compelling government purpose that can be achieved in no other way. As courts readily acknowledge, virtually no law survives review under strict scrutiny. Regulation of newspapers and Internet speech receive strict scrutiny, and thus the most protection from government intervention.

As discussed below, the distinctions make sense in light of the Madisonian goals of the First Amendment. Where the physical characteristics of the medium require the government to choose speakers (broadcast), the government must take special care that its selection does not silence other perspectives. Where the nature of the medium gives private actors a near absolute power to exclude speakers from public view (cable), the government must have the freedom to encourage diversity while leaving the private actors free to speak themselves. And where the physical nature of the medium creates no barrier to entry, government intrusion beyond enforcement of antitrust may well do more harm than good.

Newspapers and Internet Content

Newspapers have no physical limitations, since anyone can buy a printing press, ink, and paper and begin publishing. Other economic or user factors may make this an unreliable means of ensuring that the public stays informed, but the close identification of the content of a newspaper with its owner and editorial board has prompted the Court to view newspapers as an extension of unique personal expression deserving the highest protection under the First Amendment.

The Court therefore applies strict scrutiny to any attempt to provide rights of access to newspapers or to require newspapers to carry certain kinds of content. The Supreme Court, for example, has struck down a mandatory "right of reply" for anyone personally attacked in a newspaper editorial, a right explicitly upheld in the context of broadcasting.[17] Importantly, as discussed by Mark Cooper elsewhere, the Court has explicitly upheld application of the antitrust laws to newspapers as furthering the goals of the First Amendment.

For the same reason, the Supreme Court has applied strict scrutiny to Internet content.[18] The Internet can contain virtually infinite content with equal opportunities for each. The Supreme Court has reasoned that since any speaker may create a Web site, Internet content deserves the same level of protection as newspaper content. Accordingly, direct regulation of a Web site's content exceeds government authority. Although it has not been tried, it is fairly evident that a rule requiring Web sites to link to other Web sites, in a right-of-reply type scenario, would be quickly struck down by the courts.[19]

Broadcasting

By contrast to newspapers and Web sites, no one may speak using radio, television, or DBS frequencies without a license from the FCC. The government thus chooses a winning viewpoint in the marketplace of ideas. Absent government intervention, the viewer will see nothing but what the licensee wishes the viewer to see. As a consequence, the First Amendment allows the government to impose suitable safeguards to ensure the public has "suitable access to social, political, esthetic, moral, and other ideas and experiences,"[20] and indeed ought to demand so.[21]

As explained in *Red Lion Broadcasting v. FCC* and other cases,[22] the limited technology of early radio prevented anyone from effectively using radio without careful management by the government, since competing uses of the same frequencies at the same time created interference. Were it not for this unique physical restriction of radio that rendered general unregulated use impossible, requiring a license as a condition of broadcasting would have been unconstitutional. Given the need to ration access to the airwaves, Congress and the FCC found themselves doing what the First Amendment seeks to prohibit at all costs: having the government pick who speaks and thus selecting "winners" in public debate.

As the *Red Lion* Court observed, however, while the physical restraints of radio require that the FCC favor certain speakers by giving them exclusive licenses, "the people as a whole retain their interest in free speech by radio and their collective right to have the medium function consistently with the ends and purposes of the First Amendment."[23] In particular, Congress and the FCC must protect the public's "paramount" right "to receive suitable access to social, political, esthetic, moral, and other ideas and experiences." This public First Amendment right to a television and radio licensing system that fosters civic discourse and diversity of views "may not constitutionally be abridged either by Congress or by the FCC."[24]

As a consequence, regulation of television and radio has taken three forms.

Obligations to Serve the Community as a Public Trustee. First, Congress and the FCC have imposed a general duty on licensees to serve "the public interest, convenience, and necessity." Licensees do not own their licenses; they hold them as public trustees for the benefit of viewers and listeners in the geographic area covered by the license, with an obligation to provide meaningful programming that benefits the entire community. Congress requires broadcasters to undergo periodic license renewals in which the FCC considers whether broadcast licensees have met their obligation.

At one time, these obligations had considerable teeth. They played a crucial role in requiring stations in the south to carry news and other programming relating to the civil rights movement, and to air programming of relevance to African American and other minority communities ignored by programmers, since systemic failure to provide such coverage could result in license revocation.[25] Licensees were required to demonstrate that their coverage included "discussion of conflicting views on issues of public importance."

Since 1981, however, the FCC has reduced explicit public interest obligations of this nature. The FCC justified this policy change on the grounds that competition among local stations provided sufficient inducement to produce public interest programming and that licensees, rather than the FCC, were in the best position to determine the needs of their communities.[26] Only in the area of children's programming, where Congress mandated that the FCC create explicit programming requirements and consider them during license renewal,[27] have explicit mandates to create and broadcast particular types of programming remained.

Rules Creating Rights of Access. Congress and the FCC have also created explicit rights of access for those who do not have broadcast licenses. For example, Congress requires that any licensee must "allow reasonable access to or . . . permit purchase of reasonable amounts of time . . . by a legally qualified candidate for Federal elective office."[28] Similarly, if a licensee provides exposure for one candidate (other than in the context of news coverage), the licensee must make its facilities available to rival candidates.[29]

In the past, as discussed by Len Hill, the FCC has also created limited rights of access for independent programmers, such as rules requiring networks to use independent programming, and other opportunities for independent programming.[30]

Structural Rules. Structural rules prevent certain types of ownership. Of all the approaches used by Congress and the FCC to promote diverse viewpoints and news production in the media, structural rules have proved the most popular.[31] Since 1940, the FCC has limited the number of licenses and the number of programming networks any licensee may own. The FCC has also restricted the number of licenses an entity may hold in any specific market. Finally, the FCC traditionally prohibited ownership of certain combinations of media assets in the same market, such as ownership of a daily newspaper and a broadcast license in the same market. It also prohibited owning radio and television licenses in the same market.[32]

Structural rules stem from two rationales. First, they create opportunities for those who would otherwise not have an opportunity to speak.[33] Second, as discussed by Mark Cooper in chapter 8 of this book, commonly held media assets will not take positions genuinely antagonistic to one another.[34]

Cable Television

Cable lies between print and broadcast. Nothing physically stops anyone from building a competing cable system, but a combination of factors tends to make cable a "natural monopoly." In addition, if the cable system operator chooses not to carry a program on its systems, virtually no one in the viewing area can see it. By contrast, the refusal of a newspaper or Web site to carry content does not prevent a reader from finding the rival content elsewhere. This makes the cable operator the information gatekeeper to the local community, with power over what viewers see and hear. At the same time, the Supreme Court has found that the cable operator has a First Amendment interest in rejecting or promoting certain kinds of programming. The Court therefore uses intermediate scrutiny to balance the First Amendment interest of the cable operator with the broader goals of the First Amendment.[35]

To balance the First Amendment rights of cable operators with the need to promote diversity of programming, Congress and the FCC have avoided direct content mandates or full separation between content and conduit (i.e., prohibiting cable companies from having a financial stake in programming). Instead, regulators have focused on structural rules and access rules. For example, Congress has required cable systems to lease access to its system to rival programmers ("leased access") and to make channels available at the request of local governments for "public, educational, and government" use ("PEG channels").[36] Regulators have also prohibited certain forms of cross-ownership and imposed a national ownership limit.[37]

Most significantly, cable systems must carry the programming of local broadcast television stations.[38] This ensures that subscribers have access to local programming. To the extent the FCC imposes public interest obligations on local broadcasters, the "must carry" requirements ensure that subscribers will have access to public interest programming.

Satellite Broadcasting

Two forms of satellite broadcasting have developed in the last several years. Direct broadcast satellite (DBS) provides a television service similar to cable, although it also dedicates channels to music. By contrast, satellite radio provides an audio service similar to radio, but with a wider range of channels.

As services using spectrum, DBS and satellite radio receive the same level of First Amendment scrutiny as terrestrial broadcasters. The national nature of the services offered—the fact that explicit public interest mandates have fallen into political disfavor and the fact that, like cable, they primarily serve as a conduit for the speech of others—has prompted regulators to rely heavily on rules creating rights of access rather than on other public interest requirements.

Congress has explicitly required DBS to provide the same access for candidates as required by terrestrial broadcasters. In addition, Congress has required DBS broadcasters to set aside between 4 and 7 percent of their spectrum capacity for access by educational programmers. Congress has also directed the FCC to determine what other obligations would promote the public interest.[39]

At present, neither Congress nor the FCC has directed satellite radio broadcasters to provide any specific service or access.

SUBSIDY

If all else fails, the government can pay to produce sufficient news content. While the FCC and Congress have occasionally used indirect subsidies, such as a set-aside of spectrum exclusively for noncommercial educational broadcasters,[40] Congress has also relied on direct subsidies. Under the subsidy system, Congress attempts to avoid the danger of having the government directly control the flow of news by making a pool of money available for others to create educational or informative programming. In addition, Congress has created a public broadcasting system, funded in part with public money, in the expectation that this would provide citizens with perspectives unconstrained by the need to appeal to a mass market.[41]

Unfortunately, Congress has never created an independent revenue stream for these subsidies. As a result, public broadcasters and others relying on subsidies must seek additional funding from private donors and must return regularly to Congress to request new funds. This has the unfortunate effect of limiting editorial discretion. First, while the Supreme Court has held that Congress may not directly prohibit any programming activity as a condition of receiving public funds,[42] the power of the purse strings gives Congress an ability to influence the editorial direction of public broadcasting.

More significantly, however, reliance on private contributions has the same impact on noncommercial broadcasters as on commercial broadcasters. Public television and public radio stations that rely on listener contributions and donations from local businesses must shape their programming to appeal to desirable demographics in the same way commercial broadcasters do. As a result, the underserved communities that should be served by public broadcasting may not be served at all.

Also like commercial broadcasters, public broadcasters may become shy of controversy that might scare away corporate or private donors. For example, in 1994 PBS broadcast an adaptation of Armistead Maupin's *Tales of the City*, the adventures of a young woman in 1970s San Francisco. The series featured drug use, homosexuality, and promiscuity as part of the culture without any moral condemnation. When the series drew a firestorm of protest, PBS declined to finance a sequel, despite the popularity of the series with viewers.[43]

Nothing prevents Congress from creating a subsidy system designed to secure editorial independence. Indeed, proponents of the public broadcasting system initially proposed a sales tax on television sets to finance public broadcasting.[44] Since the proposal would have required imposing a new tax on television sets to create a source of independent funding, Congress declined to follow the recommendation.

THE ADVOCATE'S POLICY CHECKLIST

Now armed with an understanding of both the goals of the First Amendment and the limits on possible government action, the media advocate can formulate policies that both further these goals and survive judicial scrutiny. This checklist brings together and identifies the key differences between various media, while allowing formulation of a broader strategy on promoting First Amendment goals among all media.

1) Can the public transmit information at will via a medium, and what must the government do to realize this potential? The media requiring the least regulation are those that allow citizens to participate as both speakers and listeners, and encourage citizens to engage each other directly. Regulation would take the form of necessary safeguards to prevent parties from interfering with these activities.

2) Can distributors foreclose others from transmitting or receiving information, both technically and economically? This includes both physical limitations, such as "spectrum scarcity," and also the modern realities of the present economic system. For example, if cable becomes the dominant broadband technology, the presence of a potential competitor in DSL or wireless should not preclude imposing necessary safeguards.

3) What are the number, variety, and characteristics of actors having the ability to foreclose others' speech or others' reception of speech? This analysis shares much with standard antitrust analysis, although traditional indicia of "adequate" competition from antitrust must be further developed and made more sensitive to speech concerns. The greater the number of actors involved in dictating the speech distributed and received, the more likely that a wide variety will be produced. Advocates should look at ownership and other economic relationships to explicitly evaluate whether any actor or select group of actors can limit or foreclose the speech of others.

4) What is the present number of content creators currently available on the medium and their relative dominance on the medium? Does news or programming come from only a few sources? Even if many programming choices exist, does one source or a handful of similar sources dominate the medium? Has the condition persisted over time? All of these should raise warning flags that a bottleneck exists that may need correction. If a bottleneck does not exist, it may mean that some sort of subsidy is required to support new entrants.

5) What is the relative amount of resources and/or time dedicated to speech that promotes core First Amendment values such as news, local news and information, political speech, and editorial speech? Like the previous criteria, this criterion measures outcomes, but it focuses on the forms of speech of most concern to the First Amendment.

6) What is the importance or power of the medium to society as a whole, in both economic and social terms? This criterion recognizes that all media are not created equal. The power and influence wielded by an individual who owns one Web site is not the same as owning one network-affiliated television station. Public policy cannot be made by equating media that are not equal.

7) Do some communities remain persistently unrepresented or underrepresented? Access to the media must reflect the diversity of our society. Advocates should question why some communities remain unrepresented or underrepresented, particularly if the condition persists over time or the medium suffers from a history of discrimination. Advocates should also study carefully whether the problem should be addressed through rules directed at facilities owners (such as build-out requirements or tax incentives to sell to minorities owners) or by empowering communities directly through direct or indirect subsidies (e.g., grants, spectrum set-asides for minority owners, etc.).

8) Finally, in addition to evaluating any particular medium, should the same framework be used to evaluate whether all media, taken together, adequately perform their function as measured against historic constitutional norms that promote democracy? Too often, policymakers and advocates become so involved in a specific issue or specific medium that they do not stop to keep track of the big picture. Advocates who do not consider the media environment as a whole run the risk of settling for half measures or reforms that have only limited impact.

While always alert to new approaches, advocates will do well to consider the history of media regulation designed to further the goals of the First Amendment. This history provides valuable lessons in the virtues and shortcomings of different types of media regulation. We therefore conclude with a survey of the methods of media regulation to date and a final recommendation for FCC reform.

EVALUATING MAJOR OPTIONS FOR MEDIA REGULATION

The different regulatory treatment of various media demonstrate that the United States has pursued many mechanisms to address appropriate media regulation. The present treatments of various media are the product of a combination of the accident of history, the technological characteristics of the medium, and the political stakeholders' influence on the process. We consider below the main options for regulation and their relative merits.

Separation of Content and Conduit—the Internet Ideal

The most dramatic way to divorce content creation from distribution and thus enhance the degree to which the best content is offered to the public is to prohibit vertical integration—to separate the companies and individuals that create content from the companies and individuals who make decisions about content distribution. Alternatively, one can impose a duty to carry any and all content in a nondiscriminatory fashion (called a "common carrier" requirement). The paradigmatic example of this model is the Internet accessed over telephone lines.

FCC regulation in the early stages of the Internet prohibited the phone companies from interfering with content created by others. The FCC required phone companies to allow rival ISPs (Internet service providers) to connect to their systems, required full corporate separation between the phone company and its subsidiary ISP, and prohibited the phone company from favoring its subsidiary ISP over competitors.[45] The Internet thus evolved into its current form, where content from the network owners and content from their harshest critics is equally accessible to all.[46]

Virtues and Problems in Applying
This Approach to Other Media

A number of factors affect the plausibility and effectiveness of this approach. Extremely important is whether the technology allows large amounts of information to be presented side by side. The Internet has no technological limit on its capacity to present competing content side by side, a quality it shares with the least technological means of communication. Newspapers also do not suffer any meaningful technological limit—individuals or companies could create one thousand newspapers each, and a reader could subscribe to all of them; nothing would prevent her from doing so. Public roads and the postal service do not perform a gatekeeper role in physically delivering newspapers to readers. In these cases there is no need for any entity to perform an editing function because all information can be accommodated.

By contrast, cable systems and DBS systems carry a large—but limited—number of channels. For broadcasters, the limits for local communities are even worse. A local community will have only a handful of television broadcasters and a few dozen radio stations. In these instances, all potential speakers cannot be accommodated. Someone must make the decision regarding which channels will be placed on the menu or which television shows will be broadcast and when.

In these cases, separation of ownership between content and distribution becomes even more important than on the Internet, because it changes the financial incentives of the actors. If, for example, cable operators were prohibited from owning cable TV channels, they would select content based on what they thought would most please customers. However, when they are allowed to own cable channels as they currently are, cable operators can make profits by choosing channels that are not the most popular but that are created in-house. Thus, the cable operator has an incentive to select its own inferior programming because it could make more money with the inferior content. Similarly, if the cable operator can select which channels to distribute to the public, it can choose to ignore new competitors to its own channels, preventing them from gaining any audience. Finally, if the cable owner also controls the most popular programming, it can prevent a rival from ever getting off the ground by denying access to popular programming.

Two problems face advocates seeking such solutions. The FCC created the separation of content and conduit at the outset of the Internet, before the economic model wedding control of content to the network provider evolved. The phone companies subject to the Internet regulation already operated under a common carrier regime; they had no history or preexisting economic interest in programming content. When the FCC extended common carriage and required separation between phone companies and their ISP subsidiaries, no one knew that the Internet would become big business. All this made it politically easy for the FCC to impose these rules.

By contrast, the existing vertically integrated companies would lose billions through forced divestiture of their content holdings, and their existing business models would collapse. These companies will therefore fight tooth and nail to prevent such radical restructuring. Policymakers will question the need for radical restructuring of multibillion-dollar industries with accompanying losses of investments and threatened losses of jobs and disruptions in service. Even the modest limitations on content ownership imposed to date, such as the limited prohibition on exclusive content by cable system owners, took years of concentrated political efforts by advocates and private companies with significant financial interests in the outcome.

More important, however, broadcasting and cable do not share the property of abundance that marks the Internet. All content cannot coexist side by side, as it can online. This increases the complexity of the First Amendment analysis enormously, particularly under the intermediate scrutiny afforded to cable systems.

Courts have found a distributor's right to editorialize and to package content protected by the First Amendment.[47] Congress can require broadcasters and cable to share the microphone, as it were, but they cannot require them to keep silent.

Partial Separation and Voluntary Guidelines

Sometimes, partial separation of content and conduit can make a difference. For many years, the Financial Interest and Syndication Rules (Fin/Syn) of the FCC prohibited networks from owning a financial interest in the programs aired on the networks or from having a financial interest in the syndication rights. This differed from the full separation of content and conduit discussed above, since the network still had significant input into the production of the content. Nevertheless, as producer Len Hill writes elsewhere in this book, the rules required networks to bring in outside talent who contributed to the creation of original and thought-provoking programming.

In the area of news production, most media outlets use voluntary guidelines to separate news and financial interest to assure the public that the news is trustworthy. The evidence suggests, however, that these voluntary safeguards provide increasingly little protection. For example, in 2001 the *San Jose Mercury News* decided to pursue profit over quality news coverage, causing its editor, Jay T. Harris, to resign in protest.[48] The *Los Angeles Times* engaged in an experiment that linked news coverage and advertising.[49] Reporters surveyed indicate they believe that advertiser concerns affect news coverage.[50] And in the area of entertainment video programming, the business decisions are an integral part of content choices and are embraced and celebrated.

Advocates looking to apply the principles of common carriage or content separation to traditional media therefore face considerable hurdles. Full separation of content and conduit faces significant political and legal hurdles. Voluntary safeguards offer little assurance. Mandatory partial separation, however, may prove both achievable and useful in some cases.

Public Trustee Model

Another possibility, at least in the realm of terrestrial and satellite broadcasting, lies with the return to the public trustee model. This leaves programming decisions in the hands of local licensees, but requires them to keep the public informed of events of significance and to include alternate perspectives in their programming choices. As discussed above (and elsewhere in this book), the expectation of policymakers in the 1980s and 1990s that public interest obligations would chill innovative programming choices, and that deregulation would therefore produce higher-quality public interest programming, has proven optimistic at best and disastrous at worst.

Indeed, with the transition to digital television and in light of the current dismal programming landscape, new interest has arisen in reviving the public trustee model.[51] Interest in reviving at least the language of public trusteeship has arisen on the part of broadcasters as well—as part of staving off competitive threats. Broadcasters have invoked the public value of free radio and television as part of their efforts to secure anticompetitive legislation[52] or special privilege.[53]

However, the public trustee model is difficult to enforce. Classification of whether programming serves the public interest is highly subjective. Even for the few remaining public interest obligations, such as the obligation to create educational children's programming, broadcasters have attempted to "game the system" by claiming that television shows such as *Bugs Bunny* or *G.I. Joe* teach social values or teamwork.

Furthermore, since the scope and enforcement of public interest obligations rest entirely with the FCC, a change in administration can cause the agency to abruptly cease enforcing the obligations. Complaints by broad-casters that the license-renewal process gives the FCC too much arbitrary authority, or creates opportunities for commercial rivals to harass licensees, traditionally evoke sympathy from policymakers and lead to further erosion of the rules. Forcing unwilling corporations to engage in socially positive behavior is extremely difficult if the corporation really does not see benefit from the behavior.

Accordingly, while renewed public interest obligations should be a sig-nificant part of any effort to ensure the adequate generation of news, they should not be considered a "magic bullet." Renewed public interest obliga-tions must be part of a larger, holistic solution.

Access Rights and Structural Restrictions

Access rights and structural restrictions have the advantage of applicability across all media that contain bottlenecks. The courts have upheld requiring access on neutral terms to cable systems, television and radio stations, and DBS facilities. Similarly, courts have upheld the constitutionality of owner-ship restrictions that set absolute limits on national ownership or prevent cross-ownership of media in the same market. While both methods are useful in promoting news coverage and diversity of views, neither can be consid-ered a "magic bullet" for the problem of ensuring sufficient news and diver-sity to stimulate vigorous public debate.

ACCESS RIGHTS

Access rights can provide a direct opportunity for unaffiliated speakers to present their views by providing direct access to the physical plant. Politi-cians may speak directly to citizens because broadcasters must sell adver-tising to federal candidates. Community groups can reach cable subscribers using community access channels, and educational groups can reach DBS viewers through the noncommercial educational set-aside.

Historically, however, access rights have proved very difficult to enforce. Citizens are not informed about their rights or how to use them, and the private companies required to offer access often place significant hurdles in the way of those who wish to obtain access.[54] Because enforcement of access rights relies on federal or state authorities who may have greater sym-pathy to incumbent providers than to citizens, and because enforcement may require a significant investment of time and effort by private citizens, rights granted on the books by federal regulation may not translate into genuine citizen access.

Finally, access is not enough. Even where access exists, citizens rarely have the resources to create quality programming or news reporting that will attract the attention of fellow citizens. For access to work effectively, the programming must have some chance of attracting viewers.

STRUCTURAL RESTRICTIONS

Structural restrictions prohibiting cross-ownership of outlets or ownership of content have also played an important part in creating an environment with plentiful and diverse sources of news. Since others in this book have discussed at length the harms created by consolidated ownership, this chapter will focus on the positive effects of structural restrictions.

Restrictions on ownership can limit the number of outlets an entity can own nationally, the number of outlets an entity can own in a given market, or the types of outlets an entity can own in a given market. This creates a positive environment for the production of news for two reasons. As an initial matter, it creates greater opportunities for new voices and new perspectives by preventing larger companies from controlling all available outlets. This allows smaller companies, or companies with different and competing interests (e.g., newspaper vs. television), to offer different perspectives.

More important, it creates competition to provide news. When two television stations offer news programming, the city is covered by two news crews, each trying to "scoop" the other. Where a story is big enough to warrant coverage by both, each will try to provide a different perspective, so as to brand its station in the minds of viewers. Allow the two stations to combine, and the two news crews become one. Competition disappears, and the public loses both quantity of news coverage and alternate perspectives on the same issues.

A limit on national ownership keeps each owner focused on his or her local community. As ownership has become increasingly concentrated in the hands of a few, local programming has suffered.[55] Large group owners prefer the efficiency of centralized news coverage rather than having each station in each market spend money on developing its own news. This has the effect of homogenizing national news and eliminating local news. Thus, limiting national ownership levels creates an environment that encourages the production of more news—and more local news.

Structural restrictions, however, do not guarantee that anyone will actually want to cover the news. Nor do they provide so many opportunities for new perspectives that it guarantees genuinely diverse perspectives. Even if a market has ten different television stations and a daily newspaper, and the law requires different owners for each, that still creates only eleven opportunities for different perspectives.

Again, structural restrictions provide an important tool, and prevent possible abuses, but they cannot be the sole means of encouraging the production of news.

Require the FCC to Affirmatively and Explicitly Embrace Promotion of Civic Discourse

As Mark Cooper explains, the commission already has an obligation to promote civic discourse, diversity, and the production of news as a consequence of the statutory directive requiring the commission to ensure that all media licenses serve "the public interest, convenience, and necessity." As the Supreme Court explained, "the 'public interest' standard necessarily invites reference to First Amendment principles,"[56] and, in particular, to the First Amendment goal of achieving "the widest possible dissemination of information from diverse and antagonistic sources."[57] Most of the public interest obligations on broadcasters, cable companies, and satellite TV have their origin in the FCC's exercise of its power to ensure the public interest is served.

While the strong legal infrastructure for mass media regulation protects FCC decisions when it chooses to act, nothing requires the FCC to impose any particular regulation. Even when political activists have managed to force progressive legislation—such as the 1992 Cable Act—the FCC usually retains sufficient discretion in implementing the law that a stubborn agency can effectively undermine the intent of the legislation. There are a wide array of specific potential legislative or regulatory actions that the FCC could take to improve the public's ability to receive and transmit information. But how can activists counter a passive agency?

As a first step, the FCC could be required by law to explicitly address the factors on the policy checklist. Generally, the FCC need only justify its decision on the grounds that the decision will "serve the public interest." This broadness of this standard, while useful to convey authority to act, also allows the FCC tremendous leeway when it does not. Because so many elements go into a determination of what serves the public interest—over and above the goals of civic discourse and news production—the FCC can emphasize those factors that favor inaction and gloss over those factors that would require action. Because of the deferential review given by the courts to FCC determinations, such decisions usually survive judicial review.

If the FCC were required to address the factors in the checklist explicitly, it could no longer hide behind the vagueness of the public interest standard. This would have two positive effects. First, as a pure matter of politics, it would potentially shame the FCC into positive action. Second, it would prove an enormous benefit in judicial review. Although the FCC receives deference from the courts, the law requires the FCC to support its decisions in a rational manner based on the administrative record. If FCC action or inaction clearly runs against the goals of the First Amendment, requiring an explicit analysis will lay bare the errors in the order and make judicial reversal possible.

CONCLUSION

A wide range of regulatory models currently governs the media we see and hear. To achieve a day when all media place citizens' rights to engage each other directly at the center and supply citizens with a necessary flow of news to ensure a healthy democracy, advocates must seek to embed structural changes in the media landscape. In doing so, advocates must remain mindful of the restraints on action imposed by the First Amendment and that political currents will shift over time.

In the same way that a diversity of views strengthens civic discourse, a diversity of models brings strengths from several different disciplines, despite the fact that the current political structure cannot agree on a single model. Armed with principles for evaluating policies in light of the goals of the First Amendment, advocates can choose which approach best serves a particular technology. The principles proposed also allow advocates to evaluate the convergence of technologies and ensure that this convergence avoids the traps of the past. No system will ever be perfect, but the continuing evolution of American mass media, with multiple styles of regulation tailored to the differences among the media and grounded in political realism, can create a vibrant system that serves us well.

NOTES

1. See Cass R. Sunstein, *Democracy and the Problem of Free Speech* (New York: Free Press, 1993), p. xvii; William J. Brennan Jr., "The Supreme Court and the

Meiklejohn Interpretation of the First Amendment," *Harvard Law Review* 79 (1965): 14–16.

2. Sunstein, *Democracy and the Problem of Free Speech*, p. 18. See also C. Edwin Baker, *Media, Markets, and Democracy* (Cambridge: Cambridge University Press, 2002), pp. 129–53 (discussing elitist, pluralist, republican, and complex theories of democracy).

3. Sunstein, *Democracy and the Problem of Free Speech*, pp. 18–19.

4. See generally, C. Edwin Baker, "The Media Citizens Need," *University of Pennsylvania Law Review* 147 (1998): 317.

5. *League of Women Voters v. FCC*, 468 U.S. 364, 380 (1984). Mark Cooper examines the Court's general jurisprudence in this area in chapter 8.

6. The goal of maximum possible diversity extends to all of the electronic media under the commission's jurisdiction, not just to broadcasting. For example, the preamble of Title VI of the Communications Act, addressing cable television regulation, states that one central purpose of the subchapter is to "assure that cable communications provide and are encouraged to provide the widest possible diversity of information sources and services to the public. 47 U.S.C. §§ 521(4). Section 2 of the 1992 Cable Act also made similar findings. 47 U.S.C. §§ 521 at note. Congress has applied similar standards to direct broadcast satellites as well. See, e.g., 47 U.S.C. §§ 335 (b) (setting aside satellite capacity for additional perspectives).

7. *FCC v. WNCN Listeners Guild*, 450 U.S. 582, 604 (1981); *United States. v. Storer Broadcasting*, 351 U.S. 192, 203 (1956); *National Broadcast Co. v. U.S.*, 319 U.S. 190, 216 (1943); *National Cable Television Association, Inc. v. FCC*, 747 F.2d 1503, 1506 (D.C. Cir. 1984); *Metropolitan Council of NAACP Branches v. FCC*, 46 F.3d 1154, 1162 (D.C. Cir. 1995) (citations omitted).

8. Compare *Neimotoko v. State of Maryland*, 340 U.S. 268 (1951) (state must protect even unpopular speakers), with *Grosjean v. American Press Co.*, 297 U.S. 233 (1936) (prohibiting tax on newspapers).

9. The courts have long accepted that without careful management, those seeking to use the electromagnetic spectrum would interfere with each other. Some activists have questioned whether this remains true. We take no position either on the technical question or on what impact it would have on the existing regulatory scheme.

10. Compare *Miami Herald Publishing Co. v. Tornillo*, 418 U.S. 241 (1974), with *Turner Broadcasting System, Inc. v. FCC*, 512 U.S. 622 (1994).

11. Details of public reaction are contained elsewhere in this book. Some discussion of congressional action in the immediate wake of the FCC's 2003 actions can be found in Cheryl Leanza and Harold Feld, "More Than 'a Toaster with Pictures': Defending Media Ownership Limits," *Communications Lawyer* (Fall 2003).

12. *Office of Communication of the United Church of Christ v. FCC*, 359 F.2d 994 (D.C. Cir. 1966).

13. *FCC v. WNCN Listeners Guild*, 450 U.S. at 582.

14. Senate Report on the Public Broadcasting Act of 1967, S. Rep. 90-222, 1967

USSCAN 1772 (1967); House Report on the Public Broadcasting Act of 1967, H.R. Rep. 90-572, 1967 USSCAN 1799 (1967).

15. The nature of the First Amendment regime that applies to DBS is the same as terrestrial broadcasting. The Federal Court of Appeals for the DC Circuit has twice found DBS subject to the same level of First Amendment scrutiny as terrestrial broadcasters. See *Time Warner Entertainment Co., L.P. v. FCC*, 93 F.3d 957, 974–77 (D.C. Cir. 1996), *suggestion for reh'g en banc denied*, 105 F.3d 723 (D.C. Cir. 1997); *National Association of Broadcasters v. FCC*, 740 F.2d 1192 (D.C. Cir. 1984). However, a district court in the Fourth Circuit explicitly rejected these precedents and found the level of scrutiny applied to cable more appropriate. On appeal, however, the Fourth Circuit declined to create a circuit split and affirmed the district court without resolving the appropriate level of scrutiny. See *Satellite Broadcasting and Communications Association v. FCC*, 275 F.3d 337, 355 n.6 (4th Cir. 2001).

16. *United States v. O'Brien*, 391 U.S. 367 (1968).

17. Compare *Miami Herald Publishing Co.*, 418 U.S. at 241 (striking down a "right of reply" in newspapers under strict scrutiny) with *Red Lion Broadcasting Co. v. FCC*, 395 U.S. 367 (1969) (upholding a right of reply in broadcasting) and *Denver Area Educational Telecommunications Consortium v. FCC*, 518 U.S. 727 (1996) (discussing constitutionality of requiring cable owners to lease access to third parties).

18. *Reno v. ACLU*, 521 U.S. 844 (1997).

19. While strict scrutiny applies to regulation of Internet *content*, this does not translate into a prohibition against regulation of Internet service providers (ISPs) or others companies that sell access to the Internet. Indeed, as discussed later in this chapter, the FCC imposed regulations prohibiting the phone companies from favoring its own content or interfering with the content of others, even requiring it to separate its Internet business from its telephone business. These rules made the current, open Internet possible. See Lawrence Lessig, *Code and Other Laws of Cyberspace* (New York: Basic Books, 2000). As the Internet has evolved, some have argued that application of these rules to broadband networks violates the First Amendment. Discussion of this issue, however, exceeds the scope of this chapter. For a general discussion, compare, e.g., Justin Brown, "Fostering the Public's End-to-End: A Policy Initiative for Separating Broadband Transport From Content," *Communications Law and Policy* 8 (2003): 145 with Raymond Shih Ray Ku, "Open Internet Access and Freedom of Speech: A First Amendment Catch-22," *Tulane Law Review* 75 (2000): 87 (maintaining that ISPs are independent speakers, not merely neutral conduits, and therefore deserving of First Amendment protection). The FCC has found in the context of one merger that regulation of broadband access serves the First Amendment. *Merger of AOL and Time Warner, Inc.*, 16 FCCRcd 6547 (2001) (consolidation of dominant ISP with significant content justifies imposition of merger conditions to protect access to diverse points of view). The few courts that have considered the question of direct regulation of ISPs and the First Amendment have sent conflicting signals. Compare *AT&T Corp. v. City of Portland*, 43 F. Supp. 2d 1146, 1150 (D. Or. 1999), *rvsd on other grounds*, 216 F.3d 871, 877 (9th Cir. 2000) (no First Amendment

issue presented), and *United States v. Western Electric Co., Inc.*, 673 F. Supp. 525 (D.D.C. 1987) (regulation requiring network provider to use a separate subsidiary to engage in "electronic publishing" furthers interests of the First Amendment) with *Comcast Cable v. Broward County*, 124 F. Supp. 2d 685 (S.D. Fla. 2000) (requiring cable ISP to provide access to its plant to rivals violates First Amendment).

    20. *Red Lion Broadcasting Co.*, 395 U.S. at 367, 391.

    21. *Id.* at 400.

    22. *NBC v. FCC*, 319 U.S. 190 (1943); *Nextwave v. FCC*, 200 F.3d 43 (2nd Cir. 1999).

    23. *Red Lion*, 395 U.S. at 389–90.

    24. *Id.* at 391. As discussed in the previous section, however, Congress and the FCC have considerable—if not absolute—discretion in determining how to develop such a system. Nothing prevents the FCC from deciding that a system without regulation fosters competition that better serves the public than regulation. *Syracuse Peace Council v. FCC*, 867 F.2d 654 (D.C. Cir. 1989).

    25. *Office of Communication of the United Church of Christ*, 359 F.2d at 994.

    26. *Syracuse Peace Counsel*, 867 F.2d at 654 (upholding FCC's decision to repeal the Fairness Doctrine.) The court rejected, however, the FCC's attempts to find program mandates unconstitutional. It affirmed the FCC's policy judgment under the deferential standard described earlier.

    27. *Children's Television Act of 1990*, Public Law 101-437.

    28. *Communications Act of 1934* 47 U.S.C. §§312(7).

    29. *Id.* at §§315.

    30. *National Association of Independent Television Producers and Distributors v. FCC*, 516 F.2d 526 (2nd Cir. 1975). *Capital Cities Broadcasting/ABC, Inc. v. FCC*, 29 F.3d 309 (7th Cir. 1994).

    31. The history of the FCC's ownership rules is detailed in the *2002 Biennial Review of Broadcast Ownership Rules*, FCC Rec. 18 (2003): 13620.

    32. On June 2, 2003, the FCC eliminated its cross-ownership rules and substituted a new "diversity index," which measures the number of independent voices in a given market. The FCC also permitted ownership of three stations in many markets ("triopolies") and allowed television owners to reach up to 45 percent of the national audience through directly owned outlets. *2002 Biennial Review of the Commission's Broadcast Ownership Rules*. Congress almost immediately scaled the national audience reach back to approximately 39 percent, a level that would hold current ownership levels in place without requiring divestiture by the largest companies. *Consolidated Appropriations Act of 2004*, Public Law 108-199 §§629. The remainder of the FCC's ruling was challenged in court and, at the time of this writing, the old rules remain in effect pending resolution of the court case.

    33. *National Broadcasting Company*, 318 U.S. at 190, 218.

    34. *FCC v. National Citizens Committee for Better Broadcasting*, 436 U.S. 775 (1978).

    35. *Turner Broadcasting System, Inc.*, 512 U.S. at 622 (*Turner I*).

    36. *Communications Act of 1934*, 47 U.S.C. §§§§611, 612.

37. 47 USC §§613.

38. 47 USC §§§§614, 615.

39. 47 USC §§335. The FCC has declined to impose any public interest obligations beyond those explicitly required by Congress.

40. 47 USC 309(j)(2)(C); *National Public Radio v. FCC*, 254 F.3d 226 (D.C. Cir. 2001)

41. 47 U.S.C. §§§§390–399B. See also Senate Report on the Public Broadcasting Act of 1967, S. Rep. 90-222, 1967 USSCAN 1772 (1967); House Report on the Public Broadcasting Act of 1967, H.R. Rep. 90-572, 1967 USSCAN 1799 (1967).

42. *League of Women Voters*, 468 U.S. at 364.

43. *"More Tales of the City* Becomes Part of American Culture War," *Current*, April 25, 1994, http://www.current.org/prog/prog408g.html.

44. "Public Television: A Program for Action," *The Report of the Carnegie Commission on Educational Television* (New York: Harper & Row, 1967).

45. Lessig, *Code and Other Laws of Cyberspace*.

46. For example, SBC, Inc., owns Pacific Bell, California's predominant local telephone provider, and posts information to the Web at http://www.sbc.com/. SBC may trumpet the community service of its employees, solicit members of the public to receive e-mail from its subsidiary Pacific Bell, advocate on matters of public policy, and more. At the same time, the public can *also* obtain information from the Web site http://www.sbcsucks.com operated by a company called Sucks500.com, which allows critics to discuss the activities of various corporations.

It is important to note that the Internet's free speech nirvana is threatened as the FCC attempts to adopt rules that allow high-speed Internet distributors to control and shape content. See "Inquiry Concerning High-Speed Access to the Internet over Cable and Other Facilities," Declaratory Ruling and NPRM, FCC Rec. 17 (March 15, 2002): 4798. These decisions have been successfully challenged in the courts, but the First Amendment implications have not yet been addressed. See also Harold Feld, "Who's Line Is it Anyway" *Communications Law Conspectus* 8 (Winter 2000): 23.

47. *Turner I* (right of cable operator to select package offered); *Arkansas Educational Television Commission v. Forbes*, 523 U.S. 666 (1998) (televised debate not "public fora" and broadcaster may exclude candidates on reasonable grounds); *League of Women Voters*, 468 U.S. at 364 (right of broadcaster to editorialize).

48. Howard Kurtz, "Bottom Line News," *Washington Post*, March 20, 2001.

49. Howard Kurtz, "New Publisher at L.A. Times," *Washington Post*, June 4, 1999.

50. A survey by the Pew Research Center and the *Columbia Journalism Review* demonstrated that 25 percent of journalists have intentionally avoided newsworthy stories or softened the tone to benefit the interests of their news organizations. One-third say that the financial interests of news organizations often or sometimes go unreported. Twenty-nine percent believe stories are avoided that could affect advertisers. Pew Center for the People and the Press, "Self-Censorship: How Often and Why?" (April 30, 2000).

51. See, for example, *The Media Ownership Reform Act of 2004*, H.R. 4069 (proposing to revive public interest obligations); *Second Periodic Review of the Commission's Rules and Policies Affecting the Conversion to Digital Television*, MB 03-15 (rel. January 27, 2003).

52. Public Law 106-553 §§632 (restricting low-power FM).

53. 47 USC §§§§534-36 (cable systems must carry broadcast signals).

54. In one case, for example, a user of the DBS set-aside complained about mistreatment by Echostar, a DBS provider. Because the FCC rules allow DBS providers to select which noncommercial applicants will use the set-aside, Echostar responded by dropping the complainant from its system. Rather than punish Echostar for its retaliatory conduct, the FCC dismissed the complaint as moot. After all, now that the complainant was no longer on the system, the alleged ill-treatment by Echostar didn't matter. *American Distance Education Consortium Request for Expedited Declaratory Ruling and Informal Complaint* (rel. May 16, 2000), http://hraunfoss.fcc.gov/edocs_public/attachmatch/DA_00_973A1.pdf.

55. Project for Excellence in Journalism, "Does Ownership Matter in Local Television News: A Five-Year Study of Ownership and Quality" (February 2003), http://www.journalism.org/resources/research/reports/ownership/default.asp.

56. *Columbia Broadcasting System, Inc. v. FCC*, 412 U.S. 94, 122 (1973).

57. *FCC v. NCCB,* 436 U.S. 775, 795 (1978), (citations omitted); *Associated Press v. United States*, 326 U.S. 1, 20 (1945).

10

THE HIJACKING OF HOLLYWOOD

Corporate Control of the Creative Community

LEONARD HILL

PRODUCER, LEONARD HILL FILMS

LEONARD HILL *is a producer and founder of Leonard Hill Films, the Los Angeles–based independent television production company. He has served as vice president of Movies for Television at ABC Entertainment, manager of Primetime Series and later director of Movies for Television at NBC, and has also held positions at Paramount Television, MTM Enterprises, and Universal Television. Starting out as a writer on the series ADAM-12, he has been a member of the Writers Guild of America since 1972. Graduating summa cum laude and Phi Beta Kappa from Yale University in 1969, he received a master of arts degree from Stanford University. Mr. Hill has been a member of the board of directors of the Los Angeles Conservancy, the California Film Commission, and the Caucus for Producers, Writers, and Directors. He is also the founder and past chairman of ACI, a pioneering independent distribution company that was acquired by Pearson PLC for fifty million dollars. His production company (LHF) has produced more than 50 movies and over 160 hours of prime-time filmed entertainment and has employed such international stars as Angela Lansbury, Michael J. Fox, Kirstie Alley, Karl Malden, Ava Gardner, Brooke Shields, Ted Danson, and Jennifer Jason Leigh.*

The consolidation of media in the United States has been carried out in the name of deregulation. It is understandable that Americans share an aversion to regulation. Bureaucratic meddling too often chokes the energy of business and the imagination of innovators. But the consolidation of media ownership has not spurred competition nor has it promoted creativity. It has, instead, led to a tidal wave of self-dealing and other anticompetitive practices among the handful of companies that have come to dominate the market.

The public has been witness to the catastrophes caused by the deregulation of energy and aviation. But however troubling those meltdowns have been, the impact of media deregulation threatens to have even more pernicious effects. To fully understand the implications of such deregulation, it is useful to understand the genesis of the regulations that gave rise to broadcasting in the first place.

THE CRUX OF MEDIA REGULATION: PROTECTING THE PUBLIC INTEREST

The finite nature of the electronic spectrum requires that the government bestow regulatory privilege on designated operators. In this regard, it is important to underscore that the networks, both radio and television, were born of and nourished by government regulation. Without government intervention, broadcast signals would overlap. Absent regulation, there would be chaos.

In 1934 Congress passed legislation that enabled the creation of the Federal Communications Commission. That commission was specifically charged with protecting a most vital public asset, the electronic spectrum. In specific, the FCC was designed to order mass communication *"in the public interest, convenience, and necessity."* In seeking now to be deregulated, none of the privileged trustees of public largesse are willing to relinquish the free grant of spectrum exclusivity. They want merely to be freed of the regulatory restraints that were engineered to serve the public interest.

Not long after ordering the VHF spectrum through free grant of license, it became evident to the FCC that three national broadcasting chains had begun to use their dominion over the national airwaves to exercise cradle-to-grave control of the production, exhibition, and syndication of television programs. Observing that the networks accepted virtually no entertainment program in which they did not have a financial interest, the FCC undertook an analysis that revealed systematic extraction of rights, preferential treatment of affiliated entities, and anticompetitive warehousing of program rights. In 1965, after nearly five years of study, the commission responded to these predatory practices by proposing the Financial Interest and Syndication Rules (Fin/Syn).

After extensive hearings, Fin/Syn was adopted in 1970. Under the terms of the Fin/Syn rules, the networks were restrained from acquiring a financial interest in the off-network rights of any program not solely produced by the network and were barred from engaging in domestic syndication of off-network programs.

The purpose of Fin/Syn was summarized in the Report and Order that noted, "[I]t is not desirable for so few entities to have such a degree of power over what the American public may see and hear. . . . [A] diversification of economic interest and power in this area is a cardinal principle of the public interest standard of the Communications Act."

In 1972 the Department of Justice, in consideration of information gathered during the FCC rule making, sued the networks for restraint of trade. This suit resulted in a consent decree, promulgated in 1980. The consent decree incorporated the Fin/Syn restrictions and further determined that a network could not license a program for more than four years, could not condition production of a series on the rental of network-owned facilities, and could not produce more than two hours of weekly prime-time programming in house.

THE IMPACT OF REGULATION
ON THE CREATIVE COMMUNITY

Together, Fin/Syn and the consent decree combined to encourage the growth of independent production and syndication companies while simultaneously stimulating the growth of nonaffiliated independent television stations. The regulations were straightforward, content neutral, and self-enforcing. Their effect was immediate and salutary.

Consider that in 1970, when the rules took effect, there were about seventy-five independent television stations serving just thirty-eight markets. These stations were struggling, handicapped by an inability to acquire the rights to programs in a fair and open market. The networks had simply put an embargo on the off-network exploitation of prime-time series, choosing to warehouse these programs rather than see reruns appear on competitive channels.

By way of example, consider the case of the series *Hawaii 5-0*. CBS controlled the off-network rights to the detective show created by Leonard Freeman. CBS chose to warehouse the rerun rights to that show for thirteen straight years, much to the economic disadvantage of the creative talent responsible for the program and much to the detriment of the independent stations that clamored to acquire rights to the old episodes. The imposition of Fin/Syn changed all that.

Fin/Syn forced the broadcast chains to exit the domestic distribution business. The networks' vast warehouse of program rights was spun off into new, independent distribution companies. It is telling that one of these new distribution companies was a start-up venture named Viacom. The inherent value of off-network program rights proved to be so extraordinary that less than thirty years after its formation, Viacom was able to purchase CBS, the very network that had supplied the catalog of programs that launched the independent distribution company in the first place.

The availability of off-network programs offered to the market in open, competitive bidding spurred the growth of independent television stations. By 1982 there were 180 stations serving 88 markets and realizing combined profits of over one hundred million dollars. By 1990 there were over 340 independent stations. An energized independent station market created a dynamic market for both rerun and original made-for-syndication programming.

The unprecedented explosion of independent stations created a meaningful counterbalance to the national broadcast chains. These nonaligned stations were a boon to diversity, offering a different and decidedly local panoply of news and sports in addition to entertainment programming that had been designed and scheduled in consideration of local market tastes.

The stunning growth in the market for program rights proved to be a bonanza for the creative community. The demand for original, made-for-syndication programming skyrocketed. Regulation had rewarded the talent that drives the dream machine with unprecedented new opportunities for creative expression and a staggering growth in earnings.

The creative community was rewarded not only by the heightened demand for original programs but also by the effective marketing of off-network rights to established shows. Residual payments to actors, writers, and directors grew exponentially as programs that once were warehoused or offered on submarket terms to affiliated entities began to be actively traded in the open market.

Artists were further enriched by the license term limitation that had been imposed by the consent decree. The four-year term limit meant that hit series could be offered on the open market after the expiration of the initial license.

The creative talent would always be forced to accept minimum compensation for debuting series. The gatekeepers who control access to the national audience have extraordinary bargaining power when scheduling rookie series. But the imposition of term limits created a liberating form of free agency that allowed the market to determine fair value for those series that had earned all-star status. As a direct result of regulatory intervention, creative artists suddenly had access to the market to determine full and fair value for their services.

Regulation not only enriched the community of writers, actors, and directors; it spurred the growth of a healthy, competitive, and prolific group of independent production entities as well. The limitations that regulation had placed on in-house production and the prohibition against the extraction of financial interest made independent production a truly viable business. Inoculated against the predatory practices of unregulated networks, talented creators were encouraged to engage their entrepreneurial spirit. A dynamic community of new enterprises emerged, among them companies run by such pioneering talent as Norman Lear, Danny Arnold, Mary Tyler Moore, Aaron Spelling, Susan Harris, Steve Cannell, Diane English, Matt Williams, Susan Harris, Steven Bochco, Marcy Carsey, and David Kelley.

Significantly, these new independent production companies not only rewarded their owners with the prospect of financial gain but served to anchor true creative freedom. Producers were no longer employees, subject to the directives of corporate committees. As owners of independent companies, the best creative minds in the business had the freedom to offer their creations to a range of potential buyers.

The tribal fire burns brightest when lit by a flinty relationship between the talent that makes programs and the corporations that broadcast those shows. Fyn/Syn and the consent decree established a dynamic balance between the national networks and the community of creators who produced programming.

The rapid rise in the number of independent stations also catalyzed the creation of a fourth national network. The emergence of the Fox Network is directly attributable to the implementation of Fin/Syn and the consequences of the restraints imposed by the consent decree. The launch of a fourth network was, per se, consistent with the goal of promoting diversity in the media marketplace. Fox allowed the creative community to challenge the standard network fare with such breakthrough shows as *The Simpsons*, *Married . . . with Children*, and *Malcolm in the Middle*.

THE ASSAULT ON MEDIA REGULATION

Despite the patently procompetitive impact of Fin/Syn, the rules experienced a full frontal assault in 1983 when a newly minted FCC chair, Mark Fowler, labeled the regulations "outmoded." Invoking ideological certainty in the face of contrary historical fact, Fowler argued that only deregulation could spark market competition.

A furious debate followed Fowler's notice of proposed rule breaking. Bills were introduced in Congress to block the deregulatory juggernaut that Fowler had set in motion. In the end, the commission chair was rebuked by the very president who had appointed him. As a past president of the Screen Actors Guild (SAG), Ronald Reagan knew from firsthand experience the market-numbing implications of media concentration.

Unfortunately, President George H. W. Bush did not have the same first-hand experience as did his predecessor. When Reagan left the White House in 1988, the networks renewed their efforts to relax the rules. Their carefully coordinated efforts culminated in a special FCC en banc hearing held on December 14, 1990. The record established in that hearing is noteworthy.

The president of NBC, Robert Wright, testified (MM Docket No. 90-162) that diversity in program production was "on its deathbed . . . because the program production marketplace has become dominated by large vertically-integrated studios." Wright assuaged the commission's concern about diversity by declaring that "the networks themselves have the desire and the incentive to foster a vibrant and diverse independent production community," and he warned that "the domination of program production by a few huge conglomerates is an issue that dwarfs any Commission concern over the details of network-producer relationships."

Mr. Wright was certainly correct when he testified that "highly creative, breakthrough programs such as *All in the Family*, *Hill Street Blues*, and *Twin Peaks* have been born of the direct dealing between a network and an independent producer without the involvement of a major studio." But no credited independent program supplier would support his contention that "the natural incentives of the networks are the best guarantee that independent producers will flourish."

Given the strong commitment to deregulation voiced by Bush's chief of staff, John Sunnunu, it was presumed that the Republican-dominated FCC would ignore the dissenting testimony that had been presented and simply accept the networks' pleas as facts. It is a tribute to the thoroughness and openness of the process that the FCC finally voted to retain regulation.

The networks were shocked by the proregulatory rule making. But their assault on regulatory restraint did not abate. They challenged the FCC action in court. This time they won the lottery. The legal challenge ended up in the Seventh Circuit Court of Appeals.

The case was assigned to Judge Richard Posner. The networks had finally found a sympathetic ear. Prior to joining the bench, Judge Posner had offered counsel to CBS when the Justice Department was prosecuting the antitrust action that led to the consent decree. Despite the apparent prejudice, Posner refused to recuse himself from the case. He affirmed the conclusions that he had presented to his client years earlier and remanded the case back to the FCC.

Few people paid much attention when, in 1994, the FCC, responding to Judge Posner's decision, gutted the Financial Interest and Syndication Rules. The major newspapers certainly did not trumpet the radical revision of national broadcast policy. But then most people didn't notice that the *New York Times*, the *Washington Post*, the *Chicago Tribune*, and substantially all the other major metropolitan daily papers were themselves part of media conglomerates that had lobbied the FCC to abandon the rules.

THE CONSEQUENCES OF DEREGULATION

Just as the imposition of the Fin/Syn rules had an immediate and evident impact, so, too, did their elimination. Though the commission claimed the vacation of the rules would promote competition and diversity, the record indicates that the impact was, not surprisingly, just the opposite. In the immediate aftermath of the elimination of Fin/Syn, networks merged with studios, and, together, they began a cycle of self-dealing that would quickly decimate the community of independent suppliers.

Consider that in 1990 just 12 percent of the new series launched by the four major broadcast networks were produced in whole or in part by a network-affiliated entity. In 2002, of the forty new series that appeared on the major networks, 78 percent were supplied by network-related enterprises. And the trend is accelerating. Preferential treatment of affiliated suppliers is now the norm. The "natural incentives of the networks" that Robert Wright had assured the FCC would cradle independent suppliers were revealed to be perversely predatory.

This development should not come as a complete surprise. Jack Valenti, the head of the Motion Picture Association of America (MPAA), warned against deregulation when he testified before the FCC in 1990. Valenti observed that "[t]he networks have not been rehabilitated. They are corporate recidivists. They abused their power before. They will do it again." And they did.

Freed of Fin/Syn constraints, the networks not only engineered the annihilation of independent supply, but also worked in virtual lockstep to deny creative artists fair compensation for their labors. In conspicuously parallel practice, all the major networks revised their contracts to encompass an array of cable and other off-network rights. There was no added consideration given for these additional rights. Rights were simply extracted. There was no negotiation.

The economic impact of the extraction of nonnetwork rights on the creative community was staggering. The residual system that had been negotiated over decades by the creative guilds was premised on the assumption of off-network rights being sold in transparent, arms-length transactions. Fin/Syn had reinforced the open-market assumptions that underlay the residual structure. Freed of regulatory constraints, the networks garnished program rights in anticipation of making "synergistic" deals with related entities. The self-dealing of cable and other ancillary rights made a mockery of the residuals formulas.

A handful of the strongest members of the creative community had the resources and the guts to sue the networks for conspicuous self-dealing. Matt Williams, the creator of *Home Improvement*, sued Disney. In 1992, Williams partnered with Disney in supplying the program to ABC. In 1994, the rules fell. In 1995, Disney bought ABC for 19 billion dollars. Suddenly the renewal of *Home Improvement* saw one man, Michael Eisner, representing both the supplier and the buyer. The efficiency of the process did not maximize value for the program's creator.

The situation was much the same for Steve Bochco, the creator of *NYPD Blue*. He had partnered with Fox and sold his hit cop show to ABC. Then Fox got into the cable business. In an effort to build its nascent cable channel, FX, the studio sold the rights to *NYPD Blue* in an overly convenient deal to its sister company. The fiduciary obligation Fox owed to Bochco was subordinated to the desire to maximize interrelated corporate assets. Bochco sued and was rewarded with a huge settlement.

The same scenario played out for Alan Alda on *M*A*S*H* and Michael Moye on *Married . . . with Children*. But most artists are understandably loath to sue the hand that feeds them, even if that hand has skimmed the profits. The concentration of both carriage and content under the same corporate umbrella may have been a boon for stockholders, but it was a conspicuous bust for the creative community.

It has become increasingly unlikely that even established talent can afford to engage a media conglomerate in a legal challenge. A litigant accepts the risk that the party being sued is likely to consider the litigant as a pariah. When regulation separated studios from networks, an individual artist could reasonably afford to go after a network or a studio. But in today's deregulated climate the consequences of legal challenge are overwhelming. The artist who sues CBS today alienates not just one network but a huge piece of the entire market. Sue CBS and you have simultaneously crossed swords with Paramount Studios, Showtime, Blockbuster, UPN, MTV, Infinity, and all their distant cousins.

Beyond the evident economic harm deregulation has brought to the creative community, there is the damage that the public has suffered from the homogenization of previously antagonistic sources of content. The merger of Telemundo and NBC or the takeover of BET by Viacom not only results in a loss of jobs but leads to an erosion of diversity as well. There are fewer corporate chieftans sitting on ever-more-exalted thrones. Both style and substance are pasteurized to meet the common requirement of corporate accountancy.

THE LAST STRAW

The media meltdown that had been sparked in Judge Posner's court was further exacerbated with the passage of the Telecommunications Act of 1996. This congressional action, which Senator John McCain (R-AZ) has called "a 70 billion dollar giveaway," gave control over the digital spectrum to the stations free of either charge or public interest consideration. The Telecommunications Act also eliminated the regulatory restraints on radio and thus freed entities like Clear Channel and Infinity to aggregate endless numbers of stations under common ownership. The concepts of "diversity, localism, and competition," enshrined by Congress in the 1934 act, were either ignored or repudiated by the enactment of the 1996 act.

The elimination of Fin/Syn and the enactment of the Telecommunications Act did not merely alter the landscape of broadcast television. It was a tectonic shift in the way our national media is organized. Once the restrictions on ownership were substantially eliminated, there was a frenzy of interrelated deals. With ever-accelerating speed, networks merged with studios that had acquired book publishers and then married themselves off to cable companies that had allied with Internet service providers.

In the warm afterglow of deregulation, vertically integrated media empires celebrated newfound "efficiencies." The chairman of Disney, Michael Eisner, crowed, "There are synergies under every rock we turn over." Sumner Redstone, chair of Viacom, echoed similar sentiments when his company took control of CBS. The creative community and the public at large, however, slowly came to discover that synergy was just technospeak for the more evidently noxious concept of anticompetitive practice.

THE AXIS OF ACCESS

The extent of media consolidation has been chilling. A handful of companies control access to the national audience. Deregulation has given rise to an axis of access. AOL/Time Warner, Viacom, Disney, Newscorp, Vivendi-Universal, GE/NBC, and Liberty Media have conglomerated unprecedented power.

Consider some facts:

1. There are now ninety-one major television networks that are each available in more than sixteen million homes, but nearly 80 percent of these networks are owned or controlled by six media conglomerates.
2. In 1992 nearly 70 percent of network prime-time programming was produced by independent producers. Today more than 80 percent of prime-time is produced by companies owned or controlled by networks.
3. Just seven companies now account for over 75 percent of the income earned by all members of the Writers Guild of America.

The guarantee that Bob Wright pledged to the FCC has been voided by the sweeping consolidation of networks and the vertically integrated studios he once found to be so threatening. Freed from restraints, the large media conglomerates have used their market power and unique regulatory privileges to condition access to the national audience on the willingness of producers to relinquish control over their creations.

Independent producers are an endangered species. The network in-house production units have grown like kudzu, choking off even the strongest independent suppliers. Absent regulation, independent production will be a relic of a bygone era.

GOING FROM BAD TO WORSE

The extraordinary power of these media monoliths was evident when, in June 2003, the FCC undertook a review of the remaining media ownership rules. Under the guidance of Chair Michael Powell, the commission set out to review six key regulations. They were:

1. The newspaper/broadcast cross-ownership ban that prohibited the combined ownership of a major newspaper and broadcast station in the same urban market
2. The national television station ownership cap that prohibited any one entity from owning TV stations covering more than 35 percent of the national audience
3. The dual-network ownership rule that prohibits mergers among the four major television networks
4. The television/radio cross-ownership rule that limits the number of stations that can be jointly owned in any one market
5. The local television duopoly rule that limits common ownership of television stations in the same market
6. The local radio ownership rule that limits the number of radio stations any one entity can own in a single market

Taken together these rules provided the last remaining bulwark against the concentration of control over local media markets by large horizontally and vertically integrated media empires.

Despite the enormous importance of these regulations, Powell had little time for public input. He scheduled only one field hearing in advance of the rule making. That hearing was held in Richmond, Virginia, a place not usually considered to be the heart of the entertainment or communications industry. Richmond was, however, conveniently located near the commission's home base.

Not surprisingly, the national media did not focus on the rule making. Not that they were not interested. The *New York Times*, the *Chicago Tribune*, and the *Washington Post* all submitted extensive filings urging the commission to deregulate, but there was virtually no coverage of the issue in these newspapers. The *Times*, the *Trib*, and the *Post* stood to make windfall profits if the rules were eliminated. It seems fair to presume that the editors of these distinguished newspapers were muffled by corporate boards committed to maximizing shareholder profit.

Despite the virtual embargo on news stories that offered critical analysis of the proposed rule making, public opinion was galvanized by local organizations and Internet bloggers. The result was remarkable. Over two million comments were filed with the FCC, and most estimates suggest that 99 percent of the comments were opposed to deregulation.

A stunning array of typically antagonistic entities aligned in opposition to the relaxation of the remaining constraints on media consolidation. The American Civil Liberties Union and the National Rifle Association are seldom seen holding hands in public, but they stood side by side in opposition to Powell's determination to grant the conglomerates their deregulatory wish list. The Congressional Black Caucus joined with Senator Trent Lott (R-MS) in urging Powell to expand the proceeding.

But the cacophony of dissent fell on deaf ears. On June 2, 2003, the FCC, by a 3–2 vote (Commissioners Adelstein and Copps opposed), essentially eviscerated all six remaining regulatory safeguards. Their Report and Order was designed, per their proclamation, to set "new limits on broadcast ownership based on a thorough assessment of the impact of ownership rules on promoting competition, diversity, and localism." The report pridefully announced that the new rules would "foster a vibrant marketplace of ideas, promote vigorous competition, and ensure that broadcasters continue to serve the needs and interests of their local communities."

The report even went so far as to echo Justice Hugo Black's famous opinion (*Associated Press v. U.S.*) that affirmed "[t]he assumption that the widest possible dissemination of information from diverse and antagonistic sources is essential to the welfare of the public." No doubt a free press is a condition on which a free society is built, but though those sentiments were intoned in the report's rhetoric, the actions directed by the rule making served to promote concentration and undermine localism.*

THE DILUTION OF CONTENT
AND THE RISE OF COMMERCIALISM

The recent FCC rule making also failed completely to address the hyper-commercialism that has overtaken broadcast television. Only twenty years

---

*The FCC's proposed rules were, however, stayed by the Third US Circuit of Appeals and sent back for rewriting. But, given the disposition of the Bush administration toward media deregulation, the outcome remains very uncertain. See, in this book, the section of the editor's introduction titled "The New FCC Rules: More Deregulation, Less Democracy."—Ed.

ago the typical one-hour dramatic series episode had a running time of approximately forty-eight minutes. Today the typical episode contains roughly forty-two minutes of content.

Not content to merely increase the amount of commercial time, the networks have developed a strategy to infect the programs with commercial messages that are embedded in the actual on-screen drama or comedy. Programs have been converted into virtual infotainment by the conspicuous placement of trademarked products within scripted series.

Prior to 1990, program suppliers were required to sign affidavits confirming that they had not received any consideration for placing recognizable merchandise in the body of their productions. Once freed to engage in perpetual self-supply, the networks jettisoned any notion of opposition to plugola. By weaving commercial messages into the body of the program, networks are able to smuggle product promotion into the very fabric of a popular series and thus insidiously address viewers when they are most vulnerable to subliminal suggestion.

With flagrant disregard for even the most dilute concept of public trusteeship responsibility, the networks are currently engaged in creating "branded entertainment." This development will further weaken the separation between advertising and program content. No longer content to simply plug products through calculated set-dressing, networks now are attempting to engineer commercial messages into the very narrative of the series that are being broadcast. And this is not some dirty little secret. The influential trade journal, *Advertising Age*, in the September 15, 2003, issue, announced that ABC had launched an "Advertisers Beyond Commercials" division that was designed "to offer advertisers a vast array of opportunities to interact with our programming."

Such hypercommercialism is partly responsible for the huge boom in cheap reality programs. These inexpensive, nonscripted shows are perfectly suited for brand promotion. Consider the ABC series *Extreme Makeover: Home Edition*, a show that was sponsored by Sears and starred Sears products. The integration of Coca-Cola products on Fox's *American Idol* was equally ubiquitous.

The elimination of the rules that had separated production from distribution has fostered a whole new paradigm for media and commercialism. Where once there was the presumption that plugola was a violation of the licensee's public interest obligations, deregulated media entities are now willing to let advertisers script entire programs provided only that they are willing to pay enough for the opportunity.

The creators of content, particularly writers and directors, no longer are responsible for creating quality entertainment. Scripts were once judged solely on the quality of their characterization or the originality of plot development. The acceleration of product placement and branded entertainment have conspired to cheapen program content, forcing writers and directors to crassly manipulate commercial images with little if any regard to the integrity of the actual program content.

The commercial colonization of program content is a craven effort to use the public airwaves without any regard for the operator's responsibility to serve "the public interest, convenience, and necessity." Corporate propaganda is no longer contained in clearly understood commercial blocks but has metastasized, silently invading every organ of mass communication.

Beyond craven commercialism, program diversity and content is further diluted by decisions based on the desire of concentrated media to curry political favor with incumbent power. *Daily Variety* announced, in its May 5, 2004, issue, that "the Mouse House has moved to prevent subsid Miramax from distributing Michael Moore's controversial documentary *Fahrenheit 9/11*." Translated from industry jargon, the statement affirmed that Disney had decided to separate itself from an examination of the terrorist attacks, produced by an Academy Award–winning writer/director and financed by a Disney affiliate, simply because the film painted an unflattering portrait of the Bush administration. While the film did eventually find independent distribution, the message was clear. Big media wants to cozy up to big government.

And Disney is not alone. The decision by CBS to pull the Reagan miniseries from its prime-time schedule reflects similar concerns. Cynics have observed that big media has a new motto: if we wave the flag, then Washington will waive the rules.

THE IMPACT OF RADIO CONSOLIDATION ON CREATIVE EXPRESSION

The wholesale deregulation of radio has aroused near-universal scorn. It has seriously eroded local news, diminished the variety of music that respects local or regional tastes, and it has markedly increased raw commercialism. Deregulation of radio has undermined creative diversity. The license to operate a radio station, once given in consideration of public interest obligations, is now presumed to be a piece of corporate property to be used to profit private shareholders no matter what the public cost.

The impact of consolidation on localism has been particularly chilling. Prior to the passage of the Telecommunications Act of 1996, no one operator could own more than forty stations. The act completely eliminated the cap on ownership. A feeding frenzy followed. Only eight years later, the leading radio operator, Clear Channel, owns more than twelve hundred stations. The top two radio operators (Clear Channel and Infinity) do more business than the next twenty-five station groups combined. These companies also control concert venues, ticket sales, and promotion.

The extraordinary power to control access to the public gives Clear Channel and Infinity enormous control over both the determination of what artists get played and how those artists are compensated. It also gives these entities unnatural control over the pricing of advertising, ticketing, and music-related merchandise.

Consolidation of control over radio has also allowed the big operators to become political arms of incumbent political power. When the lead singer for the Dixie Chicks, Natalie Manes, criticized President Bush over his decision to invade Iraq without UN or even NATO support, Clear Channel pulled the Chicks from the playlist on all twelve hundred of its stations. Clear Channel disc jockeys organized mass rallies dedicated to the public destruction of Chicks' CDs. They did not wear black shirts, but armies of Clear Channel personalities were clearly marching in lockstep, each trying to please the corporate parent with ever-more-brazen demonstrations of contempt for Manes and ever-louder cheers of support for the commander in chief.

TRANSPARENCY, RESPONSIBILITY, AND CONFLICT OF INTEREST

Deregulation has allowed huge corporations to leverage conflicts of interest that were once unimaginable. But there is an inherent restraint of trade when one entity is both seller and buyer in the same transaction. The wholesale deregulation of media and the emergence of six dominant cartels make a mockery of this most basic presumption of open-market economics.

In 1962, in the case of *United States v. MCA*, the Department of Justice filed suit to prevent the then-dominant talent agency from acquiring a motion picture studio. The Department of Justice had determined that there was an incurable conflict of interest when the representatives of creative artists were empowered to employ their own clients. It was a simple principle, courageously brought to bear by Robert Kennedy against one of his brother's major benefactors, Lew Wasserman. In the face of the lawsuit, MCA did what many had thought unthinkable. They shuttered the agency.

The situation today is far different than it was in 1962. What were once seen as cancerous conflicts of interest are now promoted as entrepreneurial opportunities. In the Hollywood community, this fact is particularly evident among the dominant talent agencies.

The major Hollywood agencies, Creative Artists Agency (CAA), International Creative Management (ICM), William Morris, United Talent (UTA), and Endeavor, represent producers, advertisers, distributors, and giant corporations in addition to the creative talent that is the backbone of their business. There was a time when the individual artist was secured by the notion that an agent could only be enriched in proportion to the enrichment of the artist. That time is long ago and far away. That certainty has disappeared behind a cloud of conflicts.

It is revealing that the community of talent agents has failed to support SAG, WGA, or DGA as these creative guilds have fought against media consolidation. When the guilds were in Washington arguing against Powell's deregulatory schemes, the Association of Talent Agents (ATA) remained in Los Angeles, trying to convince SAG members to deregulate agents.

Agents chafed against the restrictions that had long been codified in guild agreements that governed the licensing of agency. They looked jealously at the windfall profits that deregulated media had enjoyed and reasoned that they, too, should be freed of restraints. Agents have unnatural influence over creative talent. And the ATA began a campaign to convince artists that there would be no harm in agents being allowed to produce programs or be involved with distribution.

There are disturbing parallels between the efforts of the media giants to be freed of regulatory restraint and the simultaneous efforts of the dominant agencies to be deregulated. Since their inception, the guilds have licensed talent agents and held them to strictly defined franchise agreements that are designed to protect the artist from otherwise predatory instincts of those who would represent them.

But the silence of the ATA on the issue of consolidation is indicative of the extent to which ingrained conflicts of interest have compromised the ability of agents to act in the best interests of talent. The concept of fiduciary obligation has been eroded by the steady growth of ever-more-incurable conflicts. Emboldened by the deregulation of media, agencies have used individual artists as a loss leader in the pursuit of a piece of the studio action.

The cynical acceptance of conflict is evident in the very leadership of

SAG. The national executive director of SAG, Robert Pisano, sits on the board of Netflix, a large, publicly traded company that is in the business of renting DVDs. He disclosed this potential conflict to the board of SAG before he was hired. The actors who sit on the SAG board agreed to waive the conflict. It is unlikely that Pisano disclosed to SAG that the Netflix IPO warned investors that "any conditions that adversely affect the movie industry, including regulatory requirement and strikes, work stoppages, or other disruptions involving writers, actors, or other essential personnel" would be detrimental to Netflix.

Though he transferred ownership of his stock options into a trust for his children, Pisano's family stands to make vastly more money from the success of Netflix than they will ever see from his SAG salary. As a director of Netflix, Pisano owes that company a fiduciary duty. Presumably, he owes SAG the same duty. But the interests of a DVD distributor and the interests of actors who are seeking to maximize the residuals they earn for DVD sales are not aligned. And therein lies the rub.

Agents, lawyers, accountants, and other professionals who represent creative talent are licensed by government authorities. Government must begin to weed out the tangle of conflicts that permeate the various component parts of the entertainment industry. The fallout from the collapse of Enron, WorldCom, and Adelphia should underscore the urgency of implementing regulations that prevent self-dealing and codify strict compliance with clearly delineated rules of ethical procedure.

The principles underlying *United States v. MCA* need to be amplified. The marriage of carriage and content is no more anticompetitive than the amalgamation of agency representation and studio production. Though the term "synergy" may have been substituted for "self-dealing," the market-numbing consequence of opaque, in-house transactions remains just as crippling.

The democratic ideals that informed the architects of the Republic are challenged by the unnatural concentration of power in the hands of either government authority or commercial enterprise. Deregulation of media has tipped the balance of power away from the public interest and in favor of shareholder profit. To restore that balance, it will be necessary to apply uniform principles of governance that promote transparency, accountability, and competition.

IGNITING A NATIONAL DEBATE

Though the FCC ignored the overwhelming display of public support for retention of media ownership rules that poured into the commission after the publication of the Notice of Proposed Rulemaking, the battle for control over mass media is far from over. What was once an abstract debate among scholars has started to sprout truly populist roots.

An array of organizations has begun to provide a meaningful forum for ventilation of public frustration. Longtime advocates such as the Consumers Union, the Media Access Project, the Center for Digital Democracy, and the AFL/CIO have found powerful new allies. The Hollywood creative guilds, SAG, WGA, DGA, and PGA, have allied with the Caucus for Producers, Writers, and Directors and the Coalition for Program Diversity in organizing to oppose the media oligopolies. New organizations such as MoveOn and Free Press have begun to stir the pot. And long-established groups such as Common Cause have come to identify media consolidation as a core issue.

Despite the fact that vertically integrated media companies have offered the public virtually no coverage of the issue, the issue of media consolidation began to capture the public's attention. In a curious way, Michael Powell's blunt indifference to democratic discourse and the wholesale elimination of rules that he pushed through served to provoke public outrage.

It certainly helped that major national figures such as Ted Turner and Barry Diller came out against Powell's reordering of the marketplace. Diller addressed the National Association of Broadcasters and, with stunning candor, observed, "I'm opposed to the changes, but I'm also upset that this has not produced enough conversation and dialogue. The way Michael Powell has gone about it is to hide the issue as much as possible. The conventional wisdom is wrong. We need more regulation, not less."

The public outrage, once ignited, is hard to extinguish. In the movie *Network*, Peter Finch spoke to his imaginary television audience and intoned, "It's time to go to your window, stick your head, out and yell, *'I'm mad as hell and I'm not going to take it anymore!'*" Almost thirty years after those prescient words, written by Paddy Chaevsky, first appeared on screen, people are beginning to follow his advice.

WHAT IS TO BE DONE?

As participants in a democratic society, citizens have the right to insist that public policy should be determined not by what conveniences incumbent power but by what enriches their Republic. They have a right to insist on a regulatory scheme that promotes a competitive marketplace of ideas in which a diversity of voices can be heard.

This isn't a utopian notion. It's a principle clearly understood by the highest court in the land. In deciding the case of *Turner Broadcasting v. FCC* in 1994, the Supreme Court asserted:

> Assuring that the public has access to a multiplicity of information sources is a governmental purpose of the highest order, for it promotes values central to the First Amendment. Indeed, it has long been a basic tenet of national communications policy that widest possible dissemination of information from diverse and antagonistic sources is essential to the welfare of the public.

The concentrated ownership of our national media makes a mockery of the public's right to a multiplicity of sources providing information and entertainment from a diverse and antagonistic array of suppliers.

Federal regulatory policy will determine whether we allow the genie that technology has unleashed to be harnessed for the public good or held captive to private interests. If the public interest is to prevail, there are a number of policy changes that must be implemented, most of which will require governmental intervention. They are the following:

1. The concept of station license in the public interest must be reaffirmed. It is outrageous that the FCC allows license holders to renew their exclusive rights every eight years merely by sending a postcard to the commission. The commission should allow scrutiny of station performance, informed by public comment, and such scrutiny should take place every five years.
2. The ban on cross-ownership of television and newspapers should be maintained. There is no public interest–based justification for allowing a full-service broadcast station and a daily newspaper to function under common ownership.
3. The station ownership caps should be reevaluated. No one entity should have the right to own more than twelve stations. Additionally, no one entity should have the right to operate multiple stations in the same market.
4. The networks should be restrained from producing prime-time entertainment programs that they broadcast. The ability to self-supply undermines competition in the marketplace of ideas and denies creative talent reasonable compensation for their labors.

5. The networks should not be allowed to have a financial interest in the off-network exploitation of programs that were initially exhibited on their systems. Since the network's leverage over the program supplier allows for the simple extraction of financial interest without due consideration, the public interest in a healthy community of diverse program suppliers is best served by prohibiting transactions that would, per se, be abusive.

6. The networks should not be allowed to function as the off-network distributor of the rights to programs that were initially exhibited on their systems. The potential for self-dealing or warehousing makes such a limitation necessary. Moreover, networks should be encouraged to schedule programs based only on consideration of the national audience in whose interest the networks are obligated to perform. Consideration of off-network values would compromise such objectivity.

7. The networks should not be allowed to license series programming for an initial term of more than four years. Since it serves the public interest for creative artists to have access to market forces to reasonably determine fair compensation for their labors, networks should be restrained from extracting perpetual renewal options.

8. The dominant cable entities (those that reach 35 percent of the national audience or more) should be defined as networks and be subject to similar prohibitions on self-supply and financial interest.

9. The regulation of radio station ownership should be maintained and it should be stated that no single entity should be allowed to control more than one hundred radio stations.

10. No network or dominant cable entity should be allowed to own a satellite broadcasting service. The potential for discriminatory treatment of competing products outweighs any public benefit that might be derived from allowing such consolidated control of terrestrial and satellite services.

11. The growth of low-power FM radio stations should be encouraged. These stations are crucial to promoting localism and diversity. The current cap on LPFM licenses should be raised to one thousand with the stipulation that no one owner may operate more than twenty such stations.

12. Grant of license should carry with it the obligation to provide free airtime to political candidates during a period of sixty days leading up to all local, state, and federal elections.

These policy changes are not definitive but begin to suggest ways in which the media playing field might be leveled to promote free and open competition. Only federal regulation can restore competition to the industries that were born of federal regulatory grant. As Alexander Hamilton observed in *The Federalist*, "Why has government been instituted at all? Because the passions of men will not conform to the dictates of reason and justice without restraint."

It is time for the government to restrain the dictates of the dominant media conglomerates in the interest of promoting fair and vigorous competition. It is time to inoculate the body politic against the contagion of self-dealing.

It is time to give meaning to the admonitions of James Madison. "A popular government without popular information or the means to acquire it is but Prologue to a Farce or a Tragedy or both."

V

THE THREAT TO A FREE INTERNET

What Corporate Media Are Doing to Undermine Democracy in Cyberspace and What Government Is *Not* Doing to Prevent It

11

PROTECTING THE FUTURE OF THE FREE INTERNET

BARRY STEINHARDT AND JAY STANLEY

AMERICAN CIVIL LIBERTIES UNION, PROGRAM ON TECHNOLOGY AND LIBERTY

BARRY STEINHARDT *is inaugural director of the Program on Technology and Liberty of the American Civil Liberties Union (ACLU). He was associate director of the ACLU between 1992 and 2002 and is a cofounder of the Global Internet Liberty Campaign (GILC), the world's first international coalition of nongovernmental organizations concerned with the rights of Internet users to privacy and free expression. A graduate of the Northeastern University School of Law, he has published widely on privacy and free expression issues in a variety of periodicals including* USA Today *and is a frequent guest on news and talk programs such as the* Today Show, *CNN's* Crossfire, *and CBS's* Face the Nation *and* Morning News.

JAY STANLEY *is the communications director of the Technology and Liberty Program of the ACLU, where he researches, writes, and speaks about privacy and technology issues. He has been an analyst at the technology research firm Forrester, focusing on public policy issues related to the Internet. A graduate of Williams College with an MA in American History from the University of Virginia, he has also been an American politics editor at* Facts on File.

INTRODUCTION

T he Internet as we have known it is going to change—the only question is how. There's a fight going on over that question, and at stake is nothing less than the Internet's potential as a medium for free expression, civic involvement, and economic innovation. Unfortunately, unless the government changes course and begins to restrain the increasingly concentrated power of the companies that sell Internet access, the Internet's vaunted freedom and openness will dissolve as these private interests gain leverage over our most precious communications medium.

Driving the change is the ongoing conversion by consumers from a dial-up Internet (based on slow modem connections over phone lines) to far-faster "broadband" connections. With dial-up, Internet access is provided over a medium that provides open, equal access to all: the telephone system. But with the shift to broadband facilities like cable, Internet access must be adapted to systems that are far more subject to centralized control.

Freedom of speech is of little value if the forums where that right is commonly exercised are not themselves free. And the Internet is without doubt the most vital and active such forum around today—a place where citizens can publish their views to be seen by a few close friends or spread around the world; where citizens can engage with others on thousands of bulletin boards and chat rooms on nearly any topic, create new communities of interest, or communicate anonymously about difficult topics. It is one of our top entertainment mediums. It is the nation's most comprehensive, flexible, and popular reference work. It is the closest thing ever invented to the vision of a true "free market" of ideas that the American Civil Liberties Union and other groups work hard to defend in so many contexts. As the Supreme Court wrote in 1997, on the Internet "any person with a phone line can become a town crier with a voice that resonates farther than it could from any soapbox."[1]

At the center of the battle over the future of the Internet is the question of whether it is a good idea for the government to impose regulations aimed at preserving the openness of the Internet. In particular, the question is whether regulators should mandate an "open access" policy that requires providers to let customers choose among multiple, competing Internet service providers (ISPs) over their broadband connections. Currently, more often than not customers who obtain broadband service from, say, Adelphia Cable, must also pay for Adelphia as their ISP; they cannot substitute any other ISPs. This raises the possibility that a broadband provider could leverage its control over the on-ramp to the Internet to interfere with the *content* of online communications.

This issue has emerged first with regard to cable Internet providers, because they have been the first dominant providers not subject to open-access regulations. Several years ago, when the ACLU first engaged in the broadband debate, cable was the dominant form of high-speed access. Today, the main alternative, DSL (digital subscriber lines, which adapt regular phone lines for high-speed use), has made substantial inroads, and several other potential alternatives loom on the horizon. Among the 24 percent of adult Americans who have broadband Internet access at home, 54 percent have cable and 42 percent have DSL.[2] Over time, most analysts expect citizens to continue gravitating toward broadband as they tire of the slow pace of the Internet delivered over phone lines. As more citizens do get broadband, Web sites will add fatter and fatter content to their pages, making dial-up even more intolerable and creating a snowball effect.

Meanwhile telephone companies are building fiber-optic connections directly to customers' homes in a few areas, while other companies are working on the possibilities of wireless systems, or using the electrical grid to provide Internet access over power lines. However, the same policy issues raised by cable are also raised by other forms of broadband access. First, few of the prospective broadband facilities will have the qualities of openness—qualities that were consciously cultivated through regulation—that dial-up access brought to the early Internet. Second, the unregulated cable model has been treated by industry and by the leadership of the Federal Communications Commission as a model for how other broadband technologies should be approached by regulators.

As more and more Americans begin accessing the Internet using broadband connections, they are moving, often unknowingly, into a new regulatory environment. The results of this shift can be seen clearly through an examination of the case of cable broadband. Regardless of whether cable wins or loses the race to become the predominant means by which Americans connect to the Internet, it has been the forerunner that raises all the key policy concerns created by the shift to broadband: how regulators have treated it, and how that treatment has differed from the old dial-up Internet; the degree of control over Internet use that cable owners have gained and asserted; and the paucity of true competition faced by providers.

THE INTERNET HAS SUCCEEDED
BECAUSE IT IS OPEN

In order to understand how it is that free expression and other liberties are endangered as the Internet shifts toward broadband, it is important to understand why the Internet grew into the free communications medium that we know today.

There is a common conception that the Internet is "free" in the sense that it is free from government regulation. But that couldn't be further from the truth.

The key characteristic of the Internet that allowed it to explode into American life almost overnight is the fact that the network serves as a neutral, nondiscriminatory "pipe" that automatically carries data from origin to destination without prejudice or interference. No company, individual, or institution has the power to decide what applications are allowed to run by users at the ends of the network, what kinds of data can be moved through the network, or whose data moves faster. This structure, referred to as "dumb" or "end-to-end" networking, allows intelligence, decision making, and innovation to take place on the edges of the network, while the network itself remains neutral. It has allowed innovation to remain in the hands of end users, allowing anyone with an idea and some technical expertise to create a new application and distribute it to anyone else on the Internet.[3]

The end-to-end process is a result of the Internet's technical design at many levels, not least the fact that the dominant means of accessing the network has always been dial-up, in which consumers access the Internet by connecting directly to their ISPs through the telephone network. Dial-up was well suited to a model of free-market competition, because every individual Internet surfer could choose which ISP to use and then connect directly to that company. If users didn't like their ISP, they could switch providers and then connect to the new provider simply by dialing a different phone number. And it was very easy to go into business as an ISP. This spurred development of an extremely healthy and competitive ISP marketplace; there are still several thousand independent ISPs in the United States.

The open rules of the telephone system helped preserve the Internet's "network neutrality," but nondiscriminatory access to the phone system was not inevitable; it was the result of government regulation—a framework consciously designed to promote the principles of openness and nondiscrimination. That framework is called "common carriage."

Common carriage policy requires that a network owner—in this case, a telephone company—not discriminate against information by halting, slowing, or otherwise tampering with the transfer of any data. The purpose of common carriage is to prevent a network owner from leveraging his network's control over the pipeline for communication to gain power or control over the actual information, products, and services that flow through it. This is not a new concept; for well over a century it has been applied in ways that have been central to the economic development of our nation, including canal systems, railroads, public highways, and the telegraph. And common carriage has been applied to the telephone system since the early twentieth century, requiring it to serve all users in an equitable and nondiscriminatory fashion.

The Internet as we now know it would never have emerged had it not been protected by telephone common carrier rules as well as other, more specific regulations issued by the FCC that curbed the power of the telephone companies:

- In 1975 the FCC issued a landmark regulation preventing telephone companies from blocking their customers from attaching their own equipment to the phone network. If the agency had decided this issue the other way, regular Americans would not have been able to use computer modems, and the explosion of online activity would have been blocked.[4]
- In 1980 the agency set out rules that required telephone companies to offer "data services" through separate affiliates because they would have had both the ability and the incentive to use their control of the telephone network to discriminate against unaffiliated, competing data services.[5]
- In 1983 the FCC issued a regulation preventing telephone companies from charging ISPs by the minute for their use of the local telephone network; if they had allowed such charges, consumers would have to pay per-minute fees for Internet access. That would have slowed the growth of the Internet, as such fees have done in Europe.[6]

In short, the impression held by some that the Internet is the product of an unregulated, "government-free zone" is mistaken. Of course, it is always possible that other counterproductive regulations *could* have blocked or stunted development of the Internet. So far, the Internet has largely escaped such harmful regulations—for example, it remains free from censorship, despite two efforts by Congress to reverse that situation (both of which have been blocked by the courts as overly broad restrictions on free speech).[7] But the addition of harmful regulation is not the only danger to the Internet—an equal danger is the *subtraction* of regulations that are vital for protecting the environment of freedom in which the online world has thrived.

THE CASE OF CABLE

Unlike phone companies, cable television providers do not have to provide nondiscriminatory access to their television subscribers, because cable TV is not subject to the common carrier regulatory regime. As a result, the content that cable TV companies deliver is largely under their control. Television content providers are forced to negotiate with cable owners to secure one of the limited number of spots in the channel lineup, while consumers are presented with little ability to customize the content and services they purchase and find themselves subject to the opportunistic pricing whims of their provider.

The Internet is fundamentally different from cable television, yet so far, the FCC is treating cable Internet the same way it treats the one-way delivery of cable television. While cable TV has traditionally been characterized by centralized control over a limited number of channels, Internet services offer access to a limitless network of distributed information sources, requiring no centralized control over content or services. When cable companies provide Internet access, they are performing a new, entirely different role that is much closer to what the phone companies do. Just as the phone companies provide a conduit or "pipe" into the global telephone network, cable broadband providers provide a pipe into the global computer network we call the Internet.

Because the technological architecture and regulatory structure of cable, unlike the dial-up Internet, does not lend itself to free-market competition, consumer and free speech advocates and many others have called for the FCC to place cable broadband under the same common carrier regime that has governed so many analogous networks for more than a century. That way, citizens who are angered by a cable operator's restrictions on content (or high fees and insulting customer service, for that matter) will have alternatives to impotently railing at their provider or giving up high-speed internet access altogether.

The FCC, however, has refused to treat cable broadband as a common carrier and has abandoned the agency's role in making sure our vital public networks remain open—in fact, it has done quite the opposite, making regulatory decisions that, if they stand, will ensure that cable Internet services are not regulated at all. Those regulatory attempts have also been fiercely opposed by the cable industry, which, for the last several years, has lobbied against open access at the federal, state, and local levels, and has fought the issue in the courts as well.

CABLE UNRESTRAINED BY REGULATION

Crucial legal battles are under way over the future of cable broadband, and the outcome may hang on a legal technicality: whether cable broadband is classified as an "information service" or a "telecommunications service."

Because the FCC has refused to require cable companies to provide open access to competing ISPs, a number of cities have tried to do so themselves. An attempt by Portland, Oregon, to mandate open access was struck down by a federal appeals court on the grounds that cable broadband is a "telecommunications service" that can only be regulated by the federal government.[8] The grounds of the court's ruling have an important implication, however, because "telecommunications services" are subject to common carriage requirements. In other words, although Portland lost the battle, the grounds of the court's opinion imply victory in the larger war.

The FCC, meanwhile, decided in March 2002 to classify broadband Internet service over cable as an "interstate information service." That technical redefinition would mean that cable broadband could be completely exempt from federal regulation such as interconnection and common carriage requirements, as well as from oversight by local cable franchising authorities.[9] The FCC's designation was challenged by public interest advocates (including the ACLU), and a federal appeals court (citing the decision in the Portland case) ruled in favor of the challenge. As of this writing, the FCC and the cable companies are expected to appeal the decision to the Supreme Court.[10]

Despite the legal uncertainty surrounding the classification of cable Internet services, and the skepticism that courts have shown so far, the FCC continues to push for deregulation of broadband. Even if cable is ultimately classified as a telecommunications service, which would allow it to be regulated, the FCC could still claim that it has the authority to voluntarily forbear from regulating it.

Another approach that has been advocated for curbing the power of broadband providers is to institute a set of "antidiscrimination" regulations which would allow providers to maintain monopolies on ISP services over their wires, but set forth a rule that bans them from interfering with most of the uses to which their customers wish to put their Internet connections. This approach has been embraced by a coalition that includes Microsoft, Amazon.com, and other companies that recognize the threat of Internet discrimination. The ultimate goal of this approach is the same as open access: keeping the Internet free and open.

In the dial-up world, then, the telephone infrastructure with its common carrier regulatory framework protected the openness of the Internet. But cable companies have never worked under that framework. They are used to the proprietary nature and total control they wield with cable television and seemingly want to extend that model to cable broadband. If cable became the dominant form of access to the Internet, that would leave consumers with dangerously little choice about how to get online.

CABLE UNRESTRAINED BY COMPETITION

The preferred check on corporate power in America is free-market competition. But cable has been sheltered from that competition because it has not been subject to regulations requiring open access to the network by competitive ISPs and because of its centralized technological architecture.

Many Americans currently face a choice between broadband access through their cable provider or no broadband access at all. Many Americans can never get DSL, in part because it is only available to those who live close to a telephone company central office, which usually means those who live in dense, urban neighborhoods.[11] And cable industry consolidation will in all likelihood continue to increase the power of each cable company. According to data provided by the National Cable and Telecommunications Association,[12] the top five cable companies in the United States control 81 percent of the market, with 52 percent of the market controlled by Comcast and Time Warner alone. Of course, from the point of view of the vast majority of individual households, 100 percent of the cable market is controlled by just one company.

Some opponents of regulation have claimed that open-access regulations are not necessary because some cable Internet providers have begun to offer access to multiple ISPs over their systems.[13] But there are several ways to provide "open access," and they are not created equal. The model of open access that many large cable operators are proposing is "rebranding and resale of wholesale services." Under rebranding, the cable operator still controls all the technical components of the Internet service, from cable modem to Internet backbone. As a result, customers get the same service that the cable operator offers—good, bad, or indifferent—and with the same potential limitations on content or services. The "competing" ISPs have no control over the quality or nature of the service provided.[14] Rebranding provides an empty shell of real competition that does little to bring about the good effects that competition is supposed to serve. It does not create pressure on providers to innovate, improve their services, or avoid steps that will anger their customers (including violating their privacy rights or their expectation of content-neutral Internet service).

In short, the cable Internet providers are not restrained effectively by either competition or regulation. The power of cable giants like Comcast over many of their customers rivals the power of Ma Bell in the days of the telephone monopoly—but Ma Bell was subject to common carrier regulations that prohibited it from abusing its monopoly to affect content.

THE POTENTIAL FOR TOTAL CONTROL OVER INTERNET USE

The lack of regulatory protection for cable broadband subscribers is all the more alarming because cable networks are subject to a nearly unlimited degree of centralized control on the technical level. When customers access the Internet using a cable modem, they are wired directly into the cable provider's system as part of one big local area network (LAN)—much the same way that computers in an office are connected together. And like an office LAN, everyone shares the same network and everyone follows the same path online—from user modem, to cable provider, to the Internet.[15]

Also like an office LAN, the administrator of a cable broadband system —the cable company—has many opportunities for interfering with online activities. In fact, cable companies have the potential for an all-seeing, all-controlling power over the activities of customers on their networks—often in ways that are invisible to their customers:[16]

- *Basic control of the service.* Providers of course have control over the fundamentals of a customer's Internet connection. For example, they can restrict the number of computers that a customer connects to the cable modem through a home network. They can control the overall speed and reliability of a customer's online experience. And they can set the price for various levels of high-speed access.

- *Control over applications.* Providers can block their customers from using particular applications, such as video conferencing, Internet telephony, and virtual private networks (which can connect far-flung individuals through a secure "private" network). Even if they don't block such uses outright, they can require that customers use the company's own, proprietary software for carrying them out (software that can in turn have any number of limitations and controls built in). In short, they can insert themselves between one end of the Internet pipe and the other by blocking particular uses of that pipe. As cable providers' dominance grows, so will their power to interfere with the innovation and experimentation that an end-to-end Internet encourages.

- *Control over access to content.* Even more frightening is the growing ability of cable providers to interfere with content. Providers can slow or block access to certain Web sites—those whose owners won't make a deal with the cable company's ISP, perhaps, or those with content considered objectionable for political or competitive reasons. At the same time they can speed up downloads from affiliated sites, or sites that have paid for the privilege. That is like the phone company being allowed to own restaurants and then providing good service and clear signals to customers who call Domino's and frequent busy signals, disconnects, and static for those calling Pizza Hut. Outrageous? It would be entirely possible if the telephone system wasn't regulated under the common carrier framework. At a time when many cable providers have assembled far-flung business empires on the premise that cross-promotion and other "synergies" will yield big profits, they will come under strong pressure to do the equivalent. And what can be done in the commercial context could be done just as easily to political content.

- *Ability to force-feed content.* Cable providers can also use their monopoly power to force-feed content to customers by requiring them to access the Internet through a particular home page containing material selected by the cable company. AOL has done something similar with its "welcome screen," which has become a powerful communications tool for the company, allowing it to plug its affiliated companies and reap advertising revenue through an often blurry mix of news stories and paid promotions.[17]

- *Ability to violate privacy.* Finally, a cable provider's absolute control over its network gives it the technical capacity to record everything its customers do online, down to the smallest mouse click. In February 2002, the nation's third-largest cable company, Comcast, without notification to its customers, began to track their Web browsing.[18] Although the practice became public and was quickly ended under a cloud of bad publicity, personal information such as Web-browsing habits is increasingly being viewed by corporations as a valuable resource to be mined and sold for marketing purposes. In addition, the efforts of media companies to keep their songs, movies, and other content from being shared over the Internet is creating strong pressures to monitor consumers' online activities. Such incentives for violating privacy aren't going to go away, and the increasing power of cable providers (combined with the lack of privacy protections in the law) makes future surveillance attempts like Comcast's inevitable.

In short, cable providers are under no obligation to remain a neutral pipe for content over an end-to-end Internet—and have many ways of interfering with that pipe. They have both the financial incentive and the technological capability to interfere with the Internet as a free and neutral medium for the exchange of information.

THE RESULTS OF THIS STATE OF AFFAIRS

The early signs of cable's monopolistic dominance are already in evidence. Cable providers have imposed numerous restrictions on the uses to which their customers can put their Internet connections. Some cable providers have issued blanket bans (unrelated to the customer's consumption of bandwidth) on the use of virtual private networks (VPNs), a common application that allows individuals to plug into secure networks from remote locations. Others have prohibited the common online activity of file sharing, which is famous for involving the trading of copyrighted music files but which also has many legal and beneficial applications.[19]

In a perfect example of the high-handedness that can result from this state of affairs, Comcast has been telling some of its customers that they must reduce their bandwidth usage, despite having provided no notice or rules on specific usage limits. In a telling detail, one customer even insisted on anonymity when making critical comments about this state of affairs to a reporter, lest Comcast retaliate against him by cutting off his service.[20] No customers of a company that actually faced competition would be afraid to exercise their free speech rights to criticize the service they've received.

The broad effect on consumers of the lack of competition in cable broadband can be seen in Tacoma, Washington. Like most American cities, Tacoma had just one cable provider, in this case AT&T. But once competition arrived there through the creation of a second, overbuilt network, the number of consumer complaints about AT&T's incumbent system dropped significantly, and it was forced to improve its services in order to compete. AT&T's network in Tacoma became significantly more advanced more quickly than most cable broadband systems in offering new services such as video-on-demand and Internet telephony. Competition also yielded lower prices for high-speed Internet access services in Tacoma.[21]

Competition in Tacoma, however, came about through overbuilding—the construction of a costly and duplicative cable network on top of the existing system—which is rare and is likely to remain so; most Americans will continue to be served by only one cable provider. But Tacoma does show the difference that true competition can make.

FACILITIES-BASED COMPETITION

Opponents of regulation, including FCC chairman Michael Powell, argue that even though particular forms of broadband access like cable may offer consumers no choice of ISP, dissatisfied consumers will always be able to go online through other means. This has been labeled "facilities-based competition."

Although DSL has recently made substantial gains in attracting customers, facilities-based competition is pure theory for the millions of Americans who currently do not have access to DSL, either because it is not technologically possible to provide it where they live or because they live in a low-income or rural area where their telephone company has decided it is not worthwhile to provide the service.

In addition, Powell and other opponents of open-access regulation, far from applying the telephone system's open-access regulatory framework to cable broadband, are actually seeking to do the opposite: using the government's hands-off approach to cable to justify an effort to dismantle the open-access approach to DSL. In February 2002 the FCC tentatively concluded that DSL broadband services are "information services," opening the legal door to such deregulation.[22] In August 2003 a divided FCC issued a new set of regulations that left in place a reduced set of open-access rules for DSL but eliminated it for advanced broadband services like fiber-optic cable.[23]

At the same time, the telephone industry undertook a tremendous lobbying effort aimed at cable-style deregulation of DSL networks, which the industry has framed as a demand for "regulatory parity" with cable. At one point the industry succeeded in convincing the US House of Representatives to pass legislation eliminating open-access requirements on DSL networks.[24]

The regulatory framework that is applied to cable needs to be changed to match the framework that has always been applied to the telephone system; unfortunately, the opposite is happening: the government's hands-off approach to cable is actually being used to justify an effort to dismantle the open-access approach to DSL.

BEYOND CABLE

The push to deregulate even DSL, which has historical ties to the common carrier phone system rather than to the entirely proprietary cable industry, makes it clear that the current policy battles are not an isolated result of unique historical factors connected to cable. Rather, they are the outcome of a broad regulatory approach that will raise the same issues when applied to other technologies that are often envisioned as "competing" with cable and DSL, such as power-line Internet service or wide-area wireless services, which could both prove equally susceptible to monopoly operation. Even visions of spontaneous, decentralized "mesh networks" of interconnected short-range Wi-Fi wireless access points still ultimately depend on fiber or other wired connections that are also subject to such control.

Even in the theoretical world where several broadband options coexist for every American, it is not likely that such a situation would long endure. One means of providing data will probably prove cheaper and better than the others; that facility will then achieve dominance, and Americans will find themselves in the same situation as those who today must accept cable broadband on the cable providers' terms or do without broadband at all.

In the event that facilities-based competition succeeded in providing equally attractive and persistent choices for all, consumers would still be left with only a handful of competitors to choose from, which does not make for healthy and vigorous competition. In those areas that do have a choice between cable and DSL, that kind of duopoly is now the reality. As antitrust experts have long noted, when an industry comes under the control of just a few players, competition is nearly always reduced, because even without explicit (and therefore illegal) agreements and collusion among the few remaining competitors, companies are often able to feel their way to anticompetitive understandings through such mechanisms as price signaling and other unspoken communications. Once cable and DSL, for example, became entrenched competitors, the competition between them would be likely to wither.

In addition, even where true competition survives, the need for open access remains. Passenger trains were never freed from common carrier obligations just because people could also fly, drive, or walk to their destinations.

In fact, the likely outcome is that just as multiple transportation modes coexist, so will multiple Internet-access modes, each of which is superior in different situations, such as rural and urban areas. But, just as in transportation, many particular individuals will be forced to rely on just the one facility that fits their needs.

THE GOVERNMENT MUST PROTECT THE INTERNET

Critics of the call for open access have charged that these concerns are "theoretical." Of course any train wreck, no matter how inevitable it appears to be, remains "theoretical" until the actual collision takes place. And the fact is, the FCC's current policy has placed communications giants on a collision course with free speech and the open Internet.

When a handful of corporations control access to the Internet, and have the technical means to interfere with the free flow of information, they will do so. That is the case, not only because they can make money by using this power to cut deals and steer their customers to particular commercial destinations, but also, potentially, because they have a political interest in certain issues or candidates, or because they have an interest in pleasing particular government officials who, for example, may have the power to decide regulatory proceedings affecting the company.[25]

Americans cannot expect major corporations—which are under intense pressure from Wall Street to meet earnings expectations every quarter, and in any case see their primary duty as serving the interests of their shareholders, not protecting free speech—to refrain from such interference on their own. So the important question becomes: what will hold them back? As we have seen, cable broadband providers are currently restrained neither by competition nor by regulation.

The broadband situation would be bad enough if it were just a case of a market where monopolistic companies are restrained neither by competition nor by the government. But Internet access is not just any business; it involves the sacred role of making available to citizens a forum for speech and self-expression—a forum that is perhaps the most valuable new civic institution to appear in the United States in the past century. An unregulated monopoly is bad for consumers; a monopoly in Internet access is far worse: it is bad for *citizens*, and therefore bad for America.

Free speech is not an economic good. That is not to say it is not economically valuable—the openness of American society in general, and free speech in particular, has played a crucial role in supporting the artistic, intellectual, and social vitality of our nation, and therefore its economic vitality as well. But like many general goods, free speech is subject to the problem of collective action—individual, profit-oriented corporations won't necessarily pay to protect it. It is not a necessary or natural result of competitive markets or other economic activity; the requirements of free speech and the requirements of profit-oriented corporations are too different. Free speech requires the protection of minority and unpopular—sometimes radically unpopular—viewpoints and expressions. Competitive businesses have no incentive to protect such voices—and indeed tend to cater to what is popular and shun what is hated or disliked. Free speech requires that no voices be permitted to dominate to the exclusion of others; businesses tend to rush toward proven successes, often sucking the oxygen out of smaller, less established voices, not only preventing them from a shot at success themselves, but also reducing the diversity of voices overall (a tendency that has long been observed, for example, in Hollywood and in the music industry).

The refusal to create competition in cable broadband and the push to dismantle it in DSL appear to be partly the product of a naive antiregulatory attitude that scorns any government rules as contrary to the "free market." What this viewpoint fails to account for is the fact that competition and regulation are not always at odds. In fact, it is often impossible to have competition *without* regulation; government intervention is needed not only to set ground rules so that competition is kept within socially desirable boundaries (for example by prohibiting cheating on measurements or gangland hits on one's competition) but sometimes to create the very arena in which competition can take place to begin with. Sometimes regulation is needed to provide a level playing field—and sometimes it is needed to create the playing field itself. For example, without government rules establishing and protecting copyrights, intellectual property would not even exist as "property," and therefore there would be no market for it. And without government rules creating and preserving broadband Internet competition, there will be no marketplace for it either, and no competitive restraint on the shrinking number of corporations that are likely to control access to the Internet.

Just as a free market of ideas requires rules in order to be effective—such

as the often complicated parliamentary rules that govern debate in any deliberative body—so, too, can an economic free market. Unless, as some have
suggested, the government simply abandons the goal of creating competition
and treats broadband as a regulated monopoly (unlikely in the current political climate), it must take regulatory steps to insure that free access to the
Internet is protected by competition. Without government interference, the
"free market" will yield monopolies that are anything but free.

If the government remains passive as the Internet shifts from the open
phone system to closed, corporate-controlled broadband networks, the online
world will be transformed in the process into a place where not all thoughts,
expressions, publications, and other content is treated equally. The ever-
more-exclusive club of cable operators must be counterbalanced by competition, which in this case can only be assured by common carrier regulations.

The wealthy and powerful cable industry has so far succeeded in blocking action to protect the openness of the Internet. Only if citizens demand
action can the precious neutrality and independence of the Internet be pre-
served. Letting access to the Internet fall under the control of a tiny cluster
of large companies would not be good for the Internet, for the free flow of
ideas and information, or for the greater good of our democratic society.

NOTES

1. *ACLU v. Reno*, 117 S. Ct. 2329 (1997).

2. John B. Horrigan, "Pew Internet Project Data Memo," Pew Internet &
American Life Project, April 19, 2004, http://www.pewinternet.org/reports/pdfs/PIP
_Broadband04.DataMemo.pdf.

3. See Lawrence Lessig, *The Future of Ideas: The Fate of the Commons in a
Connected World* (New York: Random House, 2001).

4. *Proposals for New or Revised Classes of Interstate and Foreign Message
Tolls Telephone Service (MTS) and Wide Area Telephone Service (WATS)*, 56 FCC 2.d
593 (1975), cited in Jason Oxman, "The FCC and the Unregulation of the Internet,"
Office of Plans and Policy Working Paper No. 31, FCC, July 1999.

5. *In the Matter of Amendment of Section 64.702 of the Commission's Rules
and Regulations (Second Computer Inquiry)*, 77 FCC 2.d 384, 419 (1980); cited in
Oxman, "The FCC and the Unregulation of the Internet."

6. *MTS and WATS Market Structure*, 97 FCC 2.d 682, 711–22 (1983); cited in
Oxman, "The FCC and the Unregulation of the Internet."

7. *ACLU v. Reno*, 1997; *Ashcroft v. ACLU,* 122 S. Ct. 1700 (2002).

8. *AT&T Corp. v. City of Portland*, No. 99-35609 (9th Circuit, June 22, 2000),

http://caselaw.lp.findlaw.com/cgi-bin/getcase.pl?court=9th&navby=case&no
=9935609.

9. *Appropriate Regulatory Treatment for Broadband Access to the Internet over Cable Facilities*, Notice of Proposed Rulemaking, CS Docket No. 02-52; FCC 02-77 (April 17, 2002).

10. Federal Communications Commission, *In the Matter of Inquiry Concerning High-Speed Access to the Internet over Cable and Other Facilities, Internet over Cable Declaratory Ruling, Appropriate Regulatory Treatment of Broadband Access to the Internet over Cable Facilities*, Declaratory Ruling and Notice of Proposed Rulemaking, GN Docket No. 00-185, CS Docket No. 02-52, FCC 02-77, March 12, 2002; *Brand X Internet Services v. FCC*, 345 F. 3d 1120 (9th Cir. 2003).

11. The farther away from a central officer a customer lives, the slower his or her connection speed will be. Service is not likely to be available at all to those who live farther than fifteen thousand feet away.

12. National Cable and Telecommunications Association, "Industry Overview: Top 25 MSOs as of June 2003," http://www.ncta.com/industry_overview/top50mso .cfm (accessed April 1, 2004).

13. The best example of ISP choice on cable today, AOL/Time Warner, supports just three nonaffiliated ISPs—and only because it was forced to offer a choice of ISPs by the Federal Trade Commission as a condition of its merger with AOL.

14. Columbia Telecommunications Corporation, "Technological Analysis of Open Access and Cable Television Systems," December 2001, http://www.aclu.org/ Privacy/Privacy.cfm?ID=13627&c=252. This report was commissioned by the ACLU with the Center for Digital Democracy to examine the technical feasibility of open access on cable systems. Rebranders can compete in offering proprietary content, such as chat rooms and home pages. But not in the core function of an ISP: providing a pipe with which to access the Internet.

15. Ibid.

16. Ibid.

17. See Brendan Koerner, "Click Here for Britney: AOL Muscles Its Way into Online Journalism," *Washington Monthly*, July 13, 2001, http://www.tompaine.com/ feature.cfm?ID=4428.

18. Stefanie Olsen and Rachel Konrad, "Comcast Privacy Move Its Latest Woe," CNET, February 13, 2002, http://news.com.com/2100-1023-836937.html.

19. For a survey of restrictions imposed by cable Internet providers, see Timothy Wu, "Network Neutrality, Broadband Discrimination," *Journal of Telecommunications and High Technology*, http://papers.ssrn.com/sol3/papers.cfm?abstract_id =388863. See also Chris Oakes, "Cable Net Users Feel Squeezed," *Wired News*, August 18, 2000, http://www.wired.com/news/technology/0,1282,38227,00.html, and Comcast, "Terms of Service: Acceptable Use Policy, http://www.comcast.net/ terms/use.jsp.

20. Farhad Manjoo, "One Cable Company to Rule Them All," *Salon.com*, March 17, 2004, http://www.salon.com/tech/feature/2004/03/17/comcast/.

21. CTC, "Technological Analysis of Open Access and Cable Television Systems"; Jane Hadley, "Cheaper Cable? Go to Tacoma; in Seattle, Rates Will Jump," *Seattle Post-Intelligencer*, May 29, 2002, http://seattlepi.nwsource.com/local/72341 _modem29.shtml.

22. Federal Communications Commission, *In the Matter of Appropriate Framework for Broadband Access to the Internet over Wireline Facilities*, CC Docket No. 02-33, February 15, 2002.

23. Federal Communications Commission, Triennial Review Order, August 21, 2003, http://hraunfoss.fcc.gov/edocs_public/attachmatch/FCC-03-36A1.pdf. Federal Communications Commission, "FCC Adopts New Rules for Network Unbundling Obligations of Incumbent Local Phone Carriers," press release, February 20, 2003, http://hraunfoss.fcc.gov/edocs_public/attachmatch/DOC-231344A1.pdf. In March 2004, the DC Circuit of the US Court of Appeals upheld those provisions in *United States Telecom Association v. Federal Communications Commission*, http://pacer .cadc.uscourts.gov/docs/common/opinions/200403/00-1012b.pdf.

24. *The Internet Freedom and Broadband Deployment Act* (Tauzin-Dingell bill) of 2002, HR 1542.

25. For an allegation of such political influence on a major media company, see Paul Krugman, "Channels of Influence," *New York Times*, March 25, 2003, www .nytimes.com/2003/03/25/opinion/25KRUG.html.

12

FROM BROADCAST TO BROADBAND

ON AIR WITH THE INTERNET

REED F. HUNDT
FORMER CHAIR, FCC

REED E. HUNDT, *chairman of the Federal Communications Commission (FCC) from 1993 to 1997, is presently a senior advisor on information industries to McKinsey & Company, a worldwide management consulting firm, and is a special advisor to the Blackstone Group, a New York–based private equity firm. He is also a member of the advisory committee at the Yale School of Management and is on the boards of directors of Intel, Pronto Networks, Tropos Networks, Polyserve, Megisto, and Entrisphere. In addition to being the author of* You Say You Want a Revolution: A Story of Information Age Politics *(Yale University Press, 2000), Mr. Hundt is cochairman of the Forum on Communications and Society at the Aspen Institute. Earning his Bachelor of Arts degree, magna cum laude, in history from Yale University, he also holds a JD from the Yale Law School. A member of the District of Columbia, Maryland, and California bars, he was a partner in the Washington, DC, law firm of Latham & Watkins prior to becoming FCC chairman.*

255

Broadcast television soon will be like an old grocery store or department store chain: more valuable for its real estate than for its original purpose. What the telephone did to the telegraph, the auto to the horse and buggy, the airplane to the train—that is what the broadband Internet will do to broadcast television. But it may well be that broadcast stations prove to own a phenomenally valuable asset that is best used not for broadcast television but for wireless broadband connection to the airwaves. I speak of the precious, invisible, ever replenishable airwaves.

Whether broadcast TV owners decide to use those airwaves in the most valuable possible way, and then while they still have political power get Congress to permit them to exploit those airwaves, all depends on whether broadcasters can make a compelling case for serving the nation in the manner they were originally supposed to do.

Soon after the end of the Second World War the United States embarked on an experiment the likes of which no country had ever undertaken. The plan was to tie every city and town into a common, instantaneous TV network of information. The purpose was to create a common culture, including in particular a continuing consensus for such national goals as fighting the cold war and consuming at a pace that would inevitably give American firms the scale to dominate the global economy.

The TV network would carry information, including news and entertainment, but most importantly the network would also carry advertising saturated with mainstream values from a few to the many. Two or three companies would make or buy the content and send it to the entire population. Local outlets, also called affiliates, could generate some of their own programs, but the evening for the most part was when New York City (and later Hollywood) decided what America wanted.

The local audiences could balk, presumably, but we are talking here of the magic called television. If Sid Caesar and Molly Goldberg weren't perfect for Peoria, Peoria quickly adopted them as natives. After all, TV was by far the most intrinsically fascinating medium to reach the human senses that had ever been invented in history. Even the printing press was only a modest improvement on illuminated manuscripts compared to the upgrade TV was relative to radio, not to mention vaudeville theater. In truth, TV was from the beginning a gold mine for the station owners, the investors in networks, the writers and actors, the advertisers, and the TV set manufacturers and distributors. And the consumers paid nothing beyond the price of the set, so nearly 100 percent penetration was guaranteed: there hadn't been anything better since sliced bread and sliced bread was not nearly as good.

The government, meanwhile, would supervise the creation of the TV network. It decided who would own the outlets in each city and town. Most important, it would threaten the TV network masters with numerous sanctions in the event that they displeased the government. The Janet Jackson incident at the Super Bowl—the Case of the Ripped Bustier—demonstrates that sixty years after this grand plan was initiated the government still retains a supervisory role over broadcast. This role—basically of censor, albeit an indirect one—is acknowledged by the industry, feared and loathed by what are loosely called the icons of popular culture, and welcomed by most people, other than law professors troubled by the coexistence of different First Amendment standards for competing media like broadcast and cable. For cable, not to mention the Internet, every night displays far more such and such than Janet Jackson's metallic whatever and depicts men and women acting far more violently than Justin Timberlake's campy clowning. But no one utters a peep. Only broadcast is the country's medium, and as such it must reflect in its content a base line of commonly acceptable material.

Yet on the commercial level broadcast is no longer what it was in the first fifty years of its existence. The first reason is that broadcast depends on cable and satellite to reach homes, and as a result now lacks its ability to bond the nation to its TV network of information. Cable and satellite together reach nearly 90 percent of American households. They carry the handful of broadcast channels but add to the mix another eighty-five on average for cable and well more than a hundred for satellite. As skimpy and silly as are most cable news channels, in the aggregate they do as much or more to pass on information to the country than broadcast TV does now.

Meanwhile, to compete against cable's multiple channels of saccharine and sexy, sporty and squalid, slick and simple, broadcast has had to make all its content into the one thing cable cannot easily be in its prepackaged, studioless world: namely, broadcast now always tries to appear to be absolutely immediate. Everything is news as it happens. This of course is a con. But, like Houdini's or even Shakespeare's audiences, TV audiences understand in principle that *Survivor* and *Joe Millionaire* and *60 Minutes* and *Dateline* are not really occurring in real time on the other side of the screen, but they suspend disbelief easily and cheerfully. So in millions of homes folks yell at Regis's hapless guest the answer to a truly elementary question as if the guest were in the next room eager for the help in light of a momentary fit of absolute ignorance. The news isn't really news but rather opinions (often groundless, relentlessly popular, and poorly thought through). But no matter, broadcast TV packages everything as news. Perhaps the truest statements of the way America is now can be found in the mix of lies and truth that the reality TV contestants find acceptable. Certainly the era in which broadcast TV anchors could define America for America is long gone; reality TV mocks that ancient time.

The second reason broadcast's role is irretrievably changed is the Internet. Men aged eighteen to thirty-four in the United States watched 12 percent less TV (broadcast and cable) last fall than they did the previous year. About 75 percent of them had Internet access. They are playing games, talking about sports, chilling with their buddies, but now on the Internet instead of exclusively in a group in a room vegging out in front of the boob tube.

Newspapers did not welcome radio; movies did not welcome television; broadcast TV has not been the birthplace of a Yahoo or AOL or any important TV network site. Why the old media cannot easily evolve into the owners of the new media is an important question and one perhaps best answered by Clay Christensen of the Harvard Business School or other theorists of disruptive innovation. For present purposes, it suffices to note that as broadband continues to penetrate American households, and as the actuarial tables prove to be destiny, the Internet generation will consume video, voice, information, and even advertisements from the TV network.

Broadcast television is far from dead, but it is clearly moving to its palmy retirement condo, and that isn't nearly as grand as the palatial space it used to have in American consciousness. Like anyone approaching the end of a business career, broadcast is looking now to find a way to cash out. Consolidation seems the likely answer. Some favor horizontal merging—the combining of many stations and outlets under one roof. Others favor vertical consolidation—the merging of conduit and content, such as Comcast and Disney.

These combinations are inevitable in general, although of course no specific deal is easy to predict. But they cannot halt the more important trend: the end of one-to-many broadcast as the way of tying the country together and the creation of many-to-many communications as our common fabric.

But of course this latter fabric is not intrinsically American; only by the wise action of your Federal Communications Commission coupled with the inventive spirit of hundreds of thousands of entrepreneurs did America seize the early lead in creating and defining the Internet. Broadband, or high speed Internet access, is much more a Japanese and Korean experience than American as of now, given their broadband penetration rates that are between two and three times greater than America's.

Nor does broadband yet have any intrinsically American purpose. Whereas television's birthright was to make the many one by broadcasting from one to many, the Internet from the beginning was a collective medium with no proprietor and an intense focus on the unmediated individual as the primary presence. Indeed by dint of anonymity, that presence was potentially more minatory and aloof than any audience of easily pleased television watchers ever was. If in numbers there is strength, on broadcast that is the strength of the common denominator to bring everyone to its level. On the Internet the value of the network increases exponentially according to the number of users (Metcalfe's law, named after Bob Metcalfe, an early Internet inventor), but nothing except participation makes the users have even reaction in common. On the Net, everything is always, it seems, subject to vote, and votes bind no one to anything. For this reason, Net users may see fewer reasons for society to exist than do the consumers of other mediums.

Broadcasters cannot hope to emulate the experience of the Net, any more than radio could compete with television in terms of impact on the senses. But broadcasters have the lineage of serving the public interest, notwithstanding much debate about whether Ms. Jackson was consistent with that tradition. The opportunity exists for broadcasters to find a way out of the Internet maelstrom. They could decide at the station or network level to use their spectrum—indeed only a little of it would do, since they have so much—to create a universal national wireless broadband access network. This spectrum is nice, because as everyone who has tuned in a noncable channel knows, broadcast signals go through buildings. For the lawyers in the reading audience, it is the radio waves and not the content that makes it so. These same radio waves could fairly easily carry the Internet to and from the user. Indeed television sets could be what computer folks call clients—devices that give access to the Net. With the client embedded in the TV set, and wireless connection to the Internet facilitated by using a few of the broadcast industry's channels, the broadcasters could fairly claim that they—and not cable or satellite or telephony—deserve government support for providing 100 percent Internet access at an affordable price to all Americans.

Wireless broadband will have to be proved technically for this idea to be plausible. That, however, is the easier of the problems. The harder one is finding broadcasters who would like to use some of their spectrum for the Internet instead of for sending channels of video. If they believed the Internet ruled, perhaps they could believe they need to use their spectrum while it has value as a physical medium for the Net. Barring such a change in direction for broadcasters, Net access will be provided around some other spectrum, whose owners were less unwilling, and broadcasters will find their time to be in the Net story will have passed them by.

As Thomas Hazlett has pointed out, the more than three hundred public broadcasting stations in America in fact would like to give back to the government their analog broadcasting stations. That is valuable spectrum in every city in the United States. Hazlett estimated that one TV channel in one reasonably sized city is worth up to $300 million if (and only if) the spectrum is used for some form of wireless broadband. And the PBS stations want to give it back to the government! Until folks start mailing in money because they think taxes aren't enough, you won't see this sort of generosity.

The motive of the PBS stations is this: hardly anyone watches their analog broadcasts over the air. Almost all their audience is watching them on cable or off the satellite. They are paying electricity bills for broadcasting to no one. Moreover, they are willing to broadcast digitally.

So here we are worrying about media concentration and yet some stations are trying to exit the business altogether. It seems clear that trying to bring in new broadcasters is impossible under these circumstances. But the PBS broadcasters are showing the way to a good answer for the purposes of diversity and innovation. All broadcasters should give back their analog spectrum right away, not just PBS. Then billions of dollars of spectrum would be back in the hands of the trustees of the public, the government.

The government should then regrant the spectrum for wireless broadcast. Some portion, perhaps up to thirty megahertz, should be allocated to a neutral manager for the purpose of broadband wireless on open standards. Any component maker or network service provider could use the spectrum for free, but the standards would have to be open for any hardware or software interface. The rest should not be licensed at all, even to a neutral manager. None of it needs to be auctioned to a proprietary user.

The real value of the spectrum would lie in the businesses it would incentivize.

In the wake of this spectrum grant, the government should also guarantee to wireless broadband companies the right to attach antennas to telephone poles and street lamps for minimal public charges. These are public assets and should be made available for public purposes. With this right and access to spectrum, we can assume that wireless broadband will have a chance to prove in the market that it can bring online tens of millions of homes in addition to the cable and telephone broadband subscribers.

The goal should be to bring all America into the broadband medium. After all, if this is not the goal, broadband would be the first important medium in American history that was not made, through governmental incentives, affordable to 100 percent of homes. It may prove necessary to put some extra money in the form of an assignable tax credit in the pocket of broadband subscribers. Such a subscriber could add this credit to his or her own cash for the purpose of buying broadband access. If the provider would normally charge $30 a month, a credit of $10 a month usable by the provider should cause the provider to drop the cash price to $20. At such lower levels —about the average telephone line price per month in America—we can reasonably suppose that 90 percent of all households would buy broadband.

Some say that broadband penetration is limited by the penetration of PCs, which now is about 70 percent of households. But in fact PC penetration continues to go up steadily. The reasons are twofold: PCs get cheaper and they are now also communication devices. Another way to grasp that virtually all Americans have or will have soon the willingness and interest to go on the Net is to note that close to 90 percent of all students under college age already have been online and nearly all of them want that to be a feature of their lives. As the younger generation becomes older, the demand for all to be on the Net all the time will be real. If prices are affordable, we can become a Broadband Nation.

In this event, who will care, or even remember, debates about media consolidation? The notion that a network should own only a limited amount of local TV stations will seem quaint. Instead people may care about consolidation in e-commerce or e-mail.

Imagine what an all-broadband media would feel like from the perspective of the user. First, the consumer can select among devices to access the TV network. Cell phones, personal digital assistants, notebooks, laptops, desktops, set-top boxes on TV sets, TV sets themselves, and innumerable other electronic devices will contain communication chips using standards such as Wi-Fi to send and receive radio signals establishing contact with the TV network. If the speed of transfer is fast enough, the signals can carry cinema-quality video. Under these circumstances, broadcast TV is just another method of sending information. It will compete on price and quality. Since it cannot receive information, its value is limited.

The wireless communication devices will need to reach antennas. Broadcast antennas are limited by the government. To create an open, diverse, broadband market, the government will need to order that critical antenna locations, such as hilltops and streets through canyons of rock or buildings, be shared by rival antennas or that commonly used antennas be set up.

The wireless devices will need to reach the Internet. The government will need to assure that software protocols cannot be broken or altered in order to seize competitive advantage.

Spectrum will have to be available to all user devices. To this end the government has to make sure no one corners the spectrum market.

The content on the Internet by definition cannot be limited. Anyone can put any information on a server. However, some firms may seek market power by controlling the rights to creative content or events. Government will have a role over time in assuring that monopoly not arise on the content level of the distribution system.

However, none of the concerns mentioned here is nearly as problematic as trying to maintain diversity in the analog media market. There access to spectrum and to the means of distribution is limited. The government has in some years tried to assure diversity of content and distribution. In other years it is has been indifferent. But in all circumstances, the market itself has tended toward consolidation. The Internet is not necessarily headed in that direction, provided that users can get high-speed broadband access to the Web.

The worries of a broadband age will be what they will be. What is important is to push innovation toward a broadband outcome so that the constraints on diversity of opinion, point of view, and ownership may be lessened as soon as possible. After all, it is plain already that on the Web billions, not just a handful, of sources of content may be generated. What is not so clear is whether those sources are of high enough production value to constitute true alternatives to broadcast networks. However, Clay Christensen of the Harvard Business School teaches that innovation often comes from below on the price curve. There is nothing wrong with introducing disruptive change into a consolidated media through the channel of a new medium that at least as of now appears quite resistant to consolidation.

Yet what is the government's response? So far, the FCC has done little or nothing to meet the PBS offer. What the FCC should do is simple: command by rule the turning off of all analog signals and the exclusive reliance on digital only. This was done by Germany with no ill effects that anyone has noticed. The rule should be announced now and made effective in one year. Anyone who lacks a digital TV receiver could buy a box at Radio Shack or Best Buy and put it down on the TV set—or just rely on cable and satellite as nearly 90 percent already do—and never miss a second of TV watching.

Consciously or unconsciously, the government may be concerned that as the broadcast era is overtaken by the Web and other innovations, the ability of a few to control the attitudes of the many will diminish. Indeed there is a long history of elites struggling to use mass-market media in order to maintain their status as elites in the face of the obvious problem that the masses win any contest determined by head count. Making it difficult to vote or hard to find a way to influence the votes of others are two consistent strains in the way elites have shaped and used mass media. The Internet is much more elusive than traditional media. The means of controlling it are not yet reliably determined. Even more important, the culture of the Net, at least so far, appears adamantly opposed to control by elites.

The prospect exists that just as Net users are able to coordinate their buying habits through eBay and set prices in effect by consensus, so they could also bid on political matters. It is not too fantastical to imagine deliberative software permitting voters to consider on the Net in large groups the answers to key policy questions and then reach consensus on the outcome. Certainly juries every day do the same thing to general acclaim of the process, save for exceptions that usually seem to prove the rule.

The coming of widespread deliberative democracy on the Net would be a fulfillment of the original dream for broadcast TV. With the assumption that the owners of the networks would serve the public interest, the high concept for broadcast at the time of its origin was indeed the creation of a wiser, more participatory democracy. To some extent broadcast can claim credit for achieving this result. But the current state of the industry plainly disappoints its original idealists. The Net can now step forward to keep promises technology made to democracy. It's high time.

VI

DECLINE IN LOCALISM

How Corporate Media Have Taken Over
the Public Airwaves and
What Is Being Done to Take Them Back

13

CLEAR CHANNEL
AND THE PUBLIC AIRWAVES

DOROTHY KIDD
UNIVERSITY OF SAN FRANCISCO

With research assistance from
Francisco McGee and Danielle Fairbairn
Department of Media Studies, University of San Francisco

DOROTHY KIDD, *a professor of media studies at the University of San Francisco, has worked extensively in community radio and television. In 2002 Project Censored voted her article "Legal Project to Challenge Media Monopoly" No. 1 on its Top 25 Censored News Stories list. Publishing widely in the area of community media, her research has focused on the emerging media democracy movement.*

INTRODUCTION

For a company with close ties to the Bush family, and a Wal-mart-like approach to culture, Clear Channel Communications has provided a surprising boost to the latest wave of a US media democratization movement. The media conglomerate's combination of shock jock programming, prowar interventions and canned music, anticompetitive practices, and replacement of thousands of staff by computer-driven stations has helped to mobilize a wide range of groups who normally do not seek common cause. In the last four years, Clear Channel has faced legal challenges and public criticism from politicians in both houses of Congress; regulating agencies; every class of musician, concert promoter, radio staff, and station owner; and urban and rural communities of listeners.

At root in this unlikely coalition is the concern that Clear Channel and other large media conglomerates are killing radio; they are monster chains of mega–boom boxes drowning out the multiplicity of local music, information, and conversation that Americans have come to expect from their public airwaves. In this chapter, I begin by sketching the political, economic, and media landscape that led to the Clear Channel phenomenon. The campaigns targeting Clear Channel are only one manifestation of a larger movement to take back the public spectrum. I continue by discussing the campaigns, inside and outside the dial, to remake radio as the electronic equivalent of the backyard fence, the town concert and assembly hall, providing a vital connection for people in a democratic society.

THE FCC AND CORPORATE AMERICA

While Clear Channel is taking most of the heat, it is not the only radio firm to benefit by the latest wave of megamergers. Global conglomerates Viacom, through its subsidiary Infinity Radio, and Disney-ABC both rank in radio's top ten, operating primarily in the larger US urban centers, with Citadel and Cumulus Broadcasting in the smaller markets. Clear Channel and Infinity Radio together control one-third of all radio advertising revenue, and up to 90 percent in some markets.[1]

All of them began to grow and restructure their media holdings during a conservative shift in communications regulation. During the 1980s, the Federal Communications Commission and Washington-based courts moved from the liberal focus on the "public service" responsibilities of broadcasters to an environment of "market rule" in which owners are not held accountable for their stewardship of the public airwaves.[2] Mark Fowler, President Reagan's appointee as chair of the FCC, was a firm free-marketer, and he began to remove the rules governing the structure (ownership and competition), programming content, and behavior (accountability to the public interest) of broadcasters as early as 1981.[3] As radio historian Susan Douglas has written, "The new FCC was very good for corporate America."[4]

Ownership rules were increasingly relaxed. The caps, the allowable number of stations any one company could own, were raised and cross-ownership rules altered. This led to a major buying spree that took place in the late 1980s and continued into the early 1990s. Then, under the Clinton administration, but with the same "market" mantra, the Telecommunications Act of 1996 removed the forty-station national cap and allowed companies to own up to eight stations in large markets and five in small markets, up from the previous cap of two.[5] After the act was passed, ten thousand radio stations, worth $100 billion, were sold, with Clear Channel picking up the lion's share of over twelve hundred.[6] The resulting market consolidation was enormously profitable for the biggest players, making the industry lucrative again after a significant recession in the early 1990s. However, the immediate result was a loss of 30 percent, or eleven hundred station owners, many of whom operated small, locally oriented stations, with a disproportionate number being African American. As well, ten thousand radio-related jobs were cut, with many programmers replaced by syndicated talk shows and centrally produced music. Listeners began to notice the cookie-cutter sameness and an unprecedented number of commercials per hour.

Not all of these changes were due to the removal of ownership rules. Some were due to the lessening of rules governing content and broadcaster behavior. The public service paradigm, which Fowler overturned, had been based on the idea of a social contract, established since the first Communications Act of 1927, in which broadcasters paid a minimal amount to license the public's airwaves in a local community, and in return, they promised to provide local programming in the "public interest, convenience, and necessity." Instead, Fowler argued that the idea of the FCC as trustee of the public interest was passé and bad for consumers. His commission set about to remove several of the content rules, the most important of which was the Fairness Doctrine that had required broadcasters to "present issues of concern and controversy in their programming, guarantee access to stations by candidates for political office, and ensure that informational/editorial programming was aired with a degree of fairness and balance.[7] The "indecency" rules were maintained. Susan Douglas credits the ending of the Fairness Doctrine in 1987 as a contributing factor in the rapid growth of talk radio. For radio stations could then air conservative talk show hosts such as Rush Limbaugh and not be required to provide any balance to their assertions.

Ironically, the origins of contemporary talk radio, in fact, are owed to the progressive Pacifica Radio Network and the more liberal National Public Radio. Pacifica Radio's founding mandate was to challenge the US military-industrial complex by promoting debate among people of widely different political views. During the 1960s, programmers at KPFA-FM in Berkeley, and later at sister stations WBAI-FM in New York City and KPFK in Los Angeles, experimented with a range of call-in and free-form talk shows. During the 1970s, a small number of AM commercial stations tried out a more in-your-face version of the talk form, in part to retrieve listeners who were migrating to the better music sounds on FM. Then in 1978, National Public Radio successfully demonstrated the national broadcast of syndicated programming via satellite.[8] Despite, the ideological and fiscal hostility of the Reagan administration, NPR drew millions of listeners, largely because of their informational and talk-oriented programs.[9] The format that had been developed on the progressive waves of Pacifica, and massaged on NPR, took off in the 1980s with radio deregulation, and the decline in network news, as audiences searched elsewhere for more in-depth understandings and perspectives.[10]

The Fowler FCC also eliminated many of the "behavior" rules. Stations were no longer required to regularly demonstrate their commitment to the public interest, since the licensing period was extended from every three years to every seven years. As well, the FCC abandoned the "ascertainment rules" in which broadcasters had been required to meet with community groups in their local broadcast areas to ascertain and provide programming for local concerns and interests. Finally, the requirements that stations bring their hiring practices in compliance with antidiscrimination policies were challenged in the courts.

A NEW MODEL OF CORPORATE MEDIA

Clear Channel grew from a small Texas radio chain during this shift to the market paradigm. In many respects, it epitomizes a new model of corporate media, with a consolidated global reach and few checks and balances set against its enormous power. Clear Channel now ranks among the top ten US global media conglomerates, with holdings across media industries, including more than 1,200 radio stations, 130 concert venues, as well as television stations, concert promotion companies, live theater, outdoor advertising, athlete management, film and TV production, and satellite radio in sixty-six countries. On the conglomerate's Web site, it claims to reach over half of the overall adult US population and 75 percent of the nation's people of Hispanic descent. Outside of the United States, it operates 135 concert venues and several hundred thousand outdoor displays—billboards; taxi tops; mobile truck panels; bus, train, shopping mall, and airport displays; and assorted street furniture.

Clear Channel is most visible in the radio industry. By 2001, it controlled over twelve hundred stations in clusters in all sizes of markets throughout the country, sometimes exceeding the allowable FCC ownership cap of eight stations.[11] While only 11 percent of all stations, it reaches 27 percent of all radio listeners and makes a quarter of all US radio industry revenues. In thirty-seven of the top three hundred markets, its share ranges between 50 and 99 percent. The company's biggest impact has been in the smaller markets, where Clear Channel exerts its monopoly advantages in the interconnected music, radio, and advertising markets. Clear Channel's primary focus is advertisers, and its cross-media holdings allows it to offer cross-promotion over several different media. For example, the company can book acts in its clubs and concert stadiums and then promote them on its radio and television stations, billboards, taxi tops, and airport boards. In addition to these "cluster" campaigns across multiple media platforms, it can also offer specialized campaigns across geographic areas or station music formats.[12] Clear Channel's ownership clout also allows it to lower prices below what competing advertising agencies and radio stations can offer, forcing competitors out of business, or to sell to them.

Clear Channel has so streamlined and centralized operations, sales, and management that it is known in the industry as Cheap Channel. It has replaced live talent with computer technologies that automatically program several stations from one location and with prerecorded voice tracks and program elements.[13] For example, millions of Americans in forty-eight cities listen to KISS-FM DJs Rick Dees and Sean Valentine chat about local news or promote concerts in local amphitheaters owned by Clear Channel. However, Rick and Sean were prerecorded in Los Angeles and cut and spliced. In the local KISS station down the street in Des Moines, or Jacksonville, board operators play the recorded elements for as little as six dollars per hour.[14]

While news programs were being cut during the early 1990s, Clear Channel has speeded up the process. Entire news teams have been replaced with taped feeds from CNN or other national agencies. This missing-in-action status became apparent on September 11, 2001, when the Pentagon was attacked and Clear Channel had no news team to cover it. Then in January 2002, there was a chemical spill in Minot, North Dakota, where Clear Channel owns all six radio stations, including the designated emergency broadcaster, KCJB. Yet no one responded to the call from Emergency Services because the station was on automatic, piping out a satellite feed. This was not unusual since Clear Channel only employs one full-time news employee in Minot, who rips and reads the newscasts from state and national wire services.[15] For the author of *Media Monopoly*, Ben Bagdikian, the Minot story "demonstrates the systemic negligence of the public interest throughout the country," in which the people have been "robbed of their airwaves" and have lost local programming and accountability, a hallmark of US broadcasting.[16]

SHOCK JOCKS AND BELLICOSE PROGRAMMING

Besides cutting local programming, and the thousands of staff who once produced it, Clear Channel also added a whole stable of syndicated shock talk. Its subsidiary, Premiere Radio, broadcasts one hundred programs to seventy-eight hundred stations nationwide, reaching over 180 million listeners weekly. The brand features Rush Limbaugh, Michael Savage, Dr. Laura Schlessinger, and Michael Regan, among other conservative pundits, as well as a number of hosts whose specialty is "raunch." Until recently, Premiere Radio also carried Howard Stern's show on six stations but suspended it in early 2004. Stern, who is primarily broadcast on Clear Channel's competitor, Viacom's Infinity Radio, contends that he was not dropped because of his routinely obscene programming but instead because of his opposition to the Bush reelection.

Of course, Clear Channel has not come out of nowhere. Clear Channel has particularly close ties to the Bush family, contributing to George W. Bush's private fortune and to his gubernatorial and presidential campaigns. Vice chairman of the company Texas billionaire Tom Hicks paid George Bush $15 million for the Texas Rangers.[17] In 1998, Lowry Mays, Clear Channel's CEO, gave Bush's gubernatorial campaign $51,000, while his family members have donated $160,000 to political action committees between 1999 and 2002.[18] In return, Clear Channel can count on strong representation within the Bush administration. For example, Charles James represented Clear Channel's bid for regulatory approval when it purchased AM/FM in 2000. He is the current antitrust chief in the Justice Department. The company's newly opened Washington Office includes Andrew Levin, a former top aide to Democratic Representative John Dingell, and two former telecommunications aides, one from each major party.[19] In the first year of operation, with the FCC ownership rules at stake, Clear Channel increased its lobbying expenditures more than tenfold, from $68,675 to $700,000.[20]

While Clear Channel's connections to the Bush administration are now well known, it is perhaps the media conglomerate's brazen new-money challenge to the existing rules and norms of business and government that has made it such a lighting rod for criticism. While "old network" competitors, such as ABC-Disney, and CBS-Viacom (which owns Infinity Radio) pay lip service to their public service obligations to promote the public interest, Clear Channel expresses no ambiguity. CEO Lowry Mays is notorious for saying, "We are not in the business of providing music, news, or information" but of "selling advertising to customers."[21]

Such hubris has contributed to the swath of congressional investigations, antitrust investigations, employment-related disputes, and private law suits and complaints. In 2002, Salon reporter Eric Bohlert investigated the allegations that Clear Channel was defying the FCC caps on station ownership and "parking" or "warehousing" stations that exceeded the caps. A competitor in New York said to him, "You can only own so many stations in a market. That's the spirit of the rule. Everybody else is playing by the spirit and Clear Channel is allowed to circumvent it. . . . How can they do this? What's it going to take to get the appropriate government agency to pay attention."[22] As a result of these concerns, two Democratic Party representatives, Anthony Weiner of New York and Harold Berman of California, wrote to the Justice Department and the FCC. Partly in response, in 2002, the FCC sent one of the company's requests for another station purchase to a hearing, the first to deal with market-concentration issues in a radio station since 1969.[23]

Known for its lengthy legal fights and contestative attitudes, it is perhaps no surprise that Clear Channel has played such a public role in supporting the war efforts of the Bush administration. Clear Channel's public position first became evident after 9/11 when a list was circulated to program directors of 158 songs to avoid, with such "offensive" songs as John Lennon's "Imagine," Cat Stevens' "Peace Train," and Paul Simon's "Bridge Over Troubled Water."[24] Three weeks later, on October 1, 2001, David Cook, better known as "Davey D," was fired from his position as Community Affairs Director at KMEL FM, in San Francisco, not long after he aired the Coup's Boots Riley's objections to the war and hosted Democratic Congresswoman Barbara Lee, the solitary dissenting voice in Congress against attacking Afghanistan.[25]

In 2003, Clear Channel promoted prowar rallies around the country on its radio stations.[26] While denying direct involvement, the company admitted to assisting syndicated radio talk show host Glen Beck in organizing eighteen promilitary rallies in fourteen states, primarily in the south, cosponsoring and promoting most of them on its stations and via its company Web site.[27] Rox-anne Cordonier, a former radio personality at WMYI, in South Carolina, is suing Clear Channel, claiming she was belittled by colleagues on and off air for her opposition to the war, and forced to participate in prowar rallies.[28] Charles Goyette lost his prime afternoon drive time slot at KFYI-AM in Phoenix after opposing the war in Iraq and questioning the competency of Donald Rumsfeld on air. While Goyette has a well-drafted contract, protecting him from dismissal, he has been vilified and ridiculed by radio hosts at his own station, effectively shriveling his listener base. Clear Channel's attempts at censorship extended to musicians. During a concert of indie folkie Ani DiFranco, supporters had antiwar protest materials confiscated. The Dixie Chicks were cut from the program rotation after singer Natalie Maines told British fans that she was ashamed to be from the same state as President Bush.[29] (It is only fair to note that Cumulus Media also banned the Dixie Chicks.)[30]

RECLAIMING THE SPECTRUM

Clear Channel's macho corporate business practices, and rude right-wing talk show hosts, have helped garner huge audiences. However, they have also helped galvanize a renewed campaign for free speech and corporate media accountability, remarkable in a media climate that no longer guarantees diversity in programming personnel or content. Challengers have taken on Clear Channel and the other corporate radio oligarchs on and off the radio dial. As well, the challengers have not just criticized but have worked to create new kinds of innovative radio programming, designed to meet the public interests of the multiplicity of communities who make up the American public. As Pete Tridish and Kate Coyer note in their chapter, the consolidation of ownership and the narrowing of radio programming has helped spur a movement for communities to establish their own independent low-power FM stations. Together with the growing network of campus and community stations, they have provided information and critiques of the problems of consolidated corporate media. They also have kept alive a diversity of voices in music, information, and public discussion, providing live examples of just what the public is missing in the homogenized network programs.

Another group of stations embroiled in the debate over Clear Channel, and the radio industry, have been the independent urban stations. These small commercial stations, often owned by African Americans and Hispanic Americans, have built up strong loyal followings by responding to their distinct local communities and producing programming not heard anywhere else on the dial. San Francisco KBLX radio host Lesley Stoval has worked in several. "Radio is such a wonderful medium, it's so personal, it's one-on-one. . . . And especially in the minority community, it serves as a billboard; for Black radio, Latino radio, Asian radio, it's a forum for the community. . . . But under consolidation, you can't have that, because everything is velveeta."[31]

Most of these stations have not been around very long. Until the 1970s, African Americans were systematically excluded from broadcast ownership in much of the United States. A decade earlier, after an extended civil rights media campaign initiated by the United Church of Christ, in Jackson, Mississippi, the FCC created measures to open up broadcast licenses to African Americans and others who had been systematically excluded.[32] However, many of these independent stations and small chains went under during the wave of mergers, since they could not afford to compete for advertisers when Clear Channel, and other big networks, could offer cheaper cross-media packages, concert premiums, and higher salaries.[33] As William Saunders, who owns WPAL-AM in Charleston, South Carolina, told *Black Enterprise*, "Now we have people at urban stations that don't know anyone in the community. [They] just play music and come up with new ways to make money."[34] Several of the African American station owners have begun to fight back through public discussion, lawsuits, and political lobbying. The National Association of Black-Owned Broadcasters Incorporated (NABOB), brought these station owners' concerns to Congress in a Senate Commerce Committee hearing on the radio industry in January 2003.

CALLING FOR COMMUNITY ACCOUNTABILITY

Another urban station taken over by Clear Channel was KMEL in San Francisco. KMEL called itself the "People's Station" and had developed a strong and loyal following during the 1990s as a leading independent urban music station, launching several important political rappers and DJs. The station's programs were often cutting-edge, engaging its young audience of color with fresh and local music, and talk programming that addressed the social issues of the hip-hop generation. KMEL was also very successful in the local market. After Clear Channel bought KMEL and its rival station in 1999, the conglomerate began to broadcast a shorter play list of no risk–taking tunes, removed the local community-driven music and talk programming, and replaced some of the DJs with digitally preprogrammed tapes.

When Davey D was fired from his position as community affairs director at KMEL FM, it catapulted him to the front of a community campaign to make KMEL and Clear Channel more accountable. Davey D had hosted the popular "*Street Soldiers*" program that was aimed at youths of color. He, somewhat reluctantly, began to speak out about the problems of Clear Channel and the larger problems of independent hip-hop artists trying to survive within the bottlenecks of the radio and music industries. In the last three years, he has toured the country, speaking to colleges and other groups. He has also expanded his own Web site, and helped start a new program for youth of color, *Hard Knock Radio*, on the Pacifica station KPFA.

At the same time, a number of groups from KMEL's audience base, young people of color and their allies, formed the Community Coalition for Media Accountability. They approached the station, demanding redress for the firing of Davy and another popular host, the cutting of hip-hop programs of social issues, and the replacement of local music by preprogrammed "top hits." They researched and published a content analysis of the programming. Their report, "Is KMEL the People's Station? A Community Assessment of 106.1," found that KMEL "routinely excludes the voices of youth organizers and local artists, neglects discussion of policy debates affecting youth and people of color, focuses disproportionately on crime and violence, and has no clear avenues for listeners to hold the station accountable."[35] After many months, KMEL met with them and made some concessions, including the addition of a new local music program.[36] In addition, in June 2003, KMEL agreed to cohost a community forum, featuring young people talking about policy and community solutions to street violence with Let's Get Free, one of the coalition partners.

MAKING CLEAR CHANNEL THE
POSTER CHILD OF DEREGULATION

Another effective group of critics of Clear Channel, and the music and radio industries, has been the Washington-based Future of Music. In 2002 this nonprofit advocacy group released "Radio Deregulation: Has It Served Citizens and Musicians?" which documents the way that radio's oligopolies, interacting with the five-company recording industry, hurt both musicians and citizens. Four radio oligopolies control "almost every geographic market" and "virtually every music format,"[37] and program 80 to 100 percent of the radio charts with songs from the major labels. This "twin bottleneck" makes access to the airwaves exceedingly difficult for musicians—and reduces choice for citizens."[38]

Future of Music wanted to effect change for the benefit of "middle-class" musicians and for citizens. Working with Washington advocates, the Media Access Project, the Center for Public Integrity, and the Recording Artists Coalition, the group successfully approached both the FCC and Congress. In late 2002 they presented their findings to the FCC, helping convince the two Democratic Party commissioners and some staff to conduct field hearings and to participate in media forums around the nation. With the support of other musicians organizations, AFTRA—the union that represents on-air talent—the American Federation of Musicians (AFM), the Recording Academy, Just Plain Folks, the Artists Empowerment Coalition, and the Recording Artists Coalition, Future of Music executive director Jenny Toomey testified before the influential Senate Commerce Committee, which is chaired by Republican Senator John McCain, on January 30, 2003.[39]

Toomey and Future of Music contradicted many of the orthodoxies of the market paradigm, which had successfully ruled Washington media policy in the 1980s and 1990s. Using empirical data, they debunked one of the pillars of the market argument, that consolidation would benefit consumers. The radio industry had claimed that consolidation provided consumers an increase in the varieties of music formats. Future of Music pointed out that this apparent increase is the result of two related phenomena, with shared roots in consolidated ownership. While there were new formats, most were subclassifications of existing formats, such as adding Hot AC, Rock AC, Urban AC, Mix AC, Soft AC, Light AC, and Bright AC to Adult Contemporary (AC). The new subclassified formats did not necessarily feature a different set of songs, since there was an overlap of as much as 76 percent between formats.[40] In addition to this "faux-mat" variety, Future of Music argued that the networks had not used their increased resources to create more diversity for citizens and consumers, but instead routinely operated two or more stations with the same format in the same community.

At the congressional hearing, Democratic Senator Russ Feingold from Wisconsin, reinforced the arguments of Future of Music and their allies. Earlier, in 2002, Senator Feingold had introduced the "Competition in Radio and Concert Industries Act," designed to help independent radio station owners, promoters, and consumers.[41] He testified that many singers, musicians, and managers have told him that

> play lists are no longer based on quality—subjective as that is—but are sold to the highest bidder instead. They told me how, in the past, if you couldn't

get a DJ to play your song in Cleveland, perhaps you could try in Pittsburgh, and if the song was a hit in Pittsburgh, the Cleveland DJ would probably hear about it. . . . I am told [that] that doesn't happen anymore. It really
can't. The same companies own stations in both markets. If they don't want
to play a song, they don't—anywhere. Opportunities for artists to try their
music somewhere else just doesn't exist [*sic*].[42]

Both Future of Music and Senator Feingold also criticized Clear
Channel's practice of "pay-for-play." After the first "payola" scandal in the
late 1950s, in which recording companies paid radio stations directly for airplay, the practice was deemed illegal because of the unfair advantage it gave
to the major labels over unrepresented artists or smaller independent companies.[43] However, pay-for-play works slightly differently. Rather than paying
stations directly, record companies pay independent promoters called
"indies," who in turn pay the stations to play certain songs. Musician and
manager Don Henley told the Senate hearing that "as a result of this unprecedented consolidation, record labels must now hire independent promoters on
an even grander scale to help convince radio networks and stations to play
certain records."[44]

In April 2003, after the Senate investigation and harsh criticism from
within and outside the industry, Clear Channel publicly severed its deals with
indies.[45] "Eliminating these relationships with middlemen," said Clear
Channel Radio CEO John Hogan in a press release, " should alleviate legislators' concerns and provide opportunity for us to create better ways to
market and promote music for all concerned. . . . Clear Channel Radio would
begin working directly with the recording industry on specific group-wide
contests, promotions, and marketing opportunities."[46]

A joint statement in May 2003 from Future of Music and nine other
groups in the music industry contends that Clear Channel's decision to
abandon the "increasingly controversial practice of independent radio promotion does little to protect artists and the public from future forms of payola."[47]
Instead, Clear Channel's new "group-wide" promotional strategy will "very
likely program from a centralized location and focus on artists with group-
wide, i.e., national, appeal at the expense of artists with local appeal. This
practice ignores the FCC principle that individual radio stations in radio
groups are licensed to serve local communities. Furthermore, this practice, if
implemented, will continue to harm local artists, making it nearly impossible
for them to use their local popularity to garner local airtime and denying even
the most successful local artists legitimate access to a local audience."[48]

As well, in May, *Airplay Monitor* reported "that the Clear Channel door may not be completely closed, claiming that an independent promoter recently delivered his record to a Clear Channel station and got an add."[49] Two months after that, in July, the Department of Justice reported that one of two ongoing antitrust investigations "concerns allegations Clear Channel uses its market dominance to coerce recording artists into using its concert promotion business in return for better radio airplay."[50]

By 2003 there were several different challenges to Clear Channel across the country. In addition to those discussed above, in 2002 Democratic Representative Howard Berman of California had called for an investigation of Clear Channel's use of third parties to park radio stations, in markets where they exceeded the FCC caps, and coercion of artists.[51] The Department of Justice also instigated two antitrust investigations, one of which resulted in a consent decree that required Clear Channel to sell stations and interests in Lamar Broadcasting.[52] In Florida, Clear Channel was fined $80,000 by the attorney general, when its use of voice tracking misled listeners into thinking that a national contest was local.[53]

RECREATING THE PUBLIC FORUM

At the same time as the spotlight was being focused on Clear Channel in Washington, the company was becoming a household name during the campaign to challenge the further FCC deregulation of corporate ownership. In the fall of 2002, FCC chair Michael Powell called for a review of the last rules governing media ownership, as required by the Telecommunications Act. After his refusal to hold more than one public hearing, ten citizens' groups across the country organized their own. In the hearing in San Francisco, Clear Channel was evoked by speaker after speaker in front of FCC commissioner Jonathan Adelstein. They called on Adelstein to argue for greater accountability from the media, revoking licenses such as Clear Channel's in order to return the airwaves to public use.[54]

One of the key sets of players in expanding this public discussion of the role of the media were the noncommercial independent radio stations such as the Pacifica Network and campus and community stations on regular and low-powered FM and the Internet. For example, in the Bay Area, Pacifica Radio's Berkeley station, KPFA, had been the primary source of record and analysis on the story. The station had featured two interview panels, broadcast the first public hearing in New York in January 2003, and was cocarrier of the live feed from San Francisco City Hall, with African American–owned

KPOO-FM. With a virtual embargo of the story by corporate broadcasters, KPFA was also the most trusted source of critical information and analysis for many in the audience.[55]

On June 4, Commissioner Adelstein voted with his Democratic colleague, Michael Copps, against the new rules allowing more deregulation. However, as a result, hundreds of different groups from the entire political spectrum stepped up, lobbying their political representatives, contacting their local media, writing over two million comments to the FCC, and demonstrating in the street.[56] Finally, just before the date of the ruling, the corporate media began to cover the story. As Mark Cooper, from the Consumer Federation of America, has reported, the debate in Washington, and certainly in the mainstream press, has been to the Right of the US public, who have shown a growing concern about media concentration and its impact on programming since the first wave of corporate mergers and their regulatory approval via the Telecommunications Act of 1996.[57]

The campaign continues, as several decisions are still pending in the courts. As well, no further deregulation was allowed in radio. In fact, using the Arbitron data as a new measurement of concentration, the FCC has rewritten the ownership caps. Eighty-two Clear Channel stations are no longer in compliance. Clear Channel will be required to divest of sixteen of them and also may be required to give up those stations where it "provides programming to or sells advertising on stations it does not own."[58] Essential Information, a DC-based nonprofit organization started by Ralph Nader, filed a petition to the FCC, asking it to deny renewal to sixty-three of Clear Channel's stations in Washington DC, Virginia, West Virginia, and Maryland.[59] The newly galvanized media reform campaign is also seizing the raised public profile of a new round of officially sponsored FCC hearings on localism to raise concerns with Clear Channel. At the first hearing in San Antonio, in January 2004, many of the five-hundred-plus in attendance focused their criticism on the hometown-based Clear Channel, raising placards saying "Clear Channel Blurts the Truth" and "We're Not One Country under Clear Channel."[60]

CURRENT PROSPECTS

By the summer of 2003, the framing of the public debate finally shifted from lockstep agreement with the market paradigm's celebration of consolidation to a more nuanced concern about the impact of too much centralized control over media. At this writing, in the spring of 2004, there appeared to be a setback, as Congress and the FCC finally reacted to public concerns about the growth of "raunch" programming and fined Clear Channel $775,000. While the public concern about the media has been temporarily reframed in a much narrower concern about obscenity, it will be difficult to push the critique of corporate media consolidation back in the bag, and influential Republican senator and media critic John McCain has already drawn a connection between consolidation and obscenity. It will also be difficult to stem the growing concerns and campaigns about corporate media accountability to the public interest. Clear Channel's own public relations gesture, the "Responsible Broadcasting Initiative," opens the window for initiatives such as the Community Coalition for Media Accountability in San Francisco.

Finally, the growing public awareness of the problems of Clear Channel in particular, and the more general crisis of radio, has spurred support for independent radio and for more diverse political and cultural programming. The recent opening of frequencies to low-power FM is giving a boost to traditional community-oriented radio and its cyber version on the Internet, as Tridish and Coyer discuss in their chapter. After a lengthy crisis in the 1990s, Pacifica Radio has come back with more new programming from undercovered communities and live specials featuring critical issues of both local and national import. While most of NPR's network programming has moved from risky to safe, allowing few Left-of-center voices, local affiliate KALW-FM in San Francisco has filled in some of this gap with progressive talk programs such as Laura Flander's *It's Your Call*. A new venture, Air America, launched a twenty-four-hour Left-leaning radio network on March 31, 2004, to woo audience members from Rush Limbaugh and Clear Channel's other right-wing hosts, starting full-time on stations in New York, Chicago, Los Angeles, and San Francisco, and through individual program sales on other stations and via satellite and the Internet.[61] Air America's strategic vision is to stretch the bounds of democratic discussion and the sound possibilities of the medium by featuring comedians Al Franken, Janeane Garofalo, and Lizz Winstead, as well as Public Enemy rapper Chuck D.

Clear Channel and the other radio conglomerates have severely shrunk what counts as acceptable talk and music inside narrower, more homogenized, and conservative boxes, from its visionary origins to foster democracy and peace by connecting people around the world. However, they have not been able to still the continuing public urge to use radio to form connections between the hearts and minds of listeners, artists, and commentators. The challenge will be to move the public awareness of Clear Channel and other corporate conglomerates beyond the critique of bigness, to remake a vision of the airwaves, owned and operated by the people. With new digital technologies, the horizon has been raised, opening the available frequencies and possibilities to a wide diversity of groups, operating locally, nationally, and internationally.

NOTES

1. Eric Boehlert, "One Big Happy Channel?" *Salon.com*, June 28, 2001, http://www.salon.com/tech/feature/2001/06/28/telecom_dereg/print/html.

2. Willard D. Rowland, "U.S. Broadcasting and the Public Interest in the Multichannel Era: The Policy Heritage and Its Implications," in *Connections: A Broadcast History Reader*, ed. Michele Hilmes (Belmont, CA: Thomson Wadsworth, 2003).

3. Robert Horwitz, "On Media Concentration and the Diversity Question, http://communication.ucsd.edu/people/ConcentrationpaperICA.html, p. 8.

4. Susan J. Douglas, *Listening In: Radio and the American Imagination* (New York: Times Books, 1999), p. 296.

5.

Table 1: Local Radio Station Ownership Rules
According to the 1996 Telecom Act

In a market with . . .	A single entity can control . . .
. . . 45 or more stations	. . . up to 8, no more than 5 in same band (AM or FM)
. . . 30–44 stations	. . . up to 7, no more than 4 in same band
. . . 15–29 stations	. . . up to 6, no more than 4 in same band
. . . 14 or fewer stations	. . . up to 5, no more than 3 in same band

Source: Peter Dicola and Kristin Thomson, *Radio Deregulation: Has It Served Citizens and Musicians?* Future of Music Coalition, November 18, 2002, http://www.futureofmusic.org/images/FMCradiostudy.pdf, p. 11.

6. Boehlert, "One Big Happy Channel?"

7. Horwitz, "On Media Concentration and the Diversity Question," p. 8.

8. Douglas, *Listening In*, p. 288.

9. Ibid., pp. 322–23.

10. Ibid., p. 285.

11. In Boston, Clear Channel owns or controls 9 stations; in Louisville, KY, 10; in Atlanta, 9; in New York, 10; in Columbus, OH, 11. Of 17 stations in Mansfield,

OH, Clear Channel owns 11; in Corvallis, OR, 7 of 13; in Casper, WY, 6 of 12. John Dunbar and Aron Pilhofer, "Big Radio Rules in Small Markets," Center for Public Integrity, http://www.openairwaves.org/telecom/report.aspx?aid=63.

12. Lynnley Browning, "Making Waves on Air: Big Radio's Bad Boy," *New York Times*, June 19, 2002, p. C1.

13. Maria Figueroa, Damone Richardson, and Pam Whitefield, *The Clear Picture on Clear Channel Communications, Inc.: A Corporate Profile* (New York: Institute for Workplace Studies at Cornell University, January 28, 2004), p. 6.

14. Ibid., p. 65.

15. Jennifer Lee, "On Minot, N.D., Radio, A Single Corporate Voice," *New York Times*, March 31, 2003, p. C7.

16. "San Francisco Hearing on FCC Media Ownership Rules," April 26, 2003, unpublished transcripts, Department of Media Studies, University of San Francisco.

17. Charles Goyette, "How to Lose Your Job in Talk Radio: Clear Channel Gags an Anti-war Conservative," *American Conservative*, February 2, 2004, http://www.amconmag.com/1_19_04/article3.html.

18. Figueroa, Richardson, and Whitefield. *The Clear Picture on Clear Channel Communications, Inc.*, p. 60.

19. Ibid., p. 60.

20. Ibid., p. 59.

21. Christine Y. Chen, "The Bad Boys of Radio," *Fortune*, March 3, 1993, p. 119.

22. Eric Boehlert, "Washington Tunes In," *Salon.com*, March 27, 2002.

23. Ibid.

24. Jeff Chang, "Clear Channel Fires Davey D," *CounterPunch*, October 3, 2001, http://www.counterpunch.org/chang2.html.

25. Jeff Chang, "Urban Radio Rage," *Bay Guardian*, January 22, 2003, http://www.sfbg.com/37/18/cover_kmel.html.

26. Wayne Barrett, "Bush's Voice of America," *Village Voice*, April 8, 2003, p. 22.

27. Aria Seilgmann, "De-Reg Demons: Clear Channel Builds Conservative Airwave Monopoly," *Eugene Weekly* 22, no. 17 (April 4, 2003): 12.

28. Figueroa, Richardson, and Whitefield, *The Clear Picture on Clear Channel Communications, Inc.*, p. 57.

29. Michael Fitzgerald, "Dixie Chicks Axed by Clear Channel," *Jacksonville Business Journal*, March 17, 2003, http://jacksonville.bizjournals.com/jacksonville/stories/2003/03/17/daily14.html.

30. Associated Press, "Clear Channel Growth the Result of 1996 Deregulation," *Salt Lake Tribune*, September 21, 2003, http://www.sltrib.com/2003/Sep/09212003/business/94315.asp.

31. Public Hearing on the FCC Media Ownership Rules, April 2003, San Francisco.

32. Mark Lloyd, "Communications Policy Is a Civil Rights Issue," Civil Rights

Forum on Communications Policy, August 4, 1997, http://www.civilrightsforum.org/
foundations.html; Carrie Solages, *Crisis* 110, no. 5, (September/October 2003): 20.

33. M. Dellinger, "It's O.K. I'm with Clear Channel," *New York Times*, June 29,
2003, p. 31; Brentin Mock, "Station Identification: WAMO, the City's Historic Black
Radio Station, Once Had the Community to Itself. Now It's Counting on That Sense
of Community to Compete against Monoliths," *Pittsburgh City Paper* 13, no. 29
(July 23, 2003): 10.

34. Mock, "Station Identification: WAMO."

35. Youth Media Council, "Is KMEL the People's Station? A Community
Assessment of 106.1 KMEL," Fall 2002, http://www.youthmediacouncil.org/pdfs/
BuildAPeoplesStation.pdf.

36. Chang, "Urban Radio Rage."

37. Dicola and Thomson, *Radio Deregulation*, p. 3.

38. Ibid., p. 4.

39. Jenny Toomey, "Radio Deregulation: Has It Served Citizens and Musicians?"
testimony submitted by the Future of Music Coalition for "Media Ownership: Radio"
Hearings before the Senate Committee on Commerce, Science, and Transportation,
January 30, 2003. www.futureofmusic.org/news/senatecommercetestimony.cfm.

40. Dicola andThomson, *Radio Deregulation*, p. 4.

41. http://feingold.senate.gov/releases/02/06/062702medcon.htm (accessed
February 20, 2004).

42. Statement of Senator Feingold, "Hearing of the Senate Commerce, Science,
and Transportation Committee. Subject: Hearing on Media Ownership," January 30,
2003, Federal News Service, Inc.

43. Jack Kapica, "Edison's Noisy Children," *Digital Journal.com*, July 2003,
http://www.digitaljournal.com/news/?articleID=3630&page=3; "Announcement of
Payment for Broadcast," 47 C.F.R. § 317, subchapter Iii—Special Provisions Relating to Radio; part I—General Provisions US Communications Act of 1934; chapter
5—Wire or Radio Communication.

44. Statement of Don Henley, "Hearing of the Senate Commerce, Science, and
Transportation Committee. Subject: Hearing on Media Ownership," January 30,
2003, Federal News Service, Inc.

45. Susan Crabtree and Justin Oppelaar, "Clear Channel Snips Indie Promo
Ties," *Daily Variety*, April 10, 2003.

46. Clear Channel, "Clear Channel Cuts Ties with Independent Promoters,"
press release, April 9, 2003, http://www.clearchannel.com/documents/press_releases/
20030409_Corp_Indies.pdf.

47. "Joint Statement on Current Issues in Radio," October 8, 2003, http://
futureofmusic.org/news/radioissuesstatement03.cfm.

48. Ibid.

49. "What Effect Will CC's Indie Policy Have?" *Airplay Monitor*, May 2, 2003.

50. L. A. Lorek, "Clear Channel Sweetens Its Profit Despite Sour Economy,"
San Antonio Express-News, July 30, 2003, p. 6E.

51. http://www.house.gov/search97cgi/s97_cgi?action=View&VdkVgwKey
=http%3A%2F%2Fwww%2Ehouse%2Egov%2Fapps%2Flist%2Fpress%2Fca28%
5Fberman%2Fclear%5Fchannel%2Ehtml&DocOffset=2&DocsFound=2&QueryZip
=Clear+Channel&SourceQueryZip=vdkvgwkey+%3Csubstring%3E+%22%2
Fberman%2F%22+OR+vdkvgwkey+%3Csubstring%3E%22%2Fca28%22&
Collection=members&ViewTemplate=memberview%2Ehts&.

52. Figueroa, Richardson, and Whitefield, *The Clear Picture on Clear Channel
Communications, Inc.*, pp. 56–57.

53. Ibid., p. 54.

54. Francisco McGee, "Transcripts of the Hearings on the Federal Communications Commission Rules on Media Ownership," University of San Francisco Media
Research Group, 2003.

55. Ibid.

56. Charles Layton, "Tracking the Coverage," *American Journalism Review*
(December/January 2003).

57. Mark Cooper, *Media Ownership and Democracy in the Digital Information
Age* (Stanford, CA: Stanford Center for Internet and Society, 2003), p. 31.

58. Public hearing on the FCC Media Ownership Rules, April 2003, San Francisco, p. 50.

59. Essential Information, http://www.essentialinformation.org/features/
clearchannel.html.

60. Bill McConnell, "The Public Is Interested; In Heart of Texas, FCC Panel
Gets an Earful over Lack of Localism," *Broadcasting and Cable*. February, 2, 2004,
p. 2.

61. Russell Shorto, "Al Franken, Seriously," *New York Times Magazine*, March
21, 2004.

14

A RADIO STATION IN YOUR HANDS IS WORTH 500 CHANNELS OF MUSH!

The Role of Community Radio in the Struggle against Corporate Domination of Media

PETE TRIDISH AND KATE COYER

PROMETHEUS RADIO PROJECT

PETE TRIDISH *was a member of the founding collective of Radio Mutiny, 91.3 FM in Philadelphia. He is also a founder of the Prometheus Radio Project. In 1997 he was an organizer for Radio Mutiny's demonstrations at Benjamin Franklin's Printing Press and the Liberty Bell; on both occasions the station broadcast in open defiance of the FCC's unfair rules that prohibit low-power community broadcasting. He also worked on the first two microradio conferences on the East Coast—and organized radio barn raisings in five communities around the United States. He actively participated in the rule making that led to the adoption of low-power FM radio (LPFM). He sat on the committee that sponsored the crucial Broadcast Signal Labs study, which proved to the FCC that LPFM would not cause interference. Tridish has helped to build a number of low-power radio stations and provided advice to hundreds of interested people. He has done radio trainings in Guatemala, Colombia, Nepal, and other countries. He has spoken at colleges, coffee shops, living rooms, and even the CATO Institute. He holds a BA in appropriate technology from Antioch College.*

KATE COYER *is a refugee from commercial radio, having spent her formative years backstage with bands like Hole producing shows for Westwood One. She is currently a PhD candidate and visiting tutor in the Department of Media and Communications at Goldsmiths College, University* *of London, where she researches community radio, Internet radio, media policy, and legislation. She has been producing radio and coordinating activist media projects since 1986. Coyer has worked extensively in the nonprofit sector developing public service radio campaigns, including Rock the Vote's radio program to increase youth voter participation. She has conducted radio workshops with the Community Media Association UK and the Prometheus Radio Project, where she is also a volunteer. Her recent publications include a chapter on Indymedia in* Global Activism, Global Media, *edited by Wilma de Jong (Pluto, forthcoming 2004), and a piece on tactical communications in the* Journal of Aesthetics and Protest.

L ow-power FM (LPFM) is a crucial means of reclaiming some of the broadcast spectrum. LPFM represents a renewed appreciation of local voices, public access, and participation in community broadcasting. As activists in promoting LPFM for the Prometheus Radio Project, we will argue the significance of community radio stations for the prosperity of a more democratic media.[1] This chapter will outline the history of the movement for low-power radio and show how the stage was later set for the larger struggle against concentration of media ownership. Media consolidation in radio, with the standardization of its programming, homogenized texture, and massive reduction in local news and public affairs, sparked a low-power radio movement that rose from marginal beginnings to become a formidable opponent of powerful media corporations. In illustrating the relationship between the LPFM movement and the larger fight against media deregulation, we will consider issues of corporate consolidation and the logic of market capitalism as impacting both the movement for community radio and the need for a freer flow of news and information. We will conclude by re-examining the future outlook for LPFM amidst the changing corporate, governmental, and digital landscapes.

Low-powered FM radio stations are Federal Communications Commission–licensed stations broadcasting at under one hundred watts, which translates to a broadcast range of five to ten miles. What LPFM does is give a sliver of the radio spectrum to libraries, schools, civic groups, community organizations, and churches. Individuals cannot apply for licenses, but those applying range from the local chapter of ACT-UP to the Rotary Club. The stations must be both noncommercial and not-for-profit. License applicants must clearly state how the station will be used to further the educational mission of their organization. As of March 2004, approximately 320 LPFM stations are on air, with hundreds more preparing to build. Content is not regulated, but there is a slight preference in the application process for organizations that promise to produce their content locally, and all of the typical rules of radio about indecency, slander, cursing, and so forth apply. Groups can only apply during five-day time periods, or "filing windows," which have only once been opened, and there is no schedule for when they will take place in the future. LPFM is about returning a portion of the airwaves to communities, and it is about increasing citizen participation and access to broadcasting.

Until recently, the options for local organizations to get on air were limited. The challenges and the resiliency of local community groups to gain access to the radio spectrum on both technical and political levels are well illustrated by the story of Radio Conciencia, an LPFM station on air since December 2003.

THE RADIO OF THE TOMATO PICKERS

The Coalition of Immokalee Workers (CIW) had a difficult job ahead of them. The coalition had employed various strategies on behalf of the workers in the migrant farmworking town of Immokalee, Florida, over the years: tactics such as negotiations, work stoppages, and hunger strikes to focus public attention on poverty wages and sweatshop working conditions. Several coalition members had at one time been enslaved by ruthless contractors who banked on workers' fear keeping them from reporting their captivity to authorities.

But this time, the stakes were higher. After September 11, 2001, the local sheriff was eager to take advantage of general anti-immigrant sentiments to make a power grab in his county. He asked that all local law enforcement officials be granted additional powers as Immigration and Naturalization Service (INS) agents, giving them the power to seize and deport undocumented workers. This practice has long been taboo in US law enforcement because of the difficulties such a scenario could create. For example, if undocumented immigrants saw a robbery in progress, would they dare report it to officials if they could be deported? Or, if they had evidence that could help solve a murder, would they risk contacting the police? In spite of such arguments for retaining the traditional separation of jurisdictions, the sheriff was determined to push for expansion of his authority.

In response, the coalition organized meetings and strategized to thwart the plan. It would never again be able to get farmworkers to come forward and report on South Florida's illegal slave camps if this measure went through. The members would normally have relied on their traditional organizing methods to plan a protest in front of the sheriff's office—walking house to house knocking on doors, posting fliers up around town, and passing information by word of mouth. This time, however, the coalition had an ally in mobilizing the community for the action—a local pirate radio station. The station gave the police issue a significant amount of airtime, including in-depth interviews with CIW leaders. Although the station usually steered clear of politics, and was generally left alone by the authorities, the operator of the station was convinced that this time he had to take a stand.

The word went out over the airwaves for days before the protest, and fifteen hundred farmworkers and supporters showed up to demonstrate, a far greater number than anyone expected. The sheriff dropped his plan in the face of the furor but enacted his revenge by having the pirate station shut down the following week. It had been operating for years unhindered by authorities when it stuck to playing music.

Realizing the efficacy of radio for their needs, the farmworkers raised money to buy time on a local licensed AM station. They paid two hundred and fifty dollars for an hour show each week. It was worth the steep price in terms of the show's contribution to their organizing capacity, but the cost was just too great to maintain and the workers had to discontinue the broadcast after about six months of being on air. The farmworkers concluded they were in need of a sustainable and continuous means of broadcast communication in a region where multiple languages are spoken among the significantly migratory community. The coalition decided that it was time to pursue building their own radio station.

Purchasing a station in today's marketplace dominated by conglomerates can cost millions of dollars. This was obviously not an option for the tomato pickers, who often worked from dawn to dusk for subpoverty wages. They considered starting a pirate station, but ruled out the possibility because of the vulnerability of their constituency and their high profile as an organization. They could not risk the ten-thousand-dollar fines, equipment seizures, and jail time that could accompany pirate radio operation. Unbeknownst to the farmworkers, other activists had been working on this similar problem to address the broader issue of access to the airwaves for thousands of other small community groups like themselves.

The coalition travels frequently across the country, educating communities about the living and working conditions of Florida farmworkers and the ways in which they are fighting to change those conditions. On a stop through Madison, Wisconsin, to promote their current boycott of Taco Bell,[2] they met labor radio reporters who recommended they start a radio station. The coalition was introduced to the Prometheus Radio Project. Prometheus advised them of the option to take advantage of new FCC rules won in 2000 that would allow them to apply for a low-power local radio license. The two groups worked together for several years jumping through assorted administrative hoops to finally obtain a broadcast license for the coalition in 2003.

However, it's one thing to have a radio license but another to actually have a functioning radio station. To that end, the Coalition of Immokalee Workers and the Prometheus Radio Project organized a "Radio Barn Raising" that brought together over one hundred community radio activists, broadcasters, engineers, and enthusiasts for a three-day weekend workshop and station building in December 2003. Over the weekend, the volunteers pieced together the mixing board, installed all the equipment, raised the antenna, and got Radio Conciencia on air that weekend. Radio Conciencia plans to broadcast in at least four languages—Spanish, Haitian Creole, Mam, and Quanjobal (two indigenous Guatemalan languages). In addition to music from Latin America and the Caribbean, some of the station's program themes include the rights of women, worker rights, human rights, news from the workers' countries of origin, political commentary, health education, and, if all goes as planned, even a program of jokes to give the workers a much needed break at the end of a long, hard day working in the fields.

This collaborative model of community station building has brought five new LPFM stations on air in 2002–2003 and is helping to build a growing network of radio activists. Many other groups that have participated in these events have gone back to their communities with the skills they learned and assembled their new low-power radio stations.

THE DEEP DARK HISTORY OF LOW-POWER COMMUNITY RADIO

The coalition's access to legal, low-powered community radio has come as a result of a long and arduous fight brought on by media democracy advocates, community organizers, and pirate radio operators. To the casual observer, it might be assumed that radio licensing for community organizations would be a matter of bureaucratic common sense and everyday operations for the FCC; however, winning the opportunity for organizations like the Coalition of Immokalee Workers was actually an enormous battle, which continues as this article goes to print.

The establishment of LPFM as a tier of radio did not come easily, or overnight. In 1948, with the advent of the FM band, the FCC agreed to reserve a small portion of the new spectrum for noncommercial broadcast.[3] Community groups, high schools, and colleges used to have access to local, low-power radio licenses in the early days of FM in the form of ten-watt Class D licenses, which were educational licenses issued on an as-requested basis. Class D licenses were allocated alongside full-power licenses for larger community radio stations. Ironically, these noncommercial FM licenses were not opposed by incumbent broadcasters in the beginning because of the perceived unpopularity of the FM band in an era in which AM reigned.[4]

In 1978, however, a policy change brought about by National Public Radio[5] resulted in the end of the low-power, Class D educational licenses. As NPR planned its expansion throughout the United States, it was concerned these small stations would be in the way when it wanted access to a new region that the NPR network did not yet serve. At the same time, full-power community stations were stalled in an increasingly nightmarish bureaucratic snafu—a set of rules for choosing between applicants for a frequency with an absurd gamut of comparative hearings. This system ultimately ended when the FCC realized it was not choosing the best applicants, but simply whoever had greater resources to tackle the Byzantine legal aspects of the hearings. The decision to eliminate the old rules for competing noncommercial applicants was a good one, but the FCC did not get around to issuing a new procedure until 2000. During this time it was essentially impossible to get a noncommercial radio license, and today we see the results. In the entire country, there are only about two hundred community radio stations in existence, out of about twelve thousand total stations nationwide.[6]

AVAST YE! ENTER THE PIRATES . . .

The current system of media oligopolies is far removed from the early days of radio when the airwaves were the open province of technologically savvy amateurs, much like the teenage hackers from the early days of the Internet. Virtually anyone with a transmitter and an interest in broadcasting had access to the airwaves. These hobbyists of the 1920s were instrumental in shaping the broadcast landscape and were at the forefront of developing and tweaking new broadcast equipment and technologies.[7] The term "pirate broadcaster" itself was used to describe amateurs who stepped on another hobbyist's signal and was coined at a time when there was no government or corporate regulation of the airwaves. When the government did step in and license the airwaves under the Telecommunications Act of 1934, rules were established limiting the number of stations any one company could own nationwide to seven AMs and seven FMs, thus ensuring diversity in station ownership. At the same time these safeguards were put in place, community needs were cast aside in favor of commercial interests in the allocation of broadcast licenses, especially with the elimination of amateur access. As early as 1928, the Federal Radio Commission decided to eliminate nonprofit radio stations in the interest of supporting the new, national commercial networks, claiming, falsely, that this was necessary because of concerns over broadcast scarcity. Amateurs, meanwhile, were relegated to two-way communications on a few small frequency bands.[8]

In light of the FCC's history of indifference toward community radio, a movement of pirate radio broadcasters emerged in the 1990s that directly challenged the government's policy of ignoring community radio concerns. Microbroadcasters achieved some surprising victories in the courts, which threw in to doubt the validity of the licensing system itself. Judges heard the cases put forward by microbroadcasters such as Steven Dunifer of Free Radio Berkeley and were compelled to strongly consider whether, as he claimed, under the stewardship of the FCC the public airwaves had become "a concession stand for corporate America." Though some microbroadcasting cases were ultimately lost in the courts, a great deal of momentum was created and many otherwise law-abiding citizens were taking to the airwaves without a license as a form of protest against corporate domination of media.

Dunifer's 1993 case represented a turning point in the modern United States Free Radio movement. An electrical engineer in Berkeley, California, he became disgusted with the nationalistic, pro-Pentagon reporting of the Gulf War. He built a transmitter from scratch, carried it in a backpack up to the hills of Berkeley, and took to the airwaves. After a few years of covert broadcasting, Dunifer was caught by the FCC and fined $20,000. He vowed to continue broadcasting and publicly refused to pay the fine, so the FCC took him to court seeking an injunction against him.[9]

The National Lawyer's Guild took his case, arguing that the regulations were unconstitutional on the basis of First Amendment concerns. They argued that the United States' model of telecommunication regulations allows only a wealth-based broadcasting system—that the dominance of media by corporate interests is no accident but is inherent in the design of the current regulatory framework. They also made the claim that microradio is the "leaflet of the nineties" and that to disallow it is tantamount to censorship. Free Radio Berkeley won an important Ninth Federal District Court decision in November 1997, in which Judge Claudia Wilken refused to grant an injunction against Dunifer pending review of the constitutionality of current FCC licensing practices. His case was tied up in the legal system for four years. Though Dunifer ultimately lost on a technicality, during the time his case was pending, hundreds of groups across the country flooded into the gap and took advantage of the apparent lapse in the FCC's authority to regulate the airwaves.

Accurate numbers are difficult to come by, but it appears over one thousand pirate radio stations were in operation across the country in the early 1990s, echoing Dunifer's call to see "a thousand transmitters bloom." They cast their defiant radio broadcasts as acts of civil disobedience against a corporate-based broadcast system that ignored the needs and interests of local communities. This movement of pirate radios grew as corporate influence suffused commercial radio, public radio became increasingly national in focus and "beige" in sound, and many large community radio stations experienced internal conflicts between guiding principles of community access versus encroaching corporatism.

Many consider the birth of this new wave of pirate radio to be in 1986, when Mbanna Kantako set up a radio station to serve the African American community of Springfield, Illinois. The station started out as WTRA, radio of the Tenants' Rights Association, a community organizing tool for the housing project. The station was ignored by authorities for several years, until it broke a story about what ended up being a high-profile police brutality case. When agents came to shut it down, station founder Mbanna Kantako went downtown to the federal building and the police station and dared them all to arrest him. When authorities realized such a course of action could backfire in the tense situation, they left him alone for many years—spurring many to realize the FCC was not always ready to enforce its own regulations. WTRA is now known as Human Rights Radio and continues to broadcast without a license, even after a raid of its equipment in 1999.

A BREED OF VILLAIN APART FROM OTHERS HERETOFORE DISCOVERED

The political pirates of the 1990s, like Dunifer and Kantako, were very different from anything the FCC had encountered before.[10] The difference between the political pirates and many of the earlier pirates was, as one professional radio engineer put it: "We did pirate radio and we felt like we were being mischievous, that we were getting away with something. The difference with pirates nowadays is they think they're right."[11] Political pirates brought a collective belief that a healthy democracy could not exist when corporations had exclusive control over the airwaves. Practically speaking, the political pirates also brought experience as community organizers. Tactics learned in movements for social change became useful as pirate radio became a matter of policy debate. Pirate radio broadcasters found themselves relying on campaign skills such as letter writing, protest organizing, communicating effectively with a sometimes hostile media, and the mental preparation needed to steel oneself against the prospect of getting arrested during an act of civil disobedience. Despite the lack of funding and chaotic organizational structures, the new pirates were unusually formidable opponents for an unpopular agency that had just experienced rounds of funding cuts at the hands of a Republican Congress.

Another turning point was the "Showdown at the FCC" in which 150 pirates from around the East Coast gathered in Washington, DC, in October 1998.[12] The event began with a three-day conference in a DC neighborhood youth center, where skills such as transmitter and antenna building, news reporting, and audio editing were among the workshops held. A debate took place at the Freedom Forum, a First Amendment think tank, with pirates matching wits with representatives of the broadcasting establishment. On Sunday night, a Washington, DC–based pirate radio station (Radio Libre in the Mt. Pleasant neighborhood) was launched right in the backyard of the FCC. The gathering itself culminated in a protest march from Dupont Circle to the FCC building to the National Association of Broadcasters (NAB) headquarters.

The centerpiece of the protest was a giant "meta-puppet"—a puppet controlling a puppet controlling a puppet. The corporations were represented by a twelve-foot-tall tower awash with corporate logos, topped by the Masonic all-seeing eye of the pyramid from the dollar bill. The corporations held the marionette strings that controlled the broadcasters, who were represented by a ten-foot gorilla with a television for a head sporting the logos of ABC, CBS, and NBC. The broadcasters, in turn, held the marionette strings for another puppet, the FCC, which was symbolized by an eight-foot Pinocchio (or "Kennardio," as he was called, named after William Kennard, chairman of the FCC at the time) with a giant telescoping nose that grew when he told lies about pirate radio and the public airwaves.

The highlight of the demonstration, however, was a pirate radio broadcast right from the streets. Protestors carried hidden transmitters in backpacks, which were actually broadcasting into the offices of the FCC and the NAB. Demonstrators with megaphones dared officials to come out and make arrests. When the protest reached the front of the NAB building, the crowd used the giant puppets to storm through the security guards and took over the plaza in front of the building. People surrounded the flagpole and captured the NAB flag, raising a Jolly Roger pirate flag in its place. The confrontational tactics and goofy humor caught the imagination of reporters and bystanders, and raised understanding of the issue to a new level. Unsurprisingly, the FCC found it difficult to convince the public of the necessity for the agency to protect the frequencies from the likes of the radio pirates!

For months after the incident, Chairman Kennard joked about this protest in his public appearances. Because he was often criticized by the broadcasting industry for not being sympathetic enough to their requests for regulatory favor, he enjoyed telling industry associations that crowds of rowdy pirates had accused him of being a puppet of the broadcasters.

THE FCC CAPTAIN STEERS A NEW COURSE

The new pirate operators put the relatively progressive Kennard in an awkward position. As the chief guardian of an orderly spectrum, he could not allow open rebellion against the FCC's allocation system. Kennard admitted, however, that pirates had some legitimate concerns regarding the concentration of media ownership and the lack of community access to the airwaves: "[The pirates] demonstrated that diverse voices weren't being heard on conventional radio."[13] The FCC chairman announced he would prioritize creation of legitimate opportunities for new voices on the radio dial. Media activist Robert McChesney went further in his assessment: "[The pirates] showed the FCC that low-power broadcasting is here whether you like it or not. And that they're going to have to deal with it."[14]

As a result, in conjunction with his campaign to crack down on pirates, Kennard announced he was ready to make some real changes to FCC policy regarding new applications for low-powered radio licenses. The FCC subsequently opened a rule-making proceeding in January 1999, to examine their allocation rules, and sought public comment as to what shape the new radio service should take. Kennard was particularly troubled by the effects of media consolidation on minority ownership of media, which had dwindled precipitously since passage of the 1996 Telecommunications Act. Kennard could not rewrite the act of Congress that permitted further consolidation, but he could authorize low-power radio licenses that might help to offset some of the harms from potential new media monopolies.

CARE TO COMMENT?

The FCC has two main tracks for comment from the public. Ordinary letters and phone calls are treated as informal comments and are generally filed away and ignored. Occasionally the FCC will respond to a flood of informal comments, particularly when it suits the political agenda of the commissioners or the administration. Obscenity and indecency complaints are thus looked at more closely near elections, as exemplified by the moral panic brought about by Janet Jackson's Super Bowl breast exposure that netted hundreds of thousands of complaints.

The FCC also has a formal comment process that is used to actively solicit ideas for rule making. Most people know little about this process. It is generally used only by corporate lawyers arguing for certain rule configurations pertaining to their own narrow interests. This process is very collegial and surprisingly open. If a member of the public sends in a formal comment, it gets displayed on the FCC Web site, along with all the others, so everyone can read each other's arguments. The FCC is not legally bound to use your suggestion made in a formal comment, but it is required to say why it didn't accept your suggestion. If you put in a unique idea and it was ignored in the final order and explanation of the FCC's rationale for adopting those rules, then you have standing to sue the FCC for disregarding your formal comment.

When it came time for public comments on Kennard's proposal to establish low-power FM, the FCC received more public comment than it bargained for. A new record was set for public participation in the LPFM radio proceeding. There were over 3,500 formal comments on docket 99-25,[15] overwhelmingly in favor of the new service. This figure was just a fraction of the tens of thousands of informal inquiries the FCC generally receives each year about starting a local radio station. The formal comments were often dozens and sometimes hundreds of pages long, with elaborate engineering schemes, a variety of suggested allocation methods, and documentation of enormous support for the concept. The staff at the commission was excited at the prospect of such invigorated citizen participation at the FCC and pledged they would make every effort to build such a service if the FCC's engineers found it to be technically feasible.

As part of the formal inquiry, four engineering studies were conducted to research interference to incumbent broadcasters. Interference had long been used as a red herring by the commercial broadcasters as a rationale for limiting access to unused spectrum on the radio bandwidth. Earlier low-power Class D licenses had been assigned to the portion of the FM bandwidth reserved for noncommercial broadcast, namely, the far-left-hand side of the dial. The FCC now considered opening up unused dial space situated between commercial channels, space the pirate broadcasters had demonstrated was accessible without causing interference to existing stations.

FOR ONCE, WE WIN!

After reviewing the results of the engineering studies, the FCC determined that many of the empty spots on the dial the pirates had found could, in fact, be used without creating harmful interference to existing broadcasters. The FCC understood it is common for those who control a communications industry to attempt to thwart new technologies or new stations by making claims of potential injurious interference. In spite of the considerable power and influence of the broadcast lobby, the FCC decided that the facts weighed against the case made by the commercial broadcasters. On January 26, 2000, the Federal Communications Commission voted to create a new low-power FM service. The new rules allowed small nonprofit groups, libraries, churches, and community organizations to apply for licenses to operate simple, inexpensive, noncommercial local radio stations.

OR SO WE THOUGHT . . .

Not surprisingly, the only opponents of the new low-power service were the people who already owned or worked for radio stations. Incumbent broadcasters argued that any new stations, no matter how low their power, would dramatically increase interference and result in a loss of service area for their stations. LPFM proponents claimed the amount of interference that could be caused by the new stations was so small it would make virtually no difference to the overall radio environment.

In lay terms, a low-power radio station does not interfere with incumbent radio stations any more than a streetlight in the Bronx interferes with seeing the Chrysler building in the New York City skyline. Would there be interference to your vision if you were standing five feet from the streetlight and staring straight at the lamp? Yes. If you were standing a few hundred feet from the lamppost and the streetlight happened to be lined up with your view of the Chrysler building? Maybe, though probably not. Should this be the basis for a policy decision around streetlamp allocation? No! Yet that is precisely the level of argumentation the commercial broadcasters relied upon in their quest to block community access to the airwaves, and it is this type of interference concern that swayed Congress to give special protection to the broadcasters.[16]

Congress never had the tools that the commission had to understand the miniscule scope of the phenomenon under consideration. The NAB tried to confuse the issue saying, "Any interference is unacceptable interference."[17] But they would not be willing to live up to that standard themselves, since the interference a full-power station creates as a matter of routine broadcast practice is far greater than anything that a low-power station could cause. And, in fact, the broadcast lobby has been aggressively pushing for new uses of the broadcast spectrum such as digital radio that create demonstrably far more interference to existing FM signals than low-power FM could. With new digital radio equipment rolling out in 2004, existing stations have been authorized to add digital signals on the fringe of their main channels. Many of these new digital sidebands will be more powerful then most LPFM station signals. Broadcasters are thus willing to tolerate slight increases of interference from digital stations since it suits their own financial needs. However, they remain adamant in rejecting the far-smaller amounts of interference from LPFM in their efforts to avoid more competition in the FM band, even in the form of nonprofit community radio.

DISSIMULATING SIMULATIONS

Much of the scientific basis cited by Congress in opposition to LPFM was a compact disc distributed by the NAB to members of Congress. This disc had the appearance of a scientific study, but it was in fact more of an "artist's rendering." It professed to be what two radio stations would sound like competing to be heard on the radio, but what was presented was actually the sound of two audio tracks laid on top of each other in a studio using a mixing board. In doing so, the commercial broadcasters maligned the professionalism of the FCC engineering staff. The FCC chiefs of the Office of Engineering and Technology and the Mass Media Bureau, Dale Hatfield and Roy Stewart, responded with uncharacteristic candor: "One particularly misleading disinformation effort involves a compact disc being distributed by

NAB that purports to demonstrate the type of interference to existing radio stations that NAB claims will occur from new low-power FM radio stations. This CD demonstration is misleading and is simply wrong."[18]

The NAB eventually pulled the bogus recording off of its Web site, claiming it had clearly stated that it was a simulation. Yet the NAB replaced it with alternate misleading examples of manufactured noise and hiss, or "white noise" distortion, over a recording of Mozart's Symphony 25 and a Johnny Cash song.[19] Though the NAB continued trying to make claims of interference, it became clear the numbers were simply pulling at straws because they lacked legitimate ground on which to block LPFM. Kennard summarized: "The FM service isn't rocket science . . . it's 50-year-old technology that we've studied exhaustively. This is not about technical interference, it's about incumbents trying to hoard their piece of the broadcasting pie."[20]

The NAB further resorted to emotional scare tactics about supposed threats low-power stations could pose to Reading Services for the Blind.[21] But the FCC had legally precluded low-power stations from being situated near reading services long before legislation went to Congress. To this day, broadcasters continue to cite this supposed problem to play on emotional sympathy for people with disabilities, without any basis in fact.

ALL THINGS CONSOLIDATED

Significantly, the NAB also recruited National Public Radio into the fray. Though NPR reporters and affiliate stations remain divided on the issue, the top management of NPR went all out against LPFM. NPR claimed to support the concept of LPFM, but it supported the NAB's interpretation of the engineering studies. Though NPR is public radio, it operates in many ways on a scale that makes it as cutthroat a competitor as any commercial station. Kennard himself criticized the public radio network for its lack of support for community radio: "I can only conclude that NPR is motivated by the same interests as the commercial groups—to protect their own incumbency . . . that these people see LPFM as a threat is sad. They've done much in the past to promote opportunity and a diversity of voices."[22] NPRs president, Kevin Klose, testified before Congress that NPR supported the Radio Broadcasting Preservation Act, legislation that would undermine low-power radio.

The FCC's original rules for LPFM would have opened up thousands more frequencies to community groups—but Congress, under pressure from incumbent broadcasters, sneaked the Radio Broadcasting Preservation Act into a "must-pass" spending bill in late 2000. Under the FCC rules, the largest ten cities in the country would have been granted a total of about twenty-five new stations. Under this legislation pushed by the commercial broadcasters and passed by Congress, there were no new stations allowed in any of the top fifty urban markets. The technical standards of required distance between stations were made so stringent that very few new stations were possible. These standards mandate enormous separations between radio stations, far more distance than the FCC engineers concluded was necessary to prevent interference. Smaller towns went from having five or six channels available to having just one channel that had to be shared by all the applicants. LPFM was alive, but eviscerated.

BACK IN THE SADDLE AGAIN . . .

Despite the loss in Congress, low-power advocates dusted off and started to build these radio stations in small towns across the country. These new stations are doing incredible things in their communities. The Southern Development Foundation in Opelousas, Louisiana, for example, has become the first civil rights organization in the country to own a radio station. The foundation advocates on issues of school reform, community-supported agriculture, and neighborhood economic development, and also hosts the world's largest traditional Zydeco music festival—all aspects of its work are featured in the station's programming.

Southern Arundel Citizens for Responsible Development in Churchton, Maryland, is the first radio station owned by an environmental organization. Based near the Chesapeake Bay, this station focuses on issues of the environment, development, and local maritime culture and politics, while broadcasting an eclectic mix of music played by enthusiastic DJs. Some observers questioned whether an environmental group would run the station solely as a propaganda organ for its viewpoints. WRYR, however, had a bigger plan. It has used the station to put local government meetings on the air and given airtime to many different community interests, invigorating local political culture. The group feels it benefits more from the respect it gathers by having brought the station to the community than it would by monopolizing it as a venue for its own ideas.

Another station is the Edinboro Early School, located in the Gold Coast shopping mall in Maryland. This station's goal is to recreate the flavor of an early 1950s radio station, with family-oriented programming focusing on

music of the fifties and early sixties. The station has three hours of programming a day for children from three to five years old. Other content includes
real estate and finance talk shows, an interfaith church news bulletin board,
field broadcasts from historical sites, and a music show hosted by a former
ABC executive who plays records dating back to the 1920s.

AS ANY TENANT CAN TELL YOU,
OWNERSHIP MATTERS

In short, the FCC, at the behest of Congress, watered down its original proposal to establish thousands of LPFMs and instead granted limited access in
rural communities. At the same time, an additional study on interference was
authorized by Congress. As a result, activists and organizations like the
Prometheus Radio Project did two things. First, they began helping to build
what stations were granted licenses and facilitating hopeful applicants to
negotiate the process. Second, they began to focus efforts on the broader
issue of media ownership. Low-power radio is a crucial means of setting
aside a small portion of the spectrum to communities, but it does not resolve
the larger problems stemming from a corporate-controlled media system
seeking further consolidation. Playing an active role in the fight against further media consolidation was the logical next step toward fighting for citizens' access to the airwaves and bringing together more allies in the struggle
for low-power FM.

Many community activists became deeply immersed in the politics of
telecommunications through their participation in the fight for low-power
radio. Having learned firsthand the vast political power broadcasters had,
low-power advocates were keen to act when they caught wind of the far
greater changes the FCC had planned. When the presidency changed in January 2001, Democratic FCC chairman William Kennard was replaced with
Republican Michael Powell.[23] Powell had shown little interest in LPFM. His
main focus was the cross-media ownership rules considered to be most burdensome by the media industry.

Over the years, the commission had enacted a patchwork of regulations
designed to prevent monopolization of the media by a small number of corporate entities. These rules included caps on the number of stations a single
entity could own, rules preventing networks from merging, provisions preventing newspapers and broadcast entities from owning each other, and other
similar restrictions. Powell generally believed that none of these regulations

were necessary anymore, because of the changing landscape of media created by the introduction of new technologies. With the introduction of new competing means of delivering content, such as satellite, the Internet, and cable, he argued it no longer mattered whether or not a newspaper and a television station were owned by a single owner in a given market.

The Washington, DC, circuit court had supported Powell's position by striking down several related ownership protections. The judges looked at the inconsistent mélange of communications regulations passed over the years and found some of the rules lacked a rigorous, coherent framework. Because some protections were in place, while others were not, some companies ended up with strategic advantages over others. For example, broadcast TV would often complain that cable companies competed unfairly because they faced no indecency regulations, while cable operators complained that the broadcasters did not have to pay franchise fees to municipalities. Corporations used these imbalances to argue against any rule that they felt got in the way of their profits. Powell chose to interpret these decisions to mean that the law had a "deregulatory presumption"—and that any rule that could not be justified using empirical study had to be eliminated.

The precedent for Powell's deregulatory agenda was the 1996 Telecommunications Act, which gave broadcasters the right to own up to eight stations in any single market and unlimited stations across the country. It should also be noted that until then, radio did not figure in the fiscal strategies of many large media corporations, because the financial gain of individual station ownership was just not great enough. In fact, General Electric, the parent company of NBC, sold its radio division to radio syndication company Westwood One Entertainment in 1988. It was not until the limits on national ownership were lifted that the financial stakes were raised. An acquisition frenzy ensued, resulting in the increasingly standardized and centralized nature of programming and personnel. Elimination of these protections invoked an unwelcome scenario of consolidated ownership, giving unprecedented power to media owners.

Media corporations are enormously powerful and have other business interests and interconnects. It is a strange idiosyncrasy of the American view of broadcasting that corporations can be impartial, disinterested managers and stewards of broadcast spectrum. They are in fact incredibly biased and have very large stakes in the outcomes of public policy debates. These corporations control the channels through which most Americans understand these issues. Media operates differently from other industries because it has a particular role and responsibility to a democratic society. That is why the review of media ownership standards must not only be in terms of absolute economic dominance of a particular market but also in terms of their impact on the interests of the public in general.

CARE FOR A LIGHT BULB?
OR A NEWSCAST? OR A BOMB?

In particular, antiwar activists seized the moment. Peace activists were angered by the manipulations of the media they believed had misinformed the American public during the war in Iraq. If mainstream media had greater critical integrity, they argued, far fewer people would have accepted the misleading claims about weapons of mass destruction and war might have been averted. The massive financial incentives armed conflict offers corporations provided fertile soil for a groundswell of opposition against further consolidation of media power to manipulate public opinion.

One of the most disturbing examples of this is General Electric, a major defense contractor who makes billions of dollars each year selling hardware to the US military. GE is the owner of the NBC television network, one of the major networks where Americans get their news. The power of this corporation to affect public opinion about issues of war and peace has raised serious conflict of interest concerns since the purchase in 1986. These anxieties are deepened when the corporate culture of General Electric is considered—General Electric has been convicted of seventeen felonies, ranging from tax evasion to financial impropriety on government contracts.[24]

Additionally, the wartime activities of companies like Clear Channel also raised the ire of media activists and concerned citizens. As described in detail by Dorothy Kidd elsewhere in this book, the combination of Clear Channel's aggressive business tactics, union busting, and shock jock–style management practices created widespread resentment of the company. Particularly chilling was Clear Channels "Rallies for America." Clear Channel used its considerable publicity machine (over 1,200 radio stations, over 550,000 billboards, 40 television stations, and control of hundreds of major live performance venues) to sponsor a series of rallies in support of the war in Iraq. Clear Channel became the poster child for bad corporate behavior and a telling example of what could happen to the entire media industry if further consolidation was allowed. The support Bush received in the Rallies for America is being reciprocated in the broad deregulatory agenda that the Bush-appointed FCC is pursuing, which could allow Clear Channel to expand its empire across other media platforms.[25]

With the organizing efforts refocused among low-power activists around the dangers of cross-media ownership resulting from the loss of current FCC regulations, low-power activists began focusing upon the massive dislocations in the radio industry created by companies like Clear Channel.

FCC, UNDER THE GUN

The involvement of LPFM activists in the fight against media consolidation marks a shift in the nature of the social actors who were engaged in such battles. These activists had backgrounds not in the traditional world of nonprofit, media democracy policy and legislation, but were accustomed to taking people's personal problems and recasting them as political issues. The pirate broadcasters had gained invaluable experience using the court system to argue their case, and at the same time, these were people involved in direct action and civil disobedience who were willing to take advantage of the full range of tactics at their disposal.

One of the first public salvos in the debate outside of the Washington policy circle was a demonstration by "The Angels of the Public Interest," organized by Media Tank, the Center for International Media Action, the Prometheus Radio Project, Indymedia, and others. FCC chairman Michael Powell had expressed his fervor for media consolidation in decidedly religious terms with statements such as: "The market is my religion." Going further in his dismissal of the relevance of public interest standards, he said at a meeting of the NAB: "The night after I was sworn in, I waited for a visit from the angel of the public interest. I waited all night, but she did not come."[26]

According to Media Tank's Web site, "Since he had trouble seeing one Angel that dreadful night, on March 22nd, 2001, we shall descend upon him in droves." Dressed as angels with cardboard wings and robes with tinsel on them, protesters were turned away from the FCC by police menacing with riot batons.[27]

Beyond simply raising awareness of these issues, anticonsolidation activists wanted to get the public involved in the decision-making process at the FCC. Once again, the formal FCC comment process was used, given the earlier success LPFM activists had with it. After mobilizing the relatively small mailing lists of media reform groups, several thousand comments had gotten into the FCC. Seeing the high level of interest among this relatively small constituency, larger organizations started to take an interest and mobilize.

Over the next months, the AFL-CIO, the National Organization for

Women, Common Cause, and other groups joined the outcry against media consolidation. And eventually, the appeal of the need to block further media consolidation reached across ideological lines. Brent Bozell, a prominent conservative cultural critic, brought his organization, the Parent's Television Council, to the fight. He believed that obscenity and indecency in media were on the rise because of the unaccountable, corporate bottom-line thinking about content. Describing the Left/Right coalition against the new media rules, Bozell said: "When all of us are united on an issue, then one of two things has happened. Either the earth has spun off its axis and we have all lost our minds or there is universal support for a concept."

Even the NRA turned its political gunsights on the FCC. The NRA had several times been refused the opportunity to buy political ads on major networks. Many in the NRA's membership perceive there to be a liberal bias in the media. They did not want to see a media future controlled by a small handful of politically correct corporate types in Los Angeles and New York who would be in a position to censor their grassroots campaigns for gun ownership. Once they got involved and their constituency mobilized, hundreds of thousands of comments came into the commission. By the end of the comment period on the proceeding MB 02-277, there had been an astounding new record set of more than 520,000 formal comments and millions more informal comments.

After several months, the comment period was closed, and it was time for the FCC to render its decision. On June 4, 2003, the FCC chose to almost completely ignore the public sentiment and the evidence presented by consumer advocates. The new rules dismantled most of what was left of ownership limitations. Under the new rules, in almost any city a single corporation could own up to eight radio stations, three TV stations, both competing daily newspapers (and the alternative newsweeklies), the local cable system, the billboards, the concert venues—and even the nuclear power plant down the road.

SO SUE ME[28]

On September 3, 2003, the public interest law firm Media Access Project, representing the Prometheus Radio Project and its allies, sued for a stay of implementation of the new rules. The next day the old rules would be swept aside and the new rules could go into effect. Billions of dollars were set to change hands as newspaper corporations bought TV chains, TV chains bought radio chains, and everyone bought up anything they could afford.

Public interest advocates argued that once the new ownership rules went into effect, there would be no means of repairing the damage done. The three-judge panel, after many hours of testimony, issued a stay that evening and agreed to hear the case. The mergers were stopped in their tracks and could not go forward until the judges had heard the full evidence presented by both sides and rendered their judgment.

The case was ultimately decided on June 24, 2004, when the three-judge panel ruled in favor of media activists. In a lengthy two-hundred-page decision, the court told the FCC that its attempts to further deregulate the American media system are unjustified, thus reversing the FCC's controversial 2003 decision to allow cross-platform media regulation. The court further determined the FCC relied on "irrational assumptions and inconsistencies" in determining the new cross-ownership limits, and ordered it to come up with a new proposal that adequately took into account the public interest. The judges faulted the FCC's methodology in measuring media concentration and rejected the FCC's argument that ownership limits should be removed unless evidence could be shown to warrant their retention. FCC commissioner Michael Copps (who, along with Commissioner Adelstein, both dissented on the original FCC decision) said in a released statement: "The rush to media consolidation approved by the FCC last June was wrong as a matter of law and policy. The commission has a second chance to do the right thing."[29]

What this means is that the FCC has been sent back to the drawing board to come up with a new plan based on substantive research and statistics if it wishes to pursue deregulation of media ownership. In its ruling, the court said it *may* be possible to allow cross-platform deregulation of, for example, newspaper ownership, but that the FCC *failed to justify it was necessary* at this time.[30]

Plaintiffs argued their case on technical and methodological grounds and around the issue of localism, specifically, the negative impact further media consolidation would have on *local* journalism and *local* news reporting. In the lawsuit, Media Access Project argued: "Civic participation and democracy depend on citizens' ability to find out what is going on in their hometowns and cities."[31] Ownership matters, and with increasing consolidation of national and global ownership of local media outlets, community and neighborhood-based issues get left behind.

The FCC has belatedly attempted to respond to such criticisms through the creation of a task force to study localism in television and radio. As a *New York Times* article states in its title: "Facing Criticism, FCC Is Thinking Local." The flaws of the FCC's approach to localism can be found in its

reading of local impact. For example, FCC data pertaining to New York concluded: "The Dutchess County Community College television station is fifty
percent more valuable for media diversity than the *New York Times* and equal
weight with, and just as valuable as the local ABC television affiliate."[32] It
seems implausible the FCC could sustain such logic that equates one of the
most influential and widely read newspapers in the nation with a local public
access television station.

But localism is not only a concern for commercial media. By comparison,
a typical NPR affiliate station broadcasts overwhelmingly national news and
public affairs, and depending on the station, most likely features nominal nonmusic local programming. For example, NPR affiliate KCRW in Los Angeles,
arguably one of the most high-profile and well-funded public stations in the
country, produces only thirteen hours total of in-house public affairs programming a week, as of spring 2004.[33] Aside from its weekly live coverage
of the Santa Monica City Council meeting, the station produces only three
public affairs or talk programming hours per week to issues facing Southern
Californians. Conversely, KCRW produces eighty-three hours of music programming a week and broadcasts roughly eighty-seven hours of nationally
syndicated public affairs and talk. Music is far cheaper and easier to program
then resource-laden public affairs production and often provides a welcome
alternative to corporate radio music programming. However, the disparity in
these figures nevertheless resonates a growing move away from local public
affairs and news content, and mirrors public radio around the country.

AS COMMERCIAL RADIO IS BUSY DYING,
COMMUNITY RADIO GETS BUSY BEING REBORN

Commentators have been predicting the death of radio for over fifty years,
ever since the advent of television. But radio has proven more resilient than
many of its critics. The average American home has nine radio receivers,
making it more accessible in more situations than any other medium. Its
renaissance has as much to do with the fact that it is affordable to produce,
easy to learn, and widely accessible.

Community radio is a participatory medium. It is a source of local,
neighborhood-based news and information. It is media without intermedi-
aries, a counterbalance to the world of corporatism. It is radio run for its own
sake, for the benefit of the community, rather then for the profit of station
owners. In the United Kingdom, current legislation to create an official third

tier of broadcasting for Community FM is tied in with lifelong learning initiatives and community regeneration efforts. British government supporters and media activists argue community media benefits neighborhoods and can serve as an important training ground—the idea, as Zane Ibrahim of Bush Radio South Africa asserts, that "community radio is ninety percent community and ten percent radio."

Radio is an easy medium for a group of enthusiastic amateurs. Often, ordinary people can do a better job at producing informative and entertaining radio programming than the professionals, for all their training and high-tech studios. It can serve as a great training ground for youth to learn to speak publicly, to fix things, to raise money, to plan ambitious projects. And every neighborhood has someone who can do a beautiful weekly serial reading of the *Epic of Gilgamesh*, someone with a giant collection of Slovenian music, someone who can explain the news behind the Western headlines about their home country of Egypt or Honduras or Cambodia. It was not difficult for organizers to find a group in every town that wanted to start a radio station for its community.

Noncommercial voices in media are similar to public parks or public libraries. They are public institutions that exist where the market cannot or will not provide for the common good. These voices are needed to be the experimental edge from which creativity of the rest of the media can be drawn. Young musicians that listen to Britney Spears on commercial radio will grow up to sound like Britney Spears. Young musicians exposed to a mix of Turkish folk and trance music on a noncommercial station may grow up better prepared to innovate, mix styles, and create the leading edge of music.

Low-power FM gives a sliver of the spectrum to community groups. These groups, while opinionated, tend to be more fair-minded and open to debate, and make much better stewards of broadcast frequencies. They tend to run their stations in a way that more closely approximates an open forum for the community. LPFM activists feel they have the best chance for social change in a more democratized society with a free flow of information—so even though they often have partisan perspectives on issues, they usually welcome programming from a diversity of viewpoints. These groups also do not run on a speculative market model, and thus have much greater freedom in programming choices—and also freedom not to rely on the most titillating and pandering forms of programs to bump up their audience numbers. Robert McChesney puts it this way:

> Here you have something that to every community offers the opportunity
> for people to speak to each other that's not going to be filtered by adver-

tisers . . . a chance for ideas to be heard that wouldn't pass the Rush Lim-
baugh/Howard Stern litmus test, and the Madison Avenue litmus test. A
chance for music to be heard that wouldn't be played by robots that are
responding to some demographic survey, but in fact by people who love
music and enjoy playing it.

Such stations would

bring some vitality back to the staleness of US radio, which has all the
charm of a second- or third-tier suburban shopping mall today.[34]

Or, as former FCC chairman William Kennard states simply: "[LPFM]
is an antidote to consolidation. It creates a vehicle to speak to folks that no
one is speaking to."[35]

DON'T WORRY, BE HAPPY . . . NEW TECHNOLOGIES MAY HELP, BUT WILL NOT SAVE US

Up until now, the airwaves have been regulated as if they were scarce real
estate, parceled off to different users with different compensations either
through public service or auctions of leases on their use. The scarcity model
has been the excuse that corporations have used to preserve their exclusive
use of communications channels, while ordinary citizens are excluded from
the media. There are currently much broader proceedings at the FCC that will
decide the fate of how the entire electromagnetic spectrum is used, including
radio, TV, microwaves, cellular phones, wireless Internet, and others. The
results of these decisions may be able to help dismantle the broadcast elite's
excuse of limited available channels for citizen use. If publicly minded
choices are made, we could see a future of radio that includes ubiquitous, free
internet access (and thus free online radio/audio) over the airwaves that could
replace FM radio. If corporations get their way, new technologies will continue to be commodified, constricted, metered, filtered, and narrowed to
increase commercial profitability, as happened in broadcast.

Access to communications for all citizens is at the heart of a democratic
society. There are those who claim Internet broadcasting and other digital
formats will be the great leveler of access to the airwaves. Satellite radio has
already been divided up to the highest corporate bidder through a "below-
the-radar" process among government, commercial broadcasters, and NPR,
before digital spectrum issues reached the popular vernacular. Neither is

Internet radio the panacea. At present, Internet radio is nowhere near as ubiquitous as FM listening, especially among those with low incomes. When Internet radio is offered as an alternative solution to the need for community radio on the FM band, it masks the fact that corporations are continuing to use their dominance of FM to prepare their brands for the future as they are distributed over new channels. Communities are offered futuristic "pie-in-the sky" alternatives while the present continues to be dominated by corporate interests. As one student put it: "When you hear your neighbors volunteering on the air, you feel like you know them even if you don't. I'm gung ho on the Internet, but it remains to be seen if it can foster that same feeling of intimacy. . . . Why should you use the Internet to broadcast the fact that the local church is having a bake sale or that someone's dog is lost? It just doesn't make sense."[36] At its best, radio is a local medium.

Community radio is not just about content but is also about community access and participation. The community radio institutions were built from uneasy alliances among people representing many different interests. They had no other option but to share a channel because of the expenses and the scarcity of FCC licenses. Perhaps technology may someday allow all of these people to operate a future equivalent of FM radio individually from their homes. While this may create individual convenience and allow everyone to broadcast anything they want twenty-four hours a day to anyone who cares to listen, those who focus on these dreams of eliminating technical barriers and creating infinite bandwidth miss much of the point of community radio. Ironically, the cosmopolitan sound stemming from the patched-together coalitions may turn out to be community radio's greatest asset as corporate radio starts to fade. The community form of radio will survive into the future because of the social benefits of working on projects together, cooperating, and intermingling in a community setting.

ENOUGH OF THE FUTURE, BACK TO THE PRESENT

The opportunity will arise to further open up the airwaves for low-power radio. On July 11, 2003, the FCC released a long-anticipated study, analyzing the effect of new LPFM radio stations on existing radio stations. The study, conducted by an independent testing company called the MITRE Corporation,[37] proves once again that LPFM stations do not, in fact, interfere with existing stations. In addition, the study authors recommend the lifting of burdensome restrictions imposed by Congress on the new LPFM radio service as designated in December 2000. In its testimony before Congress, the National Association of Broadcasters complained that, if the LPFM service were launched, the radio dial would be drowned in "an ocean of interference." But the study authors found so little evidence of potential interference that they chose not to implement some later stages in the study, such as an economic impact study and subjective listening tests that would only have been necessary if interference had been proven.

The release of this study is not an automatic win for community media. Some full-power broadcasters, who bitterly fought LPFM in its initial form, continue their opposition against any expansion of the service. Many members of Congress have backed the broadcast lobby—and the FCC, under Republican chairman Michael Powell, until recently has not shown the commitment to LPFM demonstrated by previous chairman William Kennard. The FCC study could lead to increased citizen access to the airwaves, but only if the public is aware of the positive study findings and is encouraged to use it as a tool to fight for an expanded LPFM service.

Signs are promising for low-power FM right now. NPR has shifted its stance and has recently stated that it does not plan further objections to the expansion of LPFM. As a result of the massive coalition that came together against the new media ownership rules pushed by Chairman Powell, and no doubt having a bit to do with the lawsuit filed by the Prometheus Radio Project and Media Access Project against these new rules, the commission has signaled it is ready to move forward on low-power radio. As part of his new "Localism in Media" initiative, Powell has promised more action on low power radio. In February of 2004, the FCC requested permission from Congress to change its rules on low-power FM, allowing hundreds of channels to be given out in the major cities across the United States. At the time of this writing, Senator John McCain is preparing to introduce legislation repealing the Radio Broadcasting Preservation Act of 2000, which would return authority over LPFM back to the FCC. The fate of low-power radio is again in the hands of Congress. Stay Tuned!

NOTES

1. Prometheus Radio Project is an activist organization that promotes a more democratic media through the establishment of community radio stations. Prometheus advocates for policies that will improve citizens' access to the airwaves and builds stations with local community groups around the world.

2. CIW has organized a boycott of Taco Bell and its parent company, Yum

Brands, the world's largest restaurant company, for their repeated refusal to take meaningful steps to improve labor standards and end labor abuses in their supply chain. The coalition has a growing list of organizations and churches supporting its efforts and college campuses following suit. Information can be found at http://www.ciw-online.org.

3. Jesse Walker, *Rebels on the Air: An Alternative History of Radio in America* (New York: New York University Press, 2001). For more history on community radio in the United States, see also Matthew Lasar, *Pacifica Radio: The Rise of An Alternative Network* (Philadelphia: Temple University Press, 2000).

4. Walker, *Rebels on the Air.*

5. See FCC Docket No. 20735, ruling to change rules related to noncommercial broadcasting: "This proceeding was . . . stimulated by a petition from the Corporation for Public Broadcasting." *Federal Register* 43, no. 173 (September 6, 1978).

6. By contrast, NPR affiliates benefited the most from the obscure rules—almost the entire US population has access to a signal that carries NPR programming, and many towns have several stations that carry NPR but no community station that carries local news.

7. Walker, *Rebels on the Air.*

8. Ibid.

9. See Dunifer's Web site for more information, http://www.freeradio.org.

10. Pete Tridish was a self-proclaimed political pirate involved with West Philadelphia's Radio Mutiny. Kate Coyer has never made an unlicensed broadcast over one hundred feet.

11. The source of this quote remains anonymous for obvious reasons.

12. Photos and more on the demonstration can be found at http://www .prometheusradio.org/pirate.shtml and http://www.sinkers.org/microradio/.

13. Alex Markels, "Radio Active," *Wired*, June 2000, http://www.wired.com/ wired/archive/8.06/radio.html?pg=1&topic=&topic_set.

14. Ibid.

15. The text of FCC docket 99-25 can be found at http://www.fcc.gov/Bureaus/ Mass_Media/Notices/1999/fcc99006.txt.

16. The text of argumentation from the National Association of Broadcasters can be found at http://www.nab.org/newsroom/issues/lpfm/responsetofcc/.

17. It should be noted that arguments surrounding questions of interference are flawed to begin with. Standards for interference date back to 1962, well before modern noise filters and digital program buttons on receivers were introduced.

18. From FCC news release located at http://ftp.fcc.gov/Bureaus/Engineering _Technology/News_Releases/2000/nret0005.html.

19. The bogus noise distortion over Mozart and Cash remain up on the NAB's Web site and can be found at http://www.nab.org/newsroom/issues/lpfm/ responsetofcc/noiseandhiss.asp.

20. Markels, "Radio Active."

21. The Reading Services to the Blind use "subcarrier" frequencies on the sides

of full-power stations to carry audio programs for the visually impaired. Volunteers read the newspapers and books, and listeners have special receivers that can receive this hidden programming.

22. Markels, "Radio Active."

23. Bush himself did not publicly speak out one way or another on the issue of deregulation, but the White House made several supporting comments toward Powell's agenda. More information on this can be found in the Media Activists Guide to the FCC at http://www.prometheusradio.org/media_activists_guide.shtml.

24. Sam Husseini, "Felons of the Air," FAIR, http://www.fair.org/extra/9411/ge-felon.html.

25. Eric Boehlert, series at http://www.salon.com.

26. Story found at http://www.mediatank.org/FaceOff.html. Quote from Powell found in the text of a speech to the American Bar Association, April 5, 1998, http://ftp.fcc.gov/Speeches/Powell/spmkp806.html.

27. Quote and story found at http://dc.indymedia.org/newswire/display/19876.

28. Hannah Sassamen especially contributed thoughtful analysis of the court decision to this section.

29. The FCC is comprised of five members, each appointed by the president, who is required to choose three from his own party and two from the opposing party. Commissioners Copps and Adelstein are the two Democrats on the commission.

30. *Prometheus Radio Project v. FCC*, 373 F.3d 372 (2004).

31. From statement found at www.mediaccessproject.org.

32. Ibid.

33. See http://www.kcrw.org for program schedule and information.

34. Fiona Morgan, "Pirate Radio Goes Legit," *Salon.com*, http://archive.salon.com/news/feature/2000/01/20/radio/.

35. Markels, "Radio Active."

36. About.com's John Anderson on the need for local FM radio.

37. The study can be found at http://www.mitre.org/work/tech_papers/tech_papers_03/caasd_fm/.

INDEX

ABC News. *See* Disney Corporation

Adelstein, Jonathan (commissioner), 172n4, 224, 279, 280, 307, 314n29. *See also* Federal Communication Commission

Ailes, Roger, 140, 182n63

Air America Radio Network, 281

Alterman, Eric, 109, 120nn5–6, 182n63

Amanpour, Christiane, 86

American Civil Liberties Union (ACLU), 24, 209n18, 224, 237, 238, 239, 243, 252nn1–7, 253n14

America Online (AOL), merger with Time Warner, 25. *See also* Time Warner

Arnett, Peter, 43, 86

AT&T, 163, 164, 174n31, 209–10n19, 247–48, 252n8

  merger with Comcast, 25

Bagdikian, Ben H., 51n5, 66, 78n29, 83, 114, 121n13, 122n29, 172nn2–8, 178n43, 179n46, 272

Brokaw, Tom, 38, 103

Bush, George W., 10, 13, 19, 23, 27, 30n5, 36, 49, 52n21, 60–61, 78n26, 81, 82–83, 85–86, 87, 88, 89, 104–105, 109, 129, 137, 140n7, 142, 143, 148, 149, 153n7, 154n30, 182n63, 218, 226, 227, 267, 272–73, 274, 283n26, 304, 314n23

Cable Act (1984), 163

CBS News. *See* Viacom

censorship, 21, 22, 28, 35, 75–77, 85–87, 99, 115–17, 121–22nn19–21, 142, 153n25, 163, 186, 211n50, 242, 274, 293–94. *See also* deception, mass

  the New American, 36–52

  defined, 39